D1527524

Hemispheric Security
and U.S. Policy in
Latin America

Hemispheric Security and U.S. Policy in Latin America

EDITED BY
Augusto Varas

Westview Press
BOULDER, SAN FRANCISCO, & LONDON

Westview Special Studies on Latin America and the Caribbean

Copyright © 1989 by Westview Press, Inc.

Published in 1989 in the United States of America by Westview Press, Inc., 5500 Central Avenue, Boulder, Colorado 80301, and in the United Kingdom by Westview Press, Inc., 13 Brunswick Centre, London WC1N 1AF, England

Library of Congress Cataloging-in-Publication Data
Hemispheric security and U.S. policy in Latin America.
   (Westview special studies on Latin America and
the Caribbean)
   Includes index.
   1. America—National security.   2. United States—
Military relations—Latin America.   3. Latin America—
Military relations—United States.   I. Varas, Augusto.
II. Title: Hemispheric security and US policy in
Latin America.   III. Series.
UA21.H39   1989   355′.0335′73098   87–14715
ISBN 0-8133-7442-1

Printed and bound in the United States of America

The paper used in this publication meets the requirements of the American National Standard for Permanence of Paper for Printed Library Materials Z39.48-1984.

10   9   8   7   6   5   4   3   2   1

Contents

Acknowledgments

The writing of this book has been made possible thanks to the support of the Joint Program of International Relations of Latin America (RIAL) and the permanent interest of Luciano Tomassini, its executive secretary, in creating and developing a regional network of specialists and scholars dedicated to security studies and peace research.

I would also like to acknowledge the institutional support provided for this editorial project by the Latin American Faculty of Social Sciences (FLACSO) in Santiago, Chile. There, with the financial support of the Ford Foundation, it has been possible to develop a long-term research effort on security affairs and Latin American international relations. Part of the effort to produce this volume has been carried out in this institutional setting. I would also like to thank the International Studies Association for its support of the initiation of this project.

I would like to thank my friends and colleagues José Miguel Insulza, Brian Loveman, and Carlos Rico for their comments and helpful advice.

Augusto Varas

Introduction

Augusto Varas

New global and regional strategic processes in the late 1980s are creating opportunities for innovation in inter-American security relations. Recent changes in U.S.-Soviet strategic behavior, surmounting previous ideological and political barriers, have increased the potential and opportunities to improve superpower cooperation in the Third World.[1] Reinvigorated multilateral organizations, like the United Nations, are thus in a good position to play crucial roles in peaceful conflict resolution. Because global security requires regional security structures,[2] a new hemispheric security order would also contribute in its turn to world peace by creating regional conditions for peaceful conflict resolution.

The current cooperative international milieu contrasts with actual hemispheric security cooperation, which has had a poor record in the 1980s. Disagreements on the Central American and South Atlantic crises introduced serious cleavages and divisions in inter-American relations. Simultaneously, the variety of regional security issues in Latin America increased, fragmentizing regional strategic interests. This situation, if it were to continue, would create a dangerous abyss between the United States and Latin American countries vis-à-vis hemispheric security issues. Accordingly, a new inter-American security system is needed to overcome this situation.

Future hemispheric security relations should be designed so as to prevent a wave of new militarization in the region and to protect Latin American countries from being drawn into East-West competition. The best way to accomplish both goals is to design a new security order able to transform the region into a *buffer zone*. But, again, this cannot be achieved without U.S. participation and/or agreement, nor can it be achieved without a Latin American convergence around these purposes.

My interest in analyzing U.S. hemispheric security policies during the Reagan administration arose in response to that need to reshape inter-

American security relations. In order to remake these linkages around new strategic concepts one must learn from previous experiences. Historically, U.S. security interests in Latin America evolved from strategic to political considerations,[3] which contrast with early U.S. professional military interests in the region.[4] As a result, the Latin American military has been detached from U.S. institutions, the inter-American military system has become bankrupt, and the Latin American armed forces have been deprofessionalized. These changes facilitated military intervention in politics, transforming the armed forces into political resources for authoritarian experiments. During the 1980s, neo-bipolar tensions restored a regional climate of cold war, but the endeavor to create an inter-American military order failed, producing the final collapse of the old system. U.S.–Latin American disagreements over how to face regional conflicts damaged not only security relations but also hemispheric political ones.[5]

Common inter-American strategic incentives and interests are crucial, for several reasons, in order for the hemisphere to move from conflictual to cooperative actions. Neither a discredited inter-American military system nor the absence of any security arrangement can produce peace in the region. Peace will depend on the development of common incentives for cooperation around specific areas of strategic and security concerns. Inter-American security cooperation should overcome its political bias and be confined within the scope of modern military professional activity. Moreover, this limitation should be the outcome of a gradually evolving set of discrete regional security regimes, as indicated in this volume.

To introduce these changes, major hemispheric obstacles that prevent a common approach to security should be identified. First, it is important to note the nature of regional conflicts. Because the region contains a variety of conflict formations—ideological and territorial—a clear separation between the two would favor new strategic relations. A second obstacle is the expansion of the military sector, which has fragmented the previous regional balance of power. In addition, a new military regional competition responding to a diversified set of strategic interests is accelerating. It is crucial to prevent this tendency's evolution into new crises. Third, U.S. presence in the region, which cannot be ignored, is currently guided by policies that are not providing foundations for a new security system. The U.S. military presence in the hemisphere should be transformed into a positive one. The recent loss of U.S. influence in the region should be enough of an incentive to strengthen the idea of partnership, which would ensure peace and security in the hemisphere.

Responding to these main obstacles, a new hemispheric security order should be single-issue oriented. The previous order was focused mainly on territorial dimensions of security (the closest to internal political control) but embraced all countries and included all aspects of national defense; it attempted to integrate different subregional and institutional realities into a single hemispheric framework. The variety of domestic and hemispheric military realities hinders the organization of a single, all-embracing system. In fact, the latter should be the final result of several discrete systems, structured around perceptions of a common threat.

New concepts and new structures for common regional security are required. Because inter-American cooperation exists among individual services,[6] new hemispheric security regimes could use the current structure of cooperation at separate security levels but in a different conceptual framework. By maintaining some continuities in hemispheric security relations, respecting some national dynamics as acceptable, and recovering the idea of security as multidimensional, a positive multilateral military posture could be developed. This would make possible the coordination of plural defense policies around a nonideological approach. Thus, a new military determination to confront common threats to peace could reconcile inter-American military interests with democracy.

Hemispheric Security and U.S. Policy in Latin America analyzes the evolution of inter-American security relations in recent decades, providing a variety of views on these topics from the United States and Latin America. Starting with an analysis of the historical development of U.S. strategic and political interests in the Third World, Thomas Bodenheimer and Robert Gould place U.S. military policy in a broader context, that of the U.S. global strategic approach. With respect to Latin America, Augusto Varas's chapter provides a historical analysis of the development of the hemispheric security system from the post–World War II period to the present. Mark Falcoff's chapter analyzes the relative military isolation of the United States in the hemisphere and deals with options for overcoming that isolation. Margaret Daly Hayes's contribution identifies major U.S. interests in the hemisphere.

The book also includes an analysis of regional security interactions around three main subregional areas: Central America, the Caribbean, and South America. Jorge Rodríguez Beruff's chapter describes the evolution of U.S. security interests in the Caribbean and provides statistical information showing the growing importance of the English-speaking Caribbean in a new subregional security scenario. Lilia Bermúdez and Raúl Benítez's chapter on U.S. policy in Central America presents an analysis of the U.S. low-intensity-conflict approach to this area. With respect to the South American subregion, Carlos Portales discusses in his chapter the most likely trends for the coming decades and defines a set of conditions for a common regional security approach. Finally, Nina Maria Serafino's chapter provides an updated discussion of the

Contadora and Esquipulas accords, showing some ways to tackle regional conflicts through negotiations.

In this volume the reader will find a diversity of regional topics, intellectual perspectives, and alternative proposals, all of which provide clues for the development of a peaceful approach to hemispheric security issues. I hope it may make possible the transition toward a new climate of cooperation for security in the Western Hemisphere.

Notes

1. Soviet, Cuban, and Vietnamese withdrawal from Afghanistan, Angola, and Cambodia and Laos, respectively; the cease-fire between Iran and Iraq; new diplomatic approaches between the USSR and China, India and Pakistan and China; the agreements between Eastern European countries and the European Economic Community; a new negotiating position of the contras and Sandinistas after the Sapoá meeting; the new attitude of the recently recognized Palestinian state toward Israel, of China toward Taiwan, and of the USSR toward Japan are clear examples of the new security climate that has emerged on the eve of the 1990s.

2. See United Nations, "Report of the Independent Commission on Disarmament and Security," United Nations, A/CN. 10/38, 1983. This report has been known as the "Palme Report."

3. According to Gen. Fred W. Woerner (USSOUTHCOM), this political interest still remains. In his opinion, Latin American armies "will be a major player in the total life of those nations. It is important to have a relationship with that. [They] stepped out from the role of arbiter or determinant of the political process and stepped into a very new role, that of guarantor." *New York Times*, April 3, 1988.

4. See Maj. T. Wyckoff, "South America's Strategic Position," *Military Review*, July 1956, quoted in this volume; and Lars Schoultz, *National Security and United States Policy Toward Latin America* (Princeton: Princeton University Press, 1987).

5. According to then–Assistant Secretary of State Elliott Abrams, a failure of U.S. policy in Nicaragua was that aid to the contras began covertly in 1981. "It was a mistake to do this through covert action," Abrams stated at a gathering at the Heritage Foundation. "We would have been better off saying in 1981, we are going to prevent the establishment of another Cuba, any way we have to." "Abrams Admits Errors in Latin America," *International Herald Tribune*, January 5, 1989, p. 3.

6. The UNITAS naval operations and air forces cooperation against disasters, "Operación Confraternidad 88," integrating Argentina, Bolivia, Brazil, Chile, Ecuador, Peru, the United States, and Uruguay.

PART ONE

Global Approaches to Hemispheric Security

1

U.S. Military Doctrines and Their Relation to Foreign Policy

Thomas S. Bodenheimer and Robert Gould

To understand past and present military doctrines, one must analyze the foreign policy objectives these doctrines are designed to implement. Since World War II, U.S. policy has had two major goals: to prevent the development of new socialist or radical nationalist nations in the world (containment), and to force existing socialist or nationalist nations back into the pro-U.S. camp (rollback). Containment involves a defense of the status quo and is compatible with the mutual coexistence of capitalism and socialism as two social systems. Rollback, in contrast, undertakes the more aggressive agenda of eliminating socialist or socialist-leaning nations altogether. Containment and rollback are by no means mutually exclusive; in fact, postwar U.S. foreign policy is best characterized as *selective rollback*—containment of the Soviet Union and Eastern Europe combined with rollback of Third World regimes that are seen by the U.S. government as unfriendly to U.S. interests.[1]

The advent of the Reagan administration marked a shift toward the rollback extreme of the foreign policy spectrum. As a consequence, U.S. military doctrines have moved from more defensive toward more aggressive postures. In three major areas military doctrine has undergone changes during the Reagan era: nuclear, conventional, and unconventional (low-intensity) war doctrine. This chapter outlines U.S. foreign and military policy since World War II and discusses recent debates over nuclear, conventional, and low-intensity war policy in the light of the 1980s shift toward rollback foreign policy goals.

U.S. Postwar Foreign Policy and Military Doctrines

Containment and Selective Rollback

Shortly after World War II, U.S. foreign policy which was most clearly enunciated by the 1947 Truman Doctrine, was based on the concept of containment. Advocates of containment viewed the world situation as an immense conflict between the United States and the expansionist Soviet Union. This conflict required the United States to do everything possible to contain the Soviet Union and to prevent the spread of socialist influence.[2] As a counterpart to containment, the Truman administration created a military doctrine elaborated in National Security Council document NSC-68. This was a plan for building up both nuclear and conventional forces to meet the "communist threat" anywhere in the world. During the Korean War both containment and the buildup of forces as specified in NSC-68 were put into practice.[3] By 1953, the end of the Korean War, the military budget had grown from 4.5 percent of gross national product (GNP) in 1948 to 13.8 percent of GNP.

President Dwight Eisenhower's foreign policy concentrated on economic rather than military strength to ensure U.S. dominance over the USSR. In order to keep the military budget down, Eisenhower built up the relatively inexpensive air force, which included nuclear weapons, while reducing more costly conventional forces. The major operative military doctrine was Secretary of State John Foster Dulles's nuclear "massive retaliation," which came out of Eisenhower's concern to maintain vast military power over a long period of time while avoiding the adverse economic consequences of a large military budget. Massive retaliation was essentially a policy of first strike, a nuclear response to any conventional aggression by communist forces.[4]

Throughout this period there was contention within U.S. leadership circles between those primarily oriented to European (Atlantic) concerns versus those more concerned with Asia and other "peripheral" areas of U.S. influence. Massive retaliation was geared for warfare against the USSR but was not appropriate in the Third World where nuclear weapons were largely useless.[5] Massive retaliation was an Atlanticist doctrine, based on the premise that containing the USSR in Europe was the number one foreign policy objective in the management of U.S. global interests. Eisenhower rejected a full mobilization of U.S. resources capable of carrying out multiple rollback actions in the world. However, he did not neglect the Third World altogether; his administration strengthened the Central Intelligence Agency (CIA) and used it to overthrow unwanted governments in Iran in 1953 and Guatemala in 1954.[6] These actions were early examples of selective Third World rollback. But Eisenhower's policies came under attack by Henry Kissinger and others in the 1950s as not sufficient in deterring revolutionary movements in the Third World. The critics asserted that a local war strategy for non-European areas of the world was needed.[7]

Under the Kennedy administration, these opponents of Eisenhower/ Dulles took on major policymaking roles, and a foreign policy shift developed with greater emphasis given to Asia and the rest of the Third World. Strong movements for decolonization and independence were viewed as threatening U.S. interests, requiring far more emphasis on conventional forces. The Kennedy administration developed the "2½" war strategy: The United States must be ready to fight two major wars (with the USSR and China) and one minor war (for example, Korea) at the same time. If John Kennedy had not built up conventional forces, Lyndon Johnson would not have been ready to intervene so massively in Vietnam.[8]

Defense Secretary Robert McNamara's military doctrine of "flexible response" was a solution to the overemphasis on nuclear war implied in massive retaliation, a doctrine that had become obsolete by the early 1960s due to Soviet advances in nuclear weaponry. As Richard Nixon later stated, massive retaliation was a doctrine reasonable to the era when the United States had overwhelming military strength in the world. However, with growing Soviet power, such a doctrine would mean either paralysis or holocaust.[9] The broad military doctrine of flexible response, which is still in force today, affirms that the United States must be prepared to use every variety of military power from Green Berets to nuclear weapons. The specific weapons depend on the conditions of war, and capability must exist to escalate the conflict from covert operations to conventional warfare to tactical nuclear battle and finally to the use of strategic nuclear weapons.[10]

Flexible response conceded the reality that Soviet nuclear power made massive retaliation impossible; accordingly, its complementary nuclear policy became McNamara's concept of Mutual Assured Destruction (MAD). Under this doctrine, the sole criterion for designing nuclear weapons was the maintenance of a capability to destroy the enemy after the enemy had launched a full-scale attack. The process of nuclear decisionmaking during such events as the Cuban missile crisis convinced McNamara and Kennedy that the risk of nuclear weapons use was far too great.[11] MAD, then, called for the deterrence and avoidance of nuclear war rather than the more aggressive policy of nuclear superiority and first strike. It is true that the United States continued to develop weaponry and targeting plans that fit with first strike scenarios.[12] But in the public policy arena, the acceptance of MAD as a military doctrine was based on a consensus that rollback of the USSR was impossible and that mutual coexistence (guaranteed by deterrent nuclear forces) was the only realistic foreign policy goal.

Within the background of this U.S.-Soviet nuclear stalemate, the Kennedy administration viewed the Third World, not Europe, as the key arena for world conflict; the main Soviet threat was seen as the fomenting of revolution in the Third World.[13] In order to meet this threat, Kennedy's pet project became special operations counterinsurgency forces—the Green Berets.[14] Kennedy also built up the capacity for rapid deployment of troops overseas, a precursor to the "rapid deployment force."[15] During the Kennedy administration, the concept of low-intensity conflict, now a centerpiece of U.S. military doctrine, assumed a new prominence.

The Johnson administration was dominated by the Vietnam War, which utilized a mix of counterinsurgency operations with conventional warfare. Vietnam could be considered as two wars, a containment action fought by ground troops in South Vietnam and a rollback campaign with air strikes against North Vietnam.[16] Vietnam was an example of the flexible response military doctrine, a doctrine implementing the overall foreign policy of containment with selective rollback. The Kennedy-Johnson era provided several examples of Third World rollback including U.S. interventions in Cuba (which failed), Brazil, the Dominican Republic, and Indonesia.[17]

The Nixon Doctrine and Détente

With the Nixon administration came a significant reformulation of containment strategy. The Nixon Doctrine of 1969 was predicated on the recognition that the era of expanding U.S. world power had come to an end.[18] The post–World War II objectives of direct U.S. containment of revolution among the have-nots, as well as the prevention of socialism in Europe, had become too costly economically. Vietnam demonstrated that the United States could be defeated militarily and that, ideologically, the United States was no longer universally perceived as the defender of freedom in the world.

Underlying these changes was the erosion of U.S. economic power, which became evident in the late 1960s. Europe and Japan had reemerged as formidable economic competitors and challenged U.S. industrial supremacy. Furthermore, U.S. military spending abroad, particularly in Vietnam, created a massive balance of payments problem. As a result of these developments, Nixon announced in 1971 the end of the 1944 Bretton Woods agreement that had institutionalized the dollar as the medium of international currency.[19]

It was the relative economic, political, and military decline of the United States that produced the Nixon Doctrine, which assumed that the United States could not sustain its intense involvment in international affairs. Détente was the Soviet Union was an expression of U.S. overextension. According to Henry Kissinger, one of détente's architects, Soviet nuclear parity made the U.S. nuclear arsenal virtually useless. In addition, Kissinger stated that the United States, faced with a relative erosion of its political and economic options, could no longer exert direct control all over the world; it had to encourage others to implement policies consistent with U.S. interests.[20]

Adding to the economic decline, the domestic political response to Vietnam (which included Watergate and the growth of congressional influence over foreign and military policy) brought forth a political environment that made leaders hesitant to further expand U.S. world power through military means. Examples of this trend were the policy of détente, the rapprochement with China, the elimination of the military draft, the SALT I (Strategic Arms Limitation Talks) nuclear arms limitation treaty, the passage of the War Powers Act in Congress, and the Clark amendment regarding noninvolvement in Angola.[21]

The military corollary of the Nixon Doctrine held that the United States could not build military forces capable of meeting the multiple global responses inherent in the flexible response concept. In this view, the United States should reduce emphasis on the military projection of power and substitute diplomatic and economic offensives. Thus the 2½ war doctrine was revised to 1½ wars, a change also linked to the rapprochement with China. And in the nuclear field, military doctrine—consistent with the political policy of détente—remained nuclear parity, not superiority.[22, 23]

A specific consequence of the Nixon Doctrine was the provision of economic aid and the growth of arms sales to friendly countries, thereby supplying the means for those countries to defend themselves from insurgency or attack without the need for U.S. troops. U.S. forces were less frequently used to deal with subversion or guerrilla warfare; rather, insurgency was supposed to be preempted by social and economic programs or defeated by the military power of local governments. The Nixon Doctrine, then, called for decentralized or proxy counterinsurgency, with the major U.S. role confined to the training and arming of others to implement U.S. political/military objectives. The 1973 CIA-assisted overthrow of the Allende government in Chile was an application of the Nixon Doctrine, utilizing covert operations and economic destabilization to project U.S. power.[24] Chile was an early example of low-intensity warfare doctrine, though with markedly less emphasis on the outright military aspects of that doctrine.

The early Carter administration went even further than the Nixon/ Ford administrations in deemphasizing military power in favor of the

Trilateral Commission's political strategies that emphasized trade rather than war. The reestablishment of U.S. power in the world was seen as integrally related to the solution of the world economic crisis. In addition, the early Carter administration, dominated by trilateralists, placed its major priority on the defense of Europe. Under Jimmy Carter, détente continued, arms sales were reduced, and the Nuclear Nonproliferation Act was passed; also, a human rights policy reduced some U.S. commitments to Third World dictators. However, the maintenance of U.S. surrogates through the world—the Nixon Doctrine—remained a cornerstone of U.S. policy.

By 1979, in response to numerous upheavals in the Third World (the U.S. defeat in Southeast Asia, the independence of Portuguese Africa, the overthrow of the Shah of Iran and of Anastasio Somoza in Nicaragua), the assumptions behind the Nixon Doctrine and the related policy of détente were fundamentally challenged. Leading this challenge was the Committee on the Present Danger (CPD), which claimed that the Soviet Union posed a major challenge to U.S. interests, and that the United States must reestablish the primacy of its military power to combat all revolutionary threats in the Third World—threats that were automatically assumed to be examples of Soviet expansionism.[25] A foreign policy shift back toward aggressive containment and rollback was evident.

Military doctrine responded accordingly. The new Carter Doctrine claimed the right to use military force in the Persian/Arabian Gulf if necessary. The rapid deployment force concept for protecting the oilfields of the Gulf was enunciated and partially developed. Draft registration began. And in the nuclear area, the increased technological capacity to accurately knock out Soviet military targets laid the groundwork for a resurgence of the belief that nuclear weapons are not simply deterrents but can actually be used.[26] Presidential Directive (PD) 59 endorsed the use of limited nuclear options and a counterforce nuclear strategy (hitting military rather than civilian targets to knock out the USSR's ability to retaliate), which were the first steps toward a more aggressive nuclear stance.[27]

The Reagan Administration and Rollback

During most of the Reagan administration, the Committee on the Present Danger strongly influenced international policy, which resulted in major alterations in foreign and military doctrine. Central to these changes was the rejection of détente as the guiding principle of international relations and its replacement with the belief that the United States should reestablish its dominant role in the world. According to this view, all unfriendly movements in the world were caused by Soviet expansionism, which must not only be contained but defeated. Such a policy entailed a rejection of the Nixon Doctrine's realpolitik of coexistence with the Soviets. The new stance of confrontation with the Soviet Union, clearly articulated by the influential right-wing think tank, the Heritage Foundation, was embraced by President Ronald Reagan himself, as the following statements indicate: "The Soviet Union underlies all the unrest that is going on. If they weren't engaged in this game of dominoes, there wouldn't be any hotspots in the world. . . . [The] final step [in] the Communist master plan is to conquer the United States. . . . The march of freedom and democracy . . . will leave Marxism-Leninism on the ash heap of history."[28, 29]

Important sectors of the right wing, with major influence within the Reagan administration, attempted to move the U.S. government from its 35-year policy of containment/selective rollback to a policy of global rollback, that is, the conversion—through political, economic, or military action—of socialist or socialist-leaning nations back to capitalism. For the most avid rollback advocates, this included the Soviet Union itself.

While the late Reagan administration moderated its foreign policy positions, the first six years of the Reagan era revealed a strong inclination to support global rollback: (1) the Reagan Doctrine held that the United States should support or foment insurgencies against socialist or radical nationalist governments. Examples of the United States actually assisting in attempts to overthrow socialist governments were the wars in Nicaragua, Angola, Afghanistan, Libya, and Grenada. The Heritage Foundation, a major adviser to the Reagan government, proposed adding Ethiopia, Iran, Laos, Vietnam, and Cambodia to this list. Ronald Reagan stated in 1980 that Cuba must be removed from the Soviet sphere. (2) There were, particularly during Reagan's first term, numerous statements from administration spokesmen calling for the rollback of the USSR and Eastern Europe. Such national security advisers as Richard Pipes developed sophisticated strategies to rollback the Soviet Union. A national security document of 1982 was reported in the press to endorse a policy to shrink the Soviet empire. Both the president and the secretary of state stated that the United States did not forever recognize Soviet domination over Eastern Europe.[30]

While an integrated rollback policy toward the Soviet Union and support for Third World revolution had a strong following among top Reagan administration policymakers, such a view was not unchallenged within the administration. A powerful sector of the business community saw trade with the East as preferable to confrontation and thus opposed any form of rollback applied directly to the Soviet Union. Those interests provided the impetus that moved the late Reagan administration toward a politics of summitry and cautious arms control.

Yet the foreign policy shift of the 1980s had important consequences for nuclear, conventional, and unconventional military doctrine. Recent debates over nuclear doctrine have challenged the concept of deterrence (Mutual Assured Destruction), moving toward the ideas of survivable or winnable nuclear war, first strike, and the militarization of space.[31] The 1½ war doctrine was challenged by the doctrine of unlimited horizontal escalation. And insurgency strategies to overthrow socialist-leaning nations of the Third World acquired a central role in the Reagan administration under the name "low-intensity conflict." The remainder of this chapter describes some of these recent debates over military doctrine and discusses in some detail the doctrine of low-intensity conflict.

The Nuclear War Debate

Under the Reagan administration, a highly significant debate took place over nuclear doctrine. The foreign policy underpinning of this debate was the controversy over containment versus rollback of the Soviet Union. The polar positions were the continuation of McNamara's Mutual Assured Destruction (containment), on the one hand, and the acceptance of the notion that nuclear war can actually be fought and won (rollback), on the other.

Paul Warnke, President Carter's Arms Control and Disarmament Agency director, referred to this debate as one between the schools of deterrence (MAD) versus nuclear utilization target selection (NUTS). The latter is more commonly called the nuclear warfighting school—proponents believe that nuclear weapons can be used with an acceptable level of destruction. The ultimate position in the nuclear warfighting school is the concept of a winnable nuclear war—that the United States can actually win a nuclear war against the USSR and can survive as a viable society. Warnke stated in 1982 that the debate betwen MAD and NUTS seemed to have been settled a decade ago, but that it reemerged in the 1980s with NUTS the apparent winner.[32]

While the policy of nuclear warfighting existed in the Eisenhower years as massive retaliation, the development of Soviet nuclear strength eclipsed that policy until the Nixon administration, when the development of highly accurate counterforce weapons had the potential of giving the United States a revived period of nuclear superiority. In the later Carter years, this policy gained influence with the promulgation of PD-59.[33, 34] Nuclear war fighting doctrine had even stronger expression under the Reagan government.[35] Fred Ikle, undersecretary of defense and a key figure in formulating Reagan's nuclear policy, argued that deterrence is an insufficient strategy. An important member of the Committee on the Present Danger, Ikle worked at the Rand Corporation, at Harvard with Kissinger, and with both right-wing and moderate corporate think tanks—the American Enterprise Institute and the Council on Foreign Relations. His major argument against deterrence held that the Soviets moved far ahead of the United States in the 1970s in military spending and preparedness (although the CIA's own estimates belied this), that the Soviets believed in winning a nuclear war against the United States, and thus that the United States must be prepared to fight and win a nuclear war in return. A corollary to the doctrine of nuclear warfighting is the goal of nuclear superiority rather than the simple parity needed for effective deterrence.[36]

Others in the Committee on the Present Danger who took a nuclear warfighting stance and who subsequently joined the Reagan administration, were Richard Perle, assistant defense secretary; Richard Pipes, National Security Council adviser specializing in Soviet affairs; and Eugene Rostow, former head of the Arms Control and Disarmament Agency. Colin Gray, another former Reagan adviser, wrote in an article in *Foreign Policy* (1980) entitled "Victory is Possible," that "the United States should plan to defeat the Soviet Union and to do so at a cost that would not prohibit U.S. recovery. Washington should identify war aims that in the last resort would contemplate the destruction of Soviet political authority and the emergence of a postwar world order compatible with Western values."[37]

George Bush has stated, "You have a capability that inflicts more damage on the opposition than it can inflict upon you. That's the way you can have a . . . winner in a nuclear exchange."[38] Reagan himself has said, "We've still been following the Mutual Assured Destruction plan that was given birth by McNamara, and it was a ridiculous plan. . . . The difficulty with that was that the Soviet Union decided some time ago that a nuclear war was possible and winnable."[39]

The rejection of deterrence by President Reagan and many of his advisers was translated into formal administration policy in National Security Decision Document (NSDD) 13, signed by Reagan in 1982. NSDD 13 represented the first time a U.S. administration has proclaimed that U.S. forces must be able to win a nuclear war.[40] According to Robert Scheer, who conducted multiple interviews with high-level Reagan officials, NSDD 13 resolved the debate between deterrence and nuclear warfighting strategies in favor of those who believed in the possibility of fighting and winning a protracted nuclear war.[41, 42]

Because this change in nuclear policy came under strong criticism, the administration sought to modify its public posture with statements that nuclear war was unthinkable and unwinnable. In addition, the administration took the public position that the Strategic Defense Initiative

(SDI) would allow an effective nuclear defense that would make offensive deterrence unnecessary. Even so, it was revealed by the *New York Times* in 1985 that the administration had developed a nuclear warfighting plan integrating SDI with a host of new offensive weaponry.[43]

Critics of the Reagan government continued to hold that its actions demonstrated a belief in survivable or winnable nuclear war. Evidence cited by such critics included the massive increase in the military budget far beyond what was needed for deterrence/parity, the advocacy of weapons such as the MX missile, which are viewed by many experts as first strike weapons, and the absolute refusal to allow great power negotiation over the Strategic Defense Initiative, seen by many experts as a destabilizing system that, when taken together with other offensive weapon development, could be an integral component of a strong first strike capability.[44, 45] Moreover, SDI has been promoted by adherents of Soviet rollback as a means of economic destabilization of the USSR; SDI would draw the Soviets into a program of costly weapons expenditures that could cripple their current drive toward economic modernization.

The centrality of SDI to the rollback enthusiasts is substantiated by events surrounding the Reagan-Gorbachev summits, in which the United States continued to hold to an uncompromising line on the SDI. Some people might argue that Reagan advocacy of mutual strategic ballistic missile reductions indicates that the late Reagan administration rejected the goal of nuclear superiority. This appearance is misleading. The SDI would be more effective as a defensive shield against Soviet attack if the Soviets have substantially fewer ballistic missiles; thus there are first strike advantages to the United States offered by an SDI developed in conjunction with sharp bilateral offensive missile cuts while retaining strategic bombers and cruise missiles. In fact, such an arrangement could conceivably bring back the U.S. nuclear superiority lost in the 1960s.[46] Secretary of State George Shultz underscored this desire for superiority when he said, "With a large inventory of aircraft and cruise missiles, the United States and NATO [North Atlantic Treaty Organization] would retain a powerful nuclear capability. In a sense, we would return to the situation of the 1950's when strategic bombers served as our primary nuclear deterrent force. . . . It would be a much more diverse and capable force than in previous decades."[47]

To summarize, the foreign policy debate over containment versus rollback of the USSR was expressed in the nuclear area with heated disagreement over parity versus superiority, deterrence versus first strike capability. While the more moderate containment advocates held the advantage at the end of the Reagan years, the promoters of nuclear superiority and warfighting had gained considerable power in nuclear decisionmaking.

Conventional War and Horizontal Escalation

In the realm of conventional warfare, an all-embracing military doctrine appeared under the Reagan government—the doctrine of horizontal escalation. Under this doctrine, according to Reagan's national security advisers, "no area of the world is beyond the scope of American interest . . . [we must have] sufficient military standing to cope with any level of violence" around the globe.[48] Horizontal escalation means that if the Soviets move in one area of the world, the United States would move somewhere else to attack an asset highly valued by the Soviets.[49] For example, if the Soviets attack Iran, the United States could go into Eastern Europe. Or if the Soviets make gains in southern Africa, the United States could move into Cuba.[50] In the words of Defense Secretary Caspar Weinberger, the United States "might choose not to restrict [itself] to meeting aggression on its own immediate front. We might decide to stretch our capabilities, to engage the enemy in many places. . . ."[51]

One proponent of horizontal escalation, Vernon Aspaturian, a Soviet expert formerly with the Rand Corporation, proposed that the best defense of Europe might be to threaten valued Soviet assets outside of Europe, for example Cuba or Vietnam. Aspaturian suggested that it was unwise to attack the Soviet empire at its strongest point, and wrote: "There is an old Russian folk-proverb that 'the cloth unravels at its edge,' and in the case of the Soviet empire, the unraveling process is most easily initiated at its margins."[52] Horizontal escalation, then, is a military doctrine designed to implement the foreign policy of global rollback.

The Background: Europe Versus the Third World

Prior to the Reagan years, foreign and military policy analysts, understanding the limitations of U.S. power, had made priorities to determine which regions of the world would be allocated the finite quantity of military resources. In its extreme form, horizontal escalation holds the view that the United States must be militarily prepared in all areas of the world at once.

The background to horizontal escalation doctrine is the major postwar debate within the foreign policy establishment over the prioritization of Europe versus other areas of the world. Initially, this debate pitted the Atlanticists against the China lobby, with the latter arguing that the rollback of the Chinese revolution was more important than the defense of Europe. During the early postwar years, the Atlanticists were often rooted in the "liberal" Eastern establishment, whereas China lobby advocates were generally conservatives from the West and the Sunbelt.[53]

For most of the postwar period, the Atlanticists have played a predominant role in U.S. foreign policy, with the consequence that U.S. military power has been concentrated in Europe to a degree far in excess of its actual utilization. The Kennedy administration made the first major challenge to this European emphasis, seeing the Third World as the main arena of importance. Currently, many military/security strategists are again moving their focus away from Europe and toward the Third World.

The U.S. Army has traditionally been oriented toward Europe, with the navy and marines more preoccupied with the Third World. According to the prominent military expert Jeffrey Record, the army should shift its emphasis and join with the navy in projecting U.S. military force toward the Third World. Record argued that during the past 30 years, the U.S. Army's main planning has been for ground combat against Soviet troops in Europe. However, two developments should alter this focus: (1) the steady disintegration of NATO as an instrument of collective security capable of mustering an adequate forward defense of Western Europe, and (2) emergence of a host of new threats to vital U.S. interests in the Persian/Arabian Gulf and other areas outside Europe.[54]

Record, echoing the concerns of many U.S. commentators, argued that Europeans must take on the task of defending themselves; the United States cannot continue to commit huge resources in countries that are less willing than is the United States to defend themselves. During the past decade, the United States has accounted for 65 percent of NATO military expenditures and has maintained 45 percent of NATO's active duty military personnel. In May 1977, NATO members pledged to increase their military budgets by 3 percent above inflation. Few have done this, while the United States has been increasing military spending by 7.5 percent above inflation. Europe also participates inadequately in the defense of the Gulf, though European nations need the oil more than the United States does.

At the same time, according to Record's argument, as colonialism has disintegrated, the Third World has become a complex unstable arena of both hostile and friendly states. In addition, U.S. dependence on foreign oil, as well as on strategic metals and minerals, has increased. Record asserted that far more likely than the need to counter direct Soviet aggression is the necessity of combating terrorism, rebellion, or revolution in Third World countries, whether this "subversion" is Soviet sponsored or purely indigenous.[55]

Furthermore, Western Europe has developed political goals distinct from those of the United States. Many European governments want to see reduced U.S. commitments in the Third World to allow the U.S. military to strengthen its defense of Europe. Europe overall did not support U.S. involvement in Vietnam, and has similarly held back from support of U.S. military involvement in Central America. Thus, why concentrate so many U.S. resources with an uncertain ally?

The counterargument is that except for the Gulf, there is no area of the world more important than Europe; if Europe went into the Soviet camp, the United States could not survive as a major economic power. Therefore, even though it may be unlikely that the Soviets would invade Western Europe, such a contingency must be prevented at all costs. This eurocentric policy has tended to be favored by some military officials in the Pentagon, who grew up on war in Europe, trained in Europe, and receive large budgets and military equipment based on conventional military methods applicable to Europe. However, the Reagan administration elevated non-European military contingencies to a priority equal to that of the NATO–Warsaw Pact scenario.[56]

A Critique of Horizontal Escalation

While the debate over Europe versus the Third World continues, the doctrine of horizontal escalation tries to beg this question, holding that the United States must be able to fight on many fronts at once. Reagan's original plan for military buildup was projected to allow for the capacity to conduct horizontal escalation.[57]

Not all military experts believe that horizontal escalation is a viable strategy. In the view of Jeffrey Record, who called Reagan's military doctrine "the strategy of worldwide war," the meeting of all U.S. commitments in the world would require greater expenditures even than the Reagan administration's creation of a 600-ship/15-carrier navy and increased number of divisions. It is also doubtful that an all-volunteer army can fulfill all U.S. commitments. Moreover, Pentagon waste means that a growing military budget is not necessarily translated into effective fighting power.[58] In 1982, U.S. Army Chief of Staff Edward Meyer said, "We are accepting tremendous risks with the size of forces that we have to do what we have pledged to do."[59]

Jeffrey Record even went so far as to say that Reagan's doctrine was dangerous and would lead to defeat because its goals far exceeded the resources available to implement them. The strategy invited a dispersion of limited resources, thereby violating the fundamental principle of concentration. According to Frederick the Great, "He who attempts to defend too much, defends nothing."[60]

Horizontal escalation is a doctrine related to the global rollback foreign policy that was pursued by major elements in the Reagan administration. The pre-Reagan selective rollback policy required the capacity for a military response in limited areas of the world at any one time. Depending on whether the emphasis was on military containment or political/economic containment, this policy was consistent with the 2½ or 1½ war capacity. A policy of generalized rollback requires military capacity not only to defend against threats to capitalist nations but also to initiate attacks on socialist or socialist-leaning governments. Eventually, opposition to horizontal escalation within the Reagan government developed as this doctrine was demonstrated to be fiscally unrealistic. While Defense Secretary Weinberger at one time officially adopted horizontal escalation as policy,[61] he later stated that the United States could not afford the capacity to intervene everywhere in the world simultaneously. Budgetary realities of the late 1980s placed global horizontal escalation on the back burner.

Low-Intensity Conflict in the Third World

To meet the challenge U.S. power posed by Third World socialist and radical nationalist regimes and revolutionary insurgencies, the 1980s witnessed a renewed emphasis on the military doctrine of low-intensity conflict.[62] Because this doctrine is so critical for the implementation of the Reagan and post-Reagan foreign policy, the remainder of this chapter will concentrate on low-intensity conflict.

A recently proposed definition of low-intensity conflict for the revised U.S. Army Field Manual on the subject reads as follows:

> The limited use of power for political purposes by nations or organizations . . . to coerce, control or defend a population, to control or defend a territory or establish or defend rights. It includes military operations by or against irregular forces, peacekeeping operations, terrorism, counter-terrorism, rescue operations and military assistance under conditions of armed conflict. This form of conflict does not include protracted engagements of opposing regular forces.[63]

To put it more succinctly, low-intensity conflict involves help to friendly nations in countering insurgencies, assistance to friendly resistance movements, and the fight against terrorism.[64]

Historical Development

The roots of the low-intensity conflict doctrine can be traced to the late 1950s and early 1960s, and its full expression came in the counterinsurgency policy of the Kennedy administration. Counterinsurgency warfare was designed to meet the challenge of the many national liberation "people's wars" taking place throughout the world, at a time when the seriousness of the breach between China and the USSR had not revealed itself in its totality.

As developed by Kennedy administration ideologues such as Walt Rostow and Roger Hilsman, counterinsurgency doctrine encompassed a number of assumptions and components:

1. That a global threat existed in the form of a unified Communist strategy to advance its cause without risking either conventional or nuclear war, exploiting the modernization process throughout the Third World, and using the proven techniques of guerrilla warfare;

2. That the United States had the duty and the power to confront and defeat this challenge, ideally without the necessity of intervening directly with military forces;

3. That in order to accomplish its task, the United States had to adopt a novel approach: both military strategy, that is, fighting against guerrilla groups, and political and economic strategy involving all agencies of the U.S. government overseas; that the central objective of the U.S. action was to improve the ability of the threatened regime to govern effectively and to help it generate sufficient popular support to thwart the Communist strategy of fomenting a people's war; and that coordination and unification of the U.S. effort both in the field and in Washington were critical to its success.[65]

Although counterinsurgency doctrine achieved successes in combating insurgencies in Latin America, it foundered in the Vietnam War, leading to its temporary eclipse and a return to traditional conventional war fighting doctrines. Counterinsurgency expert Douglas Blaufarb has commented extensively on the reasons for the Vietnam failure. The decline in counterinsurgency doctrine in the 1970s was reflected in the rapid drop of funding for Special Operations Forces (SOF), which fell from its Vietnam War peak of over $1 billion per year to under $100 million in FY 1975. With the rise of a resurgent interventionary U.S. military and foreign policy in the late Carter administration, carried through to the Reagan epoch, the SOF has undergone an unprecedented "peacetime" expansion.[66]

One key reason for the increased importance of low-intensity conflict has been the recognition of the failure or limited value of other forms of warfare for the Third World. The Carter administration placed its emphasis on the rapid deployment force (RDF), a tactic in which U.S. troops, from the U.S. mainland or forward bases, would swoop in, conduct their operations, and then either stay or leave. This concept was particularly oriented toward the protection of Middle Eastern oilfields but has historic precedents in the frequent landings of U.S. Marines in the Western Hemisphere, with recent examples including the Dominican Republic in 1965 and Grenada in 1983. The RDF has been criticized as ineffective against guerrilla units and difficult to support logistically far from the U.S. mainland in the absence of friendly military bases.[67]

The RDF has not had great success in accomplishing U.S. objectives.[68] Even about the virtually uncontested military conflict in Grenada, where special operations forces were employed within an RDF-style operation, Pentagon sources have admitted to serious mistakes; for example, 4 members of the navy's elite SEAL (Sea-Air-Land) Commando unit drowned in a preinvasion accident, several Army Rangers were killed when 2 U.S. helicopters collided, and 14 soldiers were wounded when a U.S. air strike was deployed to the wrong location.[69] The doctrine of low-intensity conflict is designed to avoid the problems of the RDF.

The development of low-intensity conflict is also related to the limited success of another military doctrine—the proxy war, which is bolstered by arms sales and military aid. This conception, although used extensively under the Truman Doctrine, is particularly derivative from the Nixon Doctrine of 1969, which held that the United States must assist local governments in fighting their own wars. Proxy wars have had a checkered record; in Vietnam, even massive U.S. economic and military support of the South Vietnamese government could not keep that government from collapsing after the withdrawal of U.S. troops. Proxy governments are often unreliable allies or have interests that diverge to some degree from those of the United States, thereby impeding U.S. objectives. For example, Guatemala and Honduras were too concerned with their own internal stability to offer their troops for an invasion of Nicaragua. Another serious problem comes about when the arms sales and military aid provided fall into the hands of an enemy force, Iran being the major example. Even when the U.S.-allied government remains in power, U.S. arms can filter to insurgent groups; according to a U.S. Defense Department spokesman, fully 50 percent of weapons used by the insurgents in El Salvador are U.S. weapons taken from the Salvadoran army.[70]

The rise in arms sales to friendly governments under the Reagan administration, including the sale of arms-producing technology,[71] shows that proxy war has by no means been eliminated from the U.S. military arsenal; however, proxy war is insufficient for handling the priority Third World arena and has become integrated into the broader conception of low-intensity conflict.

Reagan's Buildup of Special Operations

Under the Reagan administration, low-intensity conflict expanded from its previous use as a counterinsurgency strategy. This expansion was based on the needs of the foreign policy known as the Reagan Doctrine, the internationally coordinated strategy of undercutting socialist and radical nationalist nations through military, economic, and political means. Rather than counterinsurgency (action against organizations that threaten friendly governments), the Reagan Doctrine holds that the United States should assist/foment insurgencies against established governments. The Reagan Doctrine is the policy of rollback in the Third World. Its most visible example is Nicaragua, where a proxy army of Nicaraguans entirely organized by the United States has been fighting the Nicaraguan government using techniques of low-intensity warfare taught by the United States. Other examples are the U.S.-financed resistance movement in Afghanistan, and the U.S.-backed, South Africa-linked, resistance movement in Angola.

The Reagan administration considered the expansion of the U.S. Special Operations Forces—the military commando units trained for low-intensity conflict—one of its highest priorities. Low-intensity conflict has become the major way to confront anti-U.S. upheavals in the Third World. A good example of the centrality of the strategy of low-intensity conflict in the Reagan years is the following February 1984 quote from Caspar Weinberger: "The high priority we have assigned to SOF revitalization reflects our recognition that low-level conflict—for which the SOF are uniquely suited—will pose the threat we are most likely to encounter throughout the end of this century."[72]

The Pentagon acknowleges that Special Operations Forces are the most heavily used U.S. military forces today and the most likely to engage in combat in the future. Since 1981, money for SOF has more than tripled, with total FY 1986 funds for special operations running about $1.5 billion. Future Pentagon plans call for spending $7.6 billion in the five years beginning in 1988.[73] The number of active duty SOF troops has increased almost 30 percent to its current level of about 15,000, with reserves bringing the number to 32,000. By 1990, active duty manpower will be up to 20,900, an 80 percent increase over 1981, with the total forces numbering 38,400. With this expansion in personnel, there has also been an enormous expansion in the highly specialized weapons stockpile.[74]

Special Operations Forces now make up 25 to 35 percent of all U.S. Military Training Teams (MTT) abroad, and are training armies in Latin America, Africa, the Middle East, Asia and Europe; under the Reagan administration, the number of MTT work-weeks abroad increased more than fivefold since 1980. SOF affords the executive branch a distinct advantage in that unlike the CIA's covert operations, the Pentagon is not required to report details of the SOF's activities to Congress. These forces can therefore be used in clandestine activites to avoid congressional oversight. SOF have been more active in Central America than in any other region: 55 Special Forces military adviser/trainers worked in El Salvador; more than 150 Green Berets in Honduras trained over 5,000 Salvadoran and 5,000 Honduran troops; Special Forces were deployed in the almost continuous series of military exercises there; and navy SEALs conducted exercises in the Gulf of Fonseca.[75]

The use of unconventional warfare tactics in Central America is consistent with recommendations of a 1984 panel convened by Undersecretary of Defense for Policy Fred Ikle, and headed by retired Army Major General John K. Singlaub. Singlaub, as head of both the World Anti-Communist League (WACL) and its U.S. chapter, the United States Council for World Freedom (USCWF), has claimed to have raised millions of dollars in arms for the Nicaraguan contras. This has been supplemented by the tens of millions of dollars generated through the complex web of private individuals and foreign powers exposed through the "Contragate" revelations. In addition, the 1986 congressional contra aid package allowed Special Forces to provide direct training to the contra forces in Honduras and in the United States. In its full expression, low-intensity conflict involves a mix of U.S. and foreign, public and private, covert and overt resources to carry out U.S. objectives overseas.

The Role of Psychological Operations

A special role is accorded within Special Operations Forces for psychological operations ("psyops"), with activities that complement the well-known CIA activities in this area of "hearts and minds" warfare. The U.S. Army Field Manual 33-5 defines psychological operations as the use of propaganda and other means to influence opinions, attitudes, emotions, and behavior of friendly, neutral, or hostile groups. The U.S. Army Manual 100-20 states that in counterinsurgency operations, "Psyops are conducted to exploit grievances and raised expectations, to influence the populace, and to promote the loyalty of insurgent members."[76]

According to psyops teachings, "Military deception is an aspect of strategy and tactics that is often used but seldom acknowledged . . . deception is the deliberate misrepresentaiton of reality done to gain a competitive advantage . . . [the terms lying and deception] are often used interchangeably."[77]

Psyop troops have recently consisted of one active duty psyop group with 3 battalions stationed at Fort Bragg and 3 reserve psyop groups with 9 battalions and 22 companies, with another active duty battalion to be added by 1990; these troops make use of all means of mass communication in carrying out their work.

Some examples of psyops revealed to the public in the past few years include the following:

- In Grenada, after the U.S. invasion, psyop troops took control of radio stations and other communication facilities and carried out a major campaign using radio broadcasts, publications, pro-U.S. signs and other means. At the time of the Grenadian election a year later, the U.S. psyop troops backed the successful candidacy of Prime Minister Herbert Blaize;
- In Nicaragua, CIA psyops have included the *Psychological Operations in Guerrilla War* manual distributed to the contra forces. The manual includes chapters on "Combatant-Propagandist Guerrillas," "Armed Propaganda," and "Development and Control of Front Organizations." Other sections include "implicit and explicit terror" and selective use of violence, including "neutralizing" Sandinista officials, hiring professional criminals, coercing individuals to join the contras, and creating "martyrs" to inspire the contra forces. In addition, psyops against Nicaragua took on a more "subtle" context: A good example of this was the consistent use of the threat of intervention against the Nicaraguans, exemplified by the MiG crisis of November 1984. This threat had the effect of intimidating and panicking the Nicaraguans to keep them in a demoralized state of constant war preparation;
- In El Salvador, with the assistance of the U.S. Information Agency, the Salvadoran Division of Psychological Operations (D-5), directly supervised by the Salvadoran Joint Chiefs of Staff, launched a propaganda effort to attract public support away from the guerrillas to President Napoleón Duarte;
- In the summer of 1986, the Reagan administration attempted to destabilize Libya by means of a disinformation campaign conducted through the U.S. press.

Psyops has been formally used by the U.S. military since World War II, and psychological warfare units accompanied conventional ground forces both in World War II and Korea. In 1952 the Psychological Warfare Center was created at Fort Bragg. While psyops has historically been linked to Special Operations Forces, some military experts feel that all military actions—whether covert special operations or conventional warfare or preparing populations prior to war—require a psyops component.[78]

Economic Destabilization

Although not a military doctrine, economic destabilization of socialist or radical nationalist governments is a critical tactic of the Reagan Doctrine of Third World rollback and is an integral part of low-intensity conflict. This tactic is designed to prevent the necessity of direct military intervention and may use proxy armies as a central feature. Economic destabilization avoids the problem of political destabilization within the United States caused by public opposition to direct U.S. intervention. In one sense, the adoption of this tactic represents a defeat for U.S. power, with military intervention less feasible than it was prior to Vietnam. But in itself, economic destabilization is a powerful weapon of the United States to destroy a government by causing disaffection among its population.

A classic historical example of economic destabilization was the covert, CIA-planned 1973 overthrow of the Allende government in Chile.[79] A more recent example was the U.S. operation to overthrow the government of Nicaragua. In Nicaragua, unlike Chile, the Sandinista government disbanded the previous military and substituted its own loyal army. Thus, in addition to the use of economic sanctions (for example, the reduction of the sugar quota and pressure on lending institutions to cut off loans, actions that cost Nicaragua U.S.$1 billion in lost credits and exports between 1981 and 1985 and that were analogous to those sanctions used in Chile), the case of Nicaragua demonstrates economic destabilization principally conducted through armed insurgency. The CIA-run contra war reduced the harvest of crops needed for foreign exchange and cut the production of crops for internal consumption, leading to price increases, food shortages, speculation, and black marketeering. In addition, the war forced precious funds, food, medications, and personnel into the defense sector, causing shortages in the civilian economy.[80]

The result of such economic warfare was the creation of a dissatisfied middle-class fifth column within Nicaragua that could link up with the contras, weakening the society internally such that the government might either collapse or become a more susceptible target to military intervention. The strong point of this form of covert economic warfare is that—compared with an invading army—the enemy is less visible so that the people are likely to blame their own government rather than the United States for their difficulties.

Complementing the use of psychological operations, diplomatic isolation, and military threats or actions, covert economic destabilization is one of the most effective tactics of low-intensity conflict pursued by the U.S. government.

Current Limitations of Special Operations Strategies

There remain questions within the military about the present ability of the United States to engage in a sustained insurgency or counter-insurgency low-intensity conflict. According to former Deputy Assistant Defense Secretary Noel Koch, insufficient money, men, equipment, and training have been allocated; also, language and cross-cultural capabilities, extremely important for this type of warfare, have been "marginally adequate" for Spanish-speaking regions and seriously deficient for all other areas.[81]

Colonel John Waghelstein, an analyst with the Strategic Studies Institute of the U.S. Army War College, who has held a variety of command positions, including responsibility for the U.S. Army Military Group in El Salvador, believes that low-intensity conflict preparation has been given short shrift. Writing in the May 1985 issue of *Military Review*, Waghelstein stated that low-intensity conflict/counterinsurgency involves two distinct uses of the U.S. military:

1. The quick strike of the Grenada operation, for which the United States is trained and equipped.
2. The assistance of an ally in politico-military operations to combat armed insurgents, a role for which the U.S. military is unprepared, with the state of preparedness for this second role being at its lowest point in 20 years.

Waghelstein has stated that the army does have instruction in low-intensity conflict at the U.S. Army Command and General Staff College at Fort Leavenworth, Kansas, but that overall there is not enough emphasis placed on the subject. Waghelstein believes that the army failed in the early 1960s to make any serious attempt to develop counterinsurgency doctrine and training, and that the same criticisms carry over today.

Waghelstein does think that changes are being made to correct the situation—for example, the revival and expansion of the Special Forces since 1979—but that preparations remain inadequate, with the military keeping its big unit, high technology orientation.[82]

Some of the inadequate support given to low-intensity conflict may reflect the old divisions between the Third World–oriented proponents of counterinsurgency and the Atlanticists geared toward more conventional modes of warfare. According to Noel Koch, Special Operations have continued to be viewed by the latter military people as a backwater area that drains resources from what they consider to be the more important European area of conventional operations. For example, in January 1986, senior Pentagon officials and operational commanders charged that Special Forces were ill prepared because the air force had neglected them in favor of building up its force of fighter planes.

Special Operations has historically received low interest from military contractors and Congress because these programs lack "big ticket" equipment programs that provide jobs in congressional districts and high profits for defense companies.[83] Serious rifts exist between military-related industry, which is interested in more and bigger weapons at the highest possible cost, and policymakers worried about national security and the federal deficit, who want an effective fighting force, which may not involve larger weapons or higher costs. Nevertheless, Special Operations Forces have recently achieved greater status through the congressional authorization, over objections from the traditional services, to integrate all unconventional forces under the First Special Operations Command, to be headed by its own four-star general and its own assistant secretary of defense for special operations and low-intensity conflict.

Conclusion

In this chapter, we have tried to show how military doctrines of a particular period are related to the more general foreign policy objectives of that period. Within an overall postwar objective of containment and selective rollback, U.S. foreign policy has shifted from the aggressive containment of the 1946 to 1969 period to relative détente between 1969 and 1979, and then toward a greater orientation toward rollback during the 1980s. The related military doctrines have also had a certain constancy but also a variability based on the foreign policy shifts. Nuclear doctrine moved from massive retaliation based on actual superiority to deterrence/parity, and more recently back toward a still-debated goal of superiority. Nonnuclear doctrine moved from a Europe-centered World War II–type warfare toward a policy of low-intensity conflict for both insurgency and counterinsurgency.

Concurrently, as foreign policy has dictated changes in military emphasis, a steady growth of military technology—not discussed in this chapter—has had a marked impact on military doctrine.

The military doctrines described in this chapter are all based on the concept that the USSR is a likely aggressor and that the United States needs strong defense against such aggression. However, according to a Brookings Institution study, the USSR has exhibited prudence and restraint in its foreign policy,[84] and the USSR is not the prime mover of most revolutionary movements in the Third World.[85] Thus it is reasonable to consider that current U.S. military doctrines, although couched in defensive language, in fact have an offensive component designed to implement the aggressive foreign policy of rollback.

Finally, it is important to consider the relationships among the nuclear, conventional, and unconventional military postures, which are summarized in the conception of "escalation dominance." Escalation dominance refers to the ability to prevail in a war at each stage of potential or actual escalation of that war. If a low-intensity conflict erupts into a regional conventional war, the United States must be capable of winning that larger war. If the regional war spreads to other areas of the world, the United States must be able to win all the battles at the same time. And if a regional or conventional worldwide conflict escalates into nuclear war, the United States must be capable of winning the nuclear confrontation.

Therefore, an active policy of promoting low-intensity insurgencies against established socialist or radical nationalist nations ultimately dictates a doctrine of nuclear superiority rather than simple deterrent parity. In this sense there is a clear relation between aggressive low-intensity conflict, military preparation to support conventional horizontal escalation, and nuclear superiority including the militarization of space.

That this relation is paramount to U.S. policymakers was underscored by the release in January 1988 of the report of the Commission on Integrated Long-Term Strategy.[86] This commission, chaired by Fred Ikle and Albert Wohlstetter, included a broad spectrum of prominent opinionmakers such as Henry Kissinger, Zbigniew Brzezinski, John Vessey, and Samuel Huntington. Reflecting an appreciation for the nation's need to reprioritize its military strategies to correspond to the changing nature of the modern world, the report, *Discriminate Deterrence*, proposes an "integrated" approach to the military doctrines we have described, centered on the newer SDI-type technologies. Expanding on classic nuclear warfighting doctrine, the panel calls for "discriminate" use of high-tech nuclear and nonnuclear devices, both in conventional and low-intensity battlefields. And to circumvent the domestic unpopularity of most military interventions, the panel proposes further development of proxy forces backed up by high-tech U.S. firepower, avoiding if possible the direct use of U.S. troops. Without question, escalation dominance will play a central role in the evolving military doctrines of the 1990s.

Notes

1. Thomas Bodenheimer and Robert Gould, *Rollback! Right-Wing Power in U.S. Foreign Policy* (Boston: South End Press, 1989), ch. 1.

2. Franz Schurmann, *The Logic of World Power* (New York: Pantheon Books, 1974), 76–78, 91–107.

3. Daniel Kaufman, Jeffrey McKitrick, and Thomas Leney, *U.S. National Security: A Framework for Analysis* (Lexington, Mass.: Lexington Books, 1985), ch. 20.

4. Fred Kaplan, *The Wizards of Armageddon* (New York: Simon & Schuster, 1983), ch. 11.

5. Gabriel Kolko, *The Roots of American Foreign Policy* (Boston: Beacon Press, 1969), 42–43.

6. Kaufman et al, *U.S. National Security*, ch. 20.

7. Seyom Brown, *The Faces of Power* (New York: Columbia University Press, 1983), 149–152.

8. Morton Halperin, *Defense Strategies for the 70s* (Lanham, Md.: University Press of America, 1983).

9. Richard Nixon, *U.S. Foreign Policy for the 1970s: Building for Peace. A Report to the Congress*, February 25, 1971.

10. Brown, *Faces of Power*, 161–180.

11. Kaplan, *Wizards of Armageddon*, 201–306.

12. Michio Kaku and Daniel Axelrod, *To Win a Nuclear War. The Pentagon's Secret War Plans* (Boston: South End Press, 1987), ch. 6.

13. Robert Haffa, *The Half War: Planning U.S. Rapid Deployment Forces to Meet a Limited Contingency, 1960–1983* (Boulder, Colo.: Westview Press, 1984), 29.

14. Kaufman et al., *U.S. National Security*, ch. 20.

15. Haffa, *The Half War*, 29.

16. Schurmann, *Logic of World Power*, 439–456.

17. Bodenheimer and Gould, *Rollback*, ch. 1.

18. Robert Scheer, *America After Nixon* (New York: McGraw-Hill, 1974), 7–8.

19. Michael Moffitt, *The World's Money* (New York: Simon & Schuster, 1983), ch. 1.

20. Scheer, *America After Nixon*, ch. 2.

21. Kaufman et al., *U.S. National Security*, ch. 20.

22. Ibid.

23. Brown, *Faces of Power*, 337–344.

24. Seymour Hersh, *The Price of Power. Kissinger in the Nixon White House* (New York: Summit Books, 1983), ch. 22.

25. Jerry Sanders, *Peddlers of Crisis* (Boston: South End Press, 1983), ch. 6.

26. Kaplan, *Wizards of Armageddon*, 363.

27. Kaufman et al., *U.S. National Security*, ch. 20.

28. *Vital Speeches of the Day*, July 1, 1982.

29. Ronnie Dugger, *On Reagan: The Man and His Presidency* (New York: McGraw-Hill, 1983), 351–352.

30. Bodenheimer and Gould, *Rollback*, ch. 2.

31. Keith Dunn and William Staudenmeier, *Military Strategy in Transition* (Boulder, Colo.: Westview Press, 1984), ch. 8.

32. Ronald Dellums, *Defense Sense* (Cambridge, Mass.: Ballinger, 1983), 30.

33. Fred Halliday, *The Making of the Second Cold War* (London: Verso Editions, 1983), 225.

34. Robert Scheer, *With Enough Shovels* (New York: Random House, 1982), 10.

35. Sanders, *Peddlers of Crisis*, 332–336.

36. Fred C. Ikle, "Arms Control and National Defense" in Peter Duignan and Alvin Rabushka, *The United States in the 1980s* (Stanford University: Hoover Institution, 1980).

37. Colin Gray and Keith Payne, "Victory is Possible," *Foreign Policy* (Summer 1980), 27.

38. Scheer, *With Enough Shovels*, 29.

39. Ibid., 31.

40. Ibid., 8–10.

41. Ibid., 8.

42. Halliday, *Making of the Second Cold War,* 236.

43. *New York Times*, May 29, 1985.

44. Robert Aldridge, *First Strike!* (Boston: South End Press, 1983), 35–40.

45. Robert Bowman, *Star Wars: Defense or Death Star?* (Institute for Space and Security Studies, 1985), 45.

46. Bodenheimer and Gould, *Rollback*, ch. 5.

47. *New York Times*, November 18, 1986.

48. George Thibault, *The Art and Practice of Military Strategy* (Washington, D.C.: National Defense University, 1984), ch. 34.

49. Haffa, *The Half War,* 229.

50. Dunn and Staudenmaier, *Military Strategy*, ch. 9.

51. U.S. Secretary of Defense, *Report to the Congress, FY 1986* (Washington, D.C.: U.S. Government Printing Office, 1985), I-16.

52. Dunn and Staudenmaier, *Military Strategy*, ch. 6.

53. Schurmann, *Logic of World Power*, 161–162.

54. *The Military Reform Debate* (West Point, N.Y.: U.S. Military Academy, 1982), 105–141.

55. *The Military Reform Debate,* 105–141.

56. Haffa, *The Half War,* 240.

57. Dunn and Staudenmaier, *Military Strategy*, ch. 9.

58. *The Military Reform Debate*, 141; Jeffrey Record, *Revising U.S. Military Strategy: Tailoring Means to Ends* (Washington, D.C.: Pergamon Press, 1984).

59. Dunn and Staudenmaier, *Military Strategy*, ch. 9.

60. Jeffrey Record, "Jousting with Unreality," *International Security* (Winter 1983/84), 11.

61. Dunn and Staudenmaier, *Military Strategy*, ch. 9.

62. Sara Miles, "The Real War: Low Intensity Conflict in Central America," *NACLA Report on the Americas* (April/May 1986).

63. Colonel John D. Waghelstein, "Post-Vietnam Counterinsurgency Doctrine," *Military Review* 65, no. 5 (May 1985), 42–49.

64. Ross S. Kelly, "Special Operations in the '80's," *Defense and Foreign Affairs*, 12, no. 8 (August and September 1984), 32–33.

65. Douglas Blaufarb, *The Counterinsurgency Era: U.S. Doctrine and Performance* (New York: Free Press, 1977).

66. Ibid.

67. *Military Reform Debate,* 128–144; Haffa, *The Half War,* ch.4.

68. William Kaufmann, *Planning Conventional Forces 1950–80* (Washington, D.C.: Brookings Institution, 1982).

69. James Motley, "Grenada: Low-Intensity Conflict and the Use of U.S. Military Power," *World Affairs* 146 (Winter 1983/84), 221–238.

70. *New York Times,* April 11, 1984.

71. Michael Klare, *American Arms Supermarket* (Austin: University of Texas Press, 1984).

72. Center for Defense Information, *The Defense Monitor* 14, no. 2 (1985), 1–16.

73. *New York Times,* July 19, 1986.

74. Center for Defense Information, *The Defense Monitor* 14, no. 2 (1985), 1, 8.

75. Ibid., 1–16.

76. Ibid., 6–7.

77. U.S. Army, *Psychological Operations Techniques and Procedures,* Field Manual FM 33-5 (Washington, D.C.: U.S. Department of the Army, 1966).

78. Frank Barnett, Hugh Tovar, and Richard Shultz, *Special Operations in U.S. Strategy* (Washington, D.C.: National Defense University Press, 1984), ch. 7.

79. Hersh, *Price of Power,* ch. 22.

80. *New York Times,* January 23 and March 19, 1985.

81. Center for Defense Information, *The Defense Monitor* 14, no. 2 (1985), 14.

82. Waghelstein, "Post-Vietnam Counterinsurgency Doctrine," 42–49.

83. Center for Defense Information, *The Defense Monitor* 14, no. 2 (1985), 14.

84. Stephen S. Kaplan, *Diplomacy of Power* (Washington, D.C.: Brookings Institution, 1981), 667–668.

85. Marshall Shulman, *East-West Tensions in the Third World* (New York: W.W. Norton, 1986).

86. Report of the Commission on Integrated Long-Term Strategy, *Discriminate Deterrence* (Washington, D.C.: U.S. Government Printing Office, January 1988).

2

Hemispheric Relations and Security Regimes in Latin America

Augusto Varas

Western hemispheric security has a troubled long-term tradition. One hundred and sixty-five years ago, in the midst of Latin American independence wars, U.S. President James Monroe defined the terms of the exclusion of extracontinental powers in the region.[1] Since then, no stable "set of implicit or explicit principles, norms, rules and decision-making procedures around which actor's expectations converge" have been established.[2]

Pan-Americanism and the inter-American military system have not been adequate institutionalizations of common regional concerns on security. This chapter will focus on the reasons for this failure. In brief, heterogeneous structures of conflict formation and approaches to security, the self-centered approach of the United States to hemispheric security, and the recent rise of Latin American countries in world military affairs all contribute to the lack of agreement.

This analysis will concentrate, first, on the different structures of conflict formation in Latin America and the diversity of power projection of various Latin American states in the hemisphere; second, on the way that conflicts are handled according to different internal political settings and ideological frameworks; third, on the development of the hemispheric security system; and, fourth, on the way that incentives for real cooperation could be developed through specific and single security regimes.

Power Projection and Conflict Formation

Ever since their constitutions empowered Latin American societies to organize themselves, mainly from the last century to the present, these states have centralized basic responsibilities such as the total control of the armed forces, not only as one form of dissuasion and defense against outside aggression, but also as a powerful form of leverage in internal political life. This centralization has been a key factor in dealing with the development process. In this way, the state governments have taken the lead in regulating both peaceful and conflicting relations among individuals and groups within their societies and among the countries that make up the Latin American region. Due to the crisis of the hemispheric security system, however, historical tensions and conflicts have reappeared, creating a new structure of regional military developments that are as diverse as each state's own power projection in the continent.

Unlike Europe, which ways of solving its problems of political integration even though difficulties of social integration still persist, Latin America still has difficulties with integration at the international and regional levels, as well as at the social level in the interaction of its various local groups and classes. The use of force is therefore much more common in this region than in other parts of the developed world. This point is essential in order to understand why security concerns are crucial to Latin American countries and why conflicting relations persist within each country and among neighboring countries. Because such conflicts are inherent in the process of development of these as yet incompletely integrated societies, the state approach to dealing with conflict plays an important part in conflict solution or perpetuation. The policies adopted determine the nature of the conflict and the alternatives that are feasible for guaranteeing an effective and lasting peace at the national as well as at the regional level.

For example, the Latin American state projects its sovereign power to cover all domestic political activities and regulate relations among all its citizens. To that end, the state tackles the problem of internal order in a number of ways, the most objectionable of which has been militarization, with the inevitable aftermath of repression and escalation of tensions.

Furthermore, the Latin American state plays a basic role in determining the national geographical perimeter, the regional criterion for the recognition of individual countries' sovereignty. The process of state-building means entering into competition with other states that are also seeking to project their sovereignty over the same areas. This competition has generated tension among states, propelling rivalry, which in some cases has had devastating consequences for both internal and subregional equilibrium.

And also, in the economic crisis of the 1980s, the Latin American state has played, and continues to play, a central role in the process of redistributing, not so much wealth, but poverty and the effects of recession. Admittedly, not all states have responded to the crisis in the same way. While many of them have opted for recessionary policies that affect the population at large, in some states such options have been restricted by socioeconomic agreements of other kinds. In these instances one can also detect security concepts that are instrumental in preventing or, alternatively, generating internal tension and conflict.[3]

In sum, Latin American state governments have assumed basic functions that enable them to generate internal and international relations of either a conflictive or peaceful nature, depending on their respective national policies and the political implications of their views on security.

As the state itself has been the prime source of the generation and constitution of Latin American nations, one of the basic functions it has developed in the course of its history, and which it firmly continues to perform today, is to project its sovereign power both within and beyond the geographical limits by which it is circumscribed.[4] This projection of a state's power within or beyond its frontiers determines the first fundamental difference among some of the conflicts in the region. The projection of power with the aim of subjecting regional groups or dissidents who challenge the state's role as the sole organizer of a centralized and institutionalized armed force results in a traditional type of conflict. This is a nineteenth century problem of sovereignty as such, understood in simple juridical and legal terms. This type of conflict reflects a present-day manifestation of the first stage in the constitution of a developing state. The achievement of undisputed sovereignty at home and abroad by some Latin American states in the late nineteenth and early twentieth centuries is still in the late 1980s a vital question on the agenda for some countries such as Colombia or Peru. There, the process of state development has acquired an archaic content that expresses itself with great force, as I will discuss later.

The projection of a state's sovereign power within a given geographic area comes up against two material limitations. One limitation is that imposed by other states in the region or subregion, which are experiencing similar problems in the process of constituting their sovereignty, or which are at least challenging the growth of others at the other's expense. There are also the limitations imposed by states outside the region that claim sovereignty over areas in dispute. We thus see that the state power projection within a given geographic area comes up against limitations that give rise to two archaic types of conflict over sovereignty—regional territorial conflicts and colonial ones. The difference between them lies in whether the opposing state belongs to the same region or to another more developed one. This differentiation does not exhaust all possible types of interstate conflict in the hemisphere. On the contrary, I intend to show that these conflicts are the product of limitations imposed on what might be called the state sovereign power projection within a clearly defined geographic area.

Another type of conflict stems from the projection of power beyond the geographic limits required by the process of consolidating a state's sovereignty. These are conflicts with hegemonic aims in which the subject of the dispute is of greater geographic scope than a precise area that can be shown on a map. Here, the area over which control is sought does not coincide with the territory of the social groups invoked as constituent parts of the nation. The aim is not so much to expand the national frontiers as to gain control over processes and interactions that occur in distant geographic areas. This difference is vital, relating to the destruction between the age-old recurrent imperial aspirations observed in history, and the hegemonic projection of state power throughout the world, which is a process typical of our times.

There is no doubt that hegemonic conflicts characterize present-day interstate relations. These can be seen in the worldwide rivalry between the superpowers to project their influence and power all over the globe, each seeking the subordination if not the military defeat of the other. Likewise, on a continental scale, we find that some states in the region seek to project their hegemony over an indeterminate area, controlling or attempting to control processes that are much less specific than designs on a particular geographic area.

Interstate conflicts in the Latin America region can therefore be placed in two categories that correspond to the two basic criteria mentioned above. First, the projection of state power may be hegemonic or simply territorial; and second, the limitations to the projection of power may be imposed either by states belonging to the region or by states outside it. The combination of these variables can be seen in Figure 2.1, which shows different types of conflict in the region.

The Nature of Regional Conflicts

There are a number of areas and different types of conflict among states in Latin America. The differences among them throw light on the conflict in each case and suggest possibilities for peaceful solutions. The following briefly examines the different types of regional conflict from the point of view expressed above.

One type of conflict results from an incomplete development of a nation state's constitution, with opposition to that process arising from outside the region. This type of conflict imparts to certain forms of regional tension a highly archaic nature. Because such conflicts are related to the early stages of the constitution of the state, they are similar to

		TYPE	
		Territorial	Hegemonic
LIMITATIONS	Regional	Constitution of the state	Local domination by a regional power
	Extraregional	Colonial	Global domination by a hegemonic power

FIGURE 2.1 Power Projections in Latin America

those experienced by Latin America in the early nineteenth century, when it struggled for independence from colonial powers. And because these situations hark back to the period of the actual constitution of the Latin American nation state when antagonists were outside the region, the conflict has a colonial flavor.

In Latin America there are three instances that fall in this archaic colonial category. When Guatemala claimed the territory of Belize, Guatemala confronted opposition from the United Kingdom, a former power in the region. Even when the United Kingdom gave Belize its independence, its maintenance within the Commonwealth under military protection from the United Kingdom brought the latter into direct conflict with Guatemala, thereby indirectly perpetuating a colonial type of conflict.

Another instance is the current tension between the United States and the associated state of Puerto Rico regarding the real nature of the relations between them. Despite the referenda that produced the current relationship, many Latin American countries view the Puerto Rican arrangement as a manifestation of colonialism. As a result, many governments have attempted to raise the issue at the United Nations. The Nonaligned Movement's position on Puerto Rico is unequivocal in its support for the island's full independence from the United States.[5]

A third type of colonial conflict is that which continues between Argentina and the United Kingdom over the Islas Malvinas, or the Falklands Islands, which caused a large-scale military confrontation. In the absence of a United Kingdom solution to the problem along the same lines as it took with Belize and with other parts of the Caribbean, or of a joint agreement with Argentina, the islands will always be a subject of contention and on the Argentine agenda for decolonization.[6]

These cases all have one common denominator: The projection of a state's sovereign power, regarded as fundamental to the constitution within definitive frontiers of an autonomous Latin American state, cannot come about as a result of decisions or limitations imposed by a state from outside the region. Given the features of this type of regional conflict, the confrontation assumes a clearly anticolonial character in the eyes of the Latin American country or national group concerned, and the struggle they wage bears all the marks of a struggle for independence.

A second type of conflict stems from an incomplete development of a nation state's constitution, with opposition arising from within the region. The conflicts referred to here are typical of the processes of the projection of sovereignty pure and simple. Characteristic of the period that followed the independence struggles of the last century, these processes were marked by the need to secure agreement on the precise demarcation of the geographic areas over which the recently created state's sovereign power was to be exercised. Regional resistance to this process stemmed precisely from the similar constitutional development of neighboring states in the area during the colonial crisis and wars of independence.

Viewed from this standpoint, it is easy to understand interstate conflicts such as that between Ecuador and Peru, which is a dispute over the final demarcation of their frontiers that developed into a military confrontation in the Cordillera del Condor during the Paquisha incidents. The same is true of the frontier dispute between Colombia and Venezuela in the Gulf of Venezuela and Lake Maracaibo, which has been in the news due to the tensions observed in that area in August 1987. Other examples are the conflicting territorial claims on the San Andrés Islands by Colombia and Nicaragua; the Esequibo dispute between Venezuela and Guyana as a result of an international ruling considered by Venezuela to be null and void; Bolivia's long-standing aim of gaining access to the Pacific; and the territorial dispute between El Salvador and Honduras, which at one time escalated into military confrontations in the so-called football war.

All of these conflicts, which vary in intensity, are connected with each state's need to project power over a clearly defined territory. One cannot deny the material basis of this type of bilateral conflict in the region. I am not speaking of an "inevitable geopolitical expansion of the state," but rather attempting to explain that in these particular instances the conflict has a specific content resulting from an objective materiality determined by the reality of the disputed object, namely, so many square miles of territory.[7]

The materiality or specificity of this type of dispute is not necessarily related to the intensity of the bilateral conflict, but it demonstrates the nature of the particular conflict. When a clearly circumscribed territory is disputed, a zero-sum situation exists in which a gain by one party entails a corresponding loss for the other. This means that Latin American territorial conflicts are very long-lasting, and they work against stable peaceful solutions.

A third type of regional conflict is the projection of regional hegemony within Latin America. The nature of the conflicts resulting from a state's projection of power beyond its national geographic boundaries makes this type of interstate tension much more diffuse than those cited earlier. Even when the intensity of the conflict is greater, both the end sought and the parties involved are more ambiguous than in the case of a purely territorial dispute. In addition to the dispute's lack of specificity, other dimensions come into play as the struggle is waged at different levels in political, military, or economic realms.

In Latin America the only regional power that exercises regional hegemony is Brazil. It is therefore not surprising that, quite apart from the geopolitical considerations of other governments, the cases of tension confronting Brazil are related to its projection of power in scattered territorial areas in which the disputed objects are immaterial; in other words, there are no specific territorial ambitions. Rather, the disputes arise from Brazil's involvement in other areas, which are incidental to the process of the accumulation of wealth and the activity of Brazil's political, economic, or social agents in separate but connected areas.

Despite the immateriality of Brazil's involvement beyond its frontier and the multidimensional nature of its regional influence, the military implications are unmistakable. Although the recent reorganization of the Brazilian army in the Amazon region may be explained by the need to protect its western frontiers from drug traffic and guerrilla warfare, it also clearly indicates the military aspect of its projection of hegemony on the subregion.[8] The areas in which Brazil's hegemonic aims make themselves felt are as extensive and ill defined as the basin of the River Plate and the Amazon Basin, and even beyond Latin America, for example, to Africa south of the Sahara and the African Atlantic coastal states. Because of the lack of specificity of Brazil's projection of hegemony in these areas, the competition among the states in the region remains diffuse so that the degree of tension is determined by security requirements and concepts that come into conflict with these hegemonic aims. Thus the historical rivalry between Argentina and Brazil has been conflictive at times when basic concepts of security have prevailed, as I will discuss in further detail later, or has given way to cooperation, even military cooperation, at times of greater pragmatism, as is the current situation under President Raúl Alfonsín.

Finally, there is another type of conflict in the region that stems from the projection of power by a country whose hegemonic ambitions extend beyond a specific area to the entire region. Without question, the only power capable of acting in such a fashion in Latin America is the United States. Although the situation could well lead to conflicts with the Soviet Union and to tension with smaller powers, it has not yet reached such a level, but it is nonetheless fraught with important implications. The power projected by the United States over the hemisphere has produced two highly conflictive situations that provide clear evidence of the nature of the tensions involved. These are the conflict between Nicaragua and Honduras, in which the United States is using Honduras as an operational base against the Sandinista government, and the ongoing tension between Cuba and the United States resulting from the latter's refusal to acknowledge the Cuban state as it is politically and ideologically constituted at present. The conflicts involved in the projection of hegemonic power are perhaps the most typical of the international conflicts in the world today and are readily expressed in Latin America.[9]

In summary, current interstate conflicts and tensions in the region have widely varying features, the key elements of which are the projection of state power with territorial or hegemonic aims and the limits set thereto, either within or outside the region. This differentiation is vital for an understanding of how regional conflicts differing in origin can lead to military tension depending on a government's political options. Conflict is thus a product of the type of issues involved and a government's policy approach to a solution.

Conflict Management and Security Options

The tensions and conflicts described thus far have been dealt with in different ways by the states and governments in the region. Government policy plays a crucial role in escalating tension into conflict; depending on the options chosen, a government can provoke or avert military confrontation. Government policy, in turn, depends on the prevailing view within the government as to a military type of solution.

The concepts of security of the Latin American states, which play a central role in heightening or reducing tension, combine with the forms in which the states project their power to activate or prevent a conflict. Latin American approaches to conflicts are not necessarily peculiar to a single type of state, government, or period. On the contrary, a variety of doctrines frequently coexist side by side in a single country from which an overriding political choice is made. Belligerent views may originate not from the military but from civilian circles.

To analyze the reasons why any particular set of conflict-solving measures is applied within a given government or state is beyond the scope of this chapter. The point I wish to make, however, is that these choices are made in a bipolar continuum. At one extreme, the fundamentalists uphold the national interest to the exclusion of any other, making it central to the constitution of the state as a political entity. This view tends to develop in ideological and political contexts beset by major problems of systemic and social integration. The national interests expressed by the government or ruling elite are used to mask the gaps in integration; ideological and cultural pretexts hide the deep fissures that prevent integration. Social, cultural, ideological, religious, political, ethnic, regional, and other factions normally make it difficult to achieve a minimum of systemic and social integration in Third World countries and, to a lesser extent, in some industrialized countries. Fundamentalism is used to shore up or provide a basis for the principles held to be constitutive of the new political or social order.[10]

This excessive insistence on national interest clearly points up an artificial element in the social integration process. As the national interest is reaffirmed by the ruling elite, group interests are frequently favored at the expense of long-standing nationwide aspirations. Fundamentalist doctrines therefore contain a manipulative element for use in populist contexts, either civilian or military.

At the other extreme, the pragmatists do not regard the national interest as crucially linked to national identity, nor do the pragmatists represent for the ruling elite any possibility of legitimizing it or maintaining it in power. From the pragmatists' viewpoint, any type of conflict of interests between two or more states is negotiable. Pragmatism tends to prevail in contexts where the problem of social or systemic integration is moving toward a solution, or a solution is being sought through political, social, or economic processes rather than by ideological and cultural propaganda.

Whether a government's approach to a conflict is closer to one or the other of these poles will also depend on internal political factors that I will not explore here. However, it is important to emphasize that what defines the continuum is the room for maneuverability in respect to a zero-sum situation.

The central consideration is the need for a nation to identify with specific values that are considered essential for the process of nation-building and national integration. The type of fundamentalism to be found in defense policies will be determined basically by the need—assessed by those who have defined it—to achieve national identity expressed in terms of an elemental pattern of confrontation with the adversary. The siege mentality has frequently been highly productive. Because factors making for national identity are unstable, if not nonexistent and are the result of fragmentary contributions of subcultures, there is

		DOCTRINE TYPE	
		Fundamentalist	Pragmatic
STATE POWER PROJECTION	Sovereign	Geopolitical (2)	Integrationist (4)
	Hegemonic	Crusade (1)	Pacifist (3)

FIGURE 2.2 Conflict Management

a strong bias toward fundamentalism. Conversely, in states where the process of collective national identification—systemic integration—has attained a degree of stability, it is easier to find and apply more pragmatic solutions in which the zero-sum model has no place.

Therefore, it is my view that governmental approaches to the settling of conflicts will be determined by the way in which defence policies are combined with the way in which the power of the state is projected, as illustrated in Figure 2.2. A description of defense policies based on the combination of doctrines and the type of projection of state power reveals four major categories, which I analyze below in detail. This analysis will enable us to define the concepts of security prevailing in Latin America in the present decade.

The Crusade. The existence of fundamentalist views in a global projection of power context generates one of the most explosive governmental policies and is characteristic of the superpowers at times of hegemonic crisis. As only the great economic and military powers can aspire to global projection of power, the combination of fundamentalism and hegemony can manifest itself almost anywhere in the world. When this occurs at a moment of crisis for the superpower's internal or international hegemony, the result is a crusade against enemies who challenge the basic values of the order that the superpower is trying to restore or establish. Although such crusades may be observed in various parts of the world, it is in Latin America that, given the economic and military presence of the United States, they occur as a result of an attempt to regain hegemony over the hemisphere, or to maintain domination in periods of political and military crisis for the ruling power in a state.

Since 1980, with the election of the Reagan administration, the U.S. defense or security policy in the hemisphere has been highly fundamentalist. This is due to the neoconservative philosophy underlying the Republican administration, which has reaffirmed the need to reinstate not only free enterprise but anticommunist and anti-Soviet attitudes throughout the region. This alone can explain the flexing of U.S. military muscle in an area where neither the USSR nor any of the countries in the region is in a position to threaten U.S. security interests.[11]

U.S. policy in the 1980s toward Grenada, Cuba, and Nicaragua has been guided by a fundamentalist political approach to international affairs and a neoconservative bias in international economics. To date, proof of this crusade can be found not only in the inordinate use of force during the Grenada invasion, but also in the explicit policy of aid to the Nicaraguan insurgents and in the threats and actual use of force against Nicaragua. U.S. operations in Honduras and El Salvador are more than merely defensive and have transformed Honduras into one of the largest military bases on the continent. The U.S. attitude toward Cuba is similar, preventing any kind of rapprochement or détente.

The antileft crusade by the United States in Latin America has become a major factor working for conflict in the region. The militarization of antagonists has become a self-fulfilling prophecy in Central America resulting in one of the hemisphere's most acute crises in recent decades.

Geopolitics. In the 1980s, the most common approach of Latin American military establishments to their defense problems has been geopolitical. The fundamentalist element in this approach is the conviction of the military that it represents the soul of the nation in each country,[12] an idea rooted in history. Latin American military establishments were greatly influenced by the geopolitical doctrines of Germany in the nineteenth century and of the United States in the twentieth century. Another important influence was Bismarck's view of the central role of the armed forces in generating national unity. This was transferred to Latin America in the form of the military's playing a central role in determining the process of economic development. In addition to these two ideas there emerged in the mid-1950s the influence of U.S. national security with its emphasis on irreducible international antagonism to the USSR at the height of the cold war, and its corollary of anticommunism in domestic policies.

These three international influences made themselves felt without difficulty in a continent beset by century-old economic problems and the continuing problems of social and system integration. At the systemic level, the armed forces could surmount the economic crisis by showing themselves to be the moving force behind a self-sustained process. At the social level, they could claim to be the champions of nationality by affirming the fundamental values on which a new national identity would be constructed.

Because, generally speaking, Latin American countries are similar in their limited projection of power, most conflicts are generated by such action, directed against either neighboring states or powers outside the region. And because the armed forces of the region consider that national identity can only be achieved by driving home the recognition of armed might and of the possession of territory as fundamental to the constitution of nationhood, most of the military establishments in the area ultimately adhere to this doctrine. Geopolitics as official military doctrine has fueled competition among nations. Given the military fragmentation of the region, this doctrine became the engine of rivalries, exacerbating the demand for more armaments and personnel as well as the potential for intraregional conflict.

An analysis of geopolitics in each Latin American country can help reveal the special emphasis assigned to the "objective" interests that each nation has according to its specific geographic and international political position.[13] These geopolitical concerns, however, depend on how the armed forces have defined the national interest. Often, the armed forces have increased their budgets because of some perceptions of threat against their national interest,[14] which has no real basis.

A variety of geopolitical frameworks have been identified, the Brazilian school being the most important. Brazilian geopolitical analysts conceive the nation as "an archipelago consisting of a series of islands and peninsulas" (including the "aircraft carrier of the Northeast"), which must be effectively coordinated in order to make possible a rational development of Brazil's interior. The inland Matto-Grosso zone that borders Paraguay and Bolivia is thought of as a heartland or "welding zone that must come under Brazilian control to allow Brazil to play her predestined continental role."

The Argentine school, on the other hand, is characterized by its preoccupation with

Brazilian expansion and hegemony; concern over the Brazilian-U.S. alliance; Argentina's natural role as a leader of the Southern Cone; a maritime emphasis (as opposed to Brazil's more continental thrust) with focus on the South Atlantic, recovery of the Malvinas Islands from British control, and protection of Argentina's claims in the Antarctic; nuclear energy, and the possible development of nuclear technology, especially if Brazil is perceived as developing them; and the impact on national development and international relations of Argentina's seeming inability to put her internal house in order.

The Chilean geopolitical school "is strongly maritime in its orientation, especially in terms of projection power in the South Pacific, control of the Straits of Magellan, and sovereignty in its claimed Antarctic sector." Bolivia, Peru, and Ecuador represent minor geopolitical schools; their national interests are, respectively, a route to the sea, the control of the Amazon Basin, and the restoration of territories lost to Peru in 1942.[15]

It is also important to mention the geopolitical thinking of the Central American Defense Council prior to the Sandinista revolution in Nicaragua in 1979, which proclaimed that Central American unity is a logical consequence of geopolitical and strategic realities. Finally, a kind of underdeveloped geopolitical outlook is found in Mexico; its major theme is the possibility of exercising geopolitical leadership over divided Central American countries.

A geopolitical approach may be observed in all types of regional conflicts. Typical examples are the way in which some military circles in Argentina regarded the Beagle Channel dispute with Chile and the Falkland/Malvinas conflict with the United Kingdom, and of the way in which the Peruvian and Ecuadorian armed forces dealt with the tensions in the disputed Amazon area in 1942, which was lost by Ecuador. Bolivia's expectations to gain access to the Pacific is central to the military argument that lack of access violates national identity, which should be restored by armed force. The same arguments could be observed during the Colombian-Venezuelan tensions in August 1987. These situations demonstrate the way in which a geopolitical definition is transformed into an objective capable of mobilizing broad social sectors in the pursuit of goals that are perceived as crucial to national identities.

Peaceful Approach. This security or defense policy is linked to a pragmatic approach to confrontations that arise from global projections of power by a state from outside the region. Pragmatism defuses a conflict thereby enabling the parties to reach a greater level of agreement. This approach is basically a policy of peaceful coexistence.

It was used by the last United Kingdom Labour government in finding a solution to the Belize dispute. In the Falkland/Malvinas, although the problem was not solved from Guatemala's viewpoint, the United Kingdom intended to apply this pragmatic approach there, but by that time the British Labour party was on its way out.

Brazil's pacific policy is also characteristic of a state with regional hegemonic aspirations but that applies pragmatism in tackling the problems involved. Traditionally, Brazil has been able, even under military governments, to achieve stable, peaceful conditions throughout its territory without any major internal conflicts.[16]

To sum up, it is interesting to observe that a pragmatic approach of peaceful coexistence can avert conflicts, in contrast to the fundamentalist approach that creates and exacerbates them. Even when conflictive situations exist, defensive policies play a central role in either exacerbating or preventing a conflict. It is unfortunate that there are so few examples, such as those given above, of a pragmatic approach by extraregional powers to disputes with Latin American states in areas where Latin American sovereignty is projected. This may well be one of the most important tasks for cooperation among nations with a view to world peace.

Integrationism. This type of security policy has been in evidence in recent years in Latin America, though its roots go back some time. Because the military governments of the 1970s failed to create new forms of society, and their plans for opening up new horizons for their countries were overtaken by the recession, a more pragmatic approach began to appear. In addition, the new national identity created by the political content of the crisis due to the existence of the military regimes and the attempts to surmount it relegated to the background any ideological propaganda by the ruling elites. This new pragmatic line originated in Argentina, Brazil, Peru, and Uruguay and was the combined product of processes of transition to democracy and the existence of nonfundamentalist civilian governments.[17]

In Argentina, the Alfonsín government tackled the dispute over the Beagle Channel with Chile in a pragmatic way, which is now moving toward an integrationist solution, which would stress cooperative politics, common interests, and joint actions, thus countering the approach of the fundamentalist militarist groups that had predominated during the military governments from 1976 onwards. With regard to tension with Uruguay, the new civilian Argentine government took a pragmatic approach to problems in the River Plata Basin, extending bilateral relations to include objectives of greater integration.

Further examples of pragmatism are the Venezuelan approach to the Esequibo dispute and the tensions with Colombia, and the Chilean-Peruvian talks in Tacna in 1985. In Peru, President Alan García initiated a politico-diplomatic move aimed at solving a problem that went back to 1929 with Chile, as the finishing touches still had not been put to all the agreements under the peace and friendship treaty that concluded the Pacific War in 1879. Peru's policy is designed to solve the problem and alleviate tension through an interesting process of self-imposed arms limitations and mutual confidence-building with its southern neighbor. In this context, the possibilities that can be achieved by integration are beginning to be visible.

The case of Brazil is even more interesting: Despite its enormous power, there has been a prevailing trend toward pacifism, which in recent months has given way to integrationist proposals to Argentina regarding the conventional arms industry and the nuclear program of the two countries.[18] There, the pragmatic approach to disputed aims connected with the projection of sovereignty pure and simple has produced several kinds of integrationist policies and plans. The Brazilian plan to develop the Amazon Basin and the existing agreement on Antarctica are characteristic of the integrationist approach.

The Post–World War II Hemispheric Security System

After World War II, U.S.–Latin American military relations have created divergent expectations.[19] The United States has been looking for allies to defend the hemispheric perimeter against a possible Soviet threat, even though some U.S. officials have recognized the null potential support the Latin American armies could provide in an East-West confrontation.[20] Responding to this paradox, the United States has supported bilateral cooperation by strengthening the internal police roles of the Latin American military. On the contrary, the latter have been looking for military assistance and professionalization, refusing to perform as a permanent role nonprofessional tasks in internal repression. Their main aim has been to develop hemispheric institutional relations in the security field with their northern peers.

These unequal expectations have diverted hemispheric military relations toward a de facto system without creating any stable institutional setting or hemispheric security regime. Accordingly, shared security interests, as well as common and reciprocal incentives for military cooperation have been blocked, impeding the organization of military hemispheric linkages in the medium and long term.

This frustrated military brotherhood in the hemisphere has structural roots. In short, there are no incentives for common cooperation for both parties due to the different nature of power projection by the United States and Latin American countries. This diversity has led to a wide variety of international and regional military postures by all parties involved.

During the 1950s and 1960s, the level of conflict among the nations of the region was low, and the dynamics of the arms race seemed to be under control. Even during the cold war, when the Soviet Union was clearly identified as the principal U.S. rival, interstate tensions were postponed, favoring common interests of continental defense.[21] The principal expression of that period was the Inter-American Treaty for Reciprocal Assistance (ITRA).

The ITRA, or Rio Treaty, was signed after the end of World War II at the Inter-American Conference for the Consolidation of Peace, held

in Rio de Janeiro in 1947. Its most important clause, Article 6, stated
the following:

> In the event that the inviolability, territorial integrity, sovereignty or political
> independence of any American State is threatened by any form of aggression
> different from an armed attack, or by any extracontinental or intercontinental
> conflict, or by any other event or situation that may endanger the peace
> of the continent, the Consultation Committee will meet immediately in
> order to determine the measures to be taken in support of the aggressed,
> or, in any case, those suitable for the maintenance of peace and security
> in the continent.[22]

This military alliance was refined through bilateral Military Assistance
Programs (MAPs), signed by all Latin American governments and the
United States between 1951 and 1958. By participating in the Inter-
American military system, the Latin American armed forces to some
extent defined their nations' defense interests in terms of the security
system of the United States. A preliminary definition of the way MAPs
were designed to operate was indicated by one U.S. military official:

> To implement our contribution, Congress prescribed that a limited number
> of members of the military service of the United States would be detailed
> to assist those countries in an advisory capacity only. Further, the United
> States would provide for the transfer to these countries of any articles,
> services, information, instruction, and training necessary to accomplish
> our mutual objectives . . . [of] ensuring the development of self-sufficient
> national training programs and the requisite training facilities required
> therefore.[23]

This relationship was initially conceived by the U.S. military as forming
an important strategic reserve and as a special attribute of the United
States. Thus, it was stated that

> South America has the immunity of remoteness from Soviet air and missile
> power which no other place in the world can claim. . . . [A] program of
> establishing part of our fundamental industrial fighting strength in this
> continent so privileged by its immunity and remoteness should be explored.
> In cooperation with those South American nations which think most
> nearly like us, and which over the years have proved themselves to be
> our firmest friends, a coordinated industrial base for a strategic war reserve
> could be erected—a base in an area almost completely immune from air
> attack.[24]

South American armed forces shared this perception about the strategic importance of South America within the U.S. defense system. Their governments viewed association with the U.S. military as a means to modernize their equipment without having to pay the full cost as they would be subsidized by their new allies. As a Chilean military officer asserted shortly after the ratification of the ITRA, the perimeter of hemispheric defense had a "weak Southern wing, comprising all of the Chilean territory; the control of this territory is going to be essential to the invaders in order to establish and consolidate bases of operation that enable them to strike the heart of their principal adversary in the future."[25]

From a military perspective, this position entailed certain duties on the part of the Latin American countries; it also implied obligation on the part of the United States to support a coordinated program of military modernization and economic development. In this respect, it was stipulated that "the arms should be provided with the corresponding factories of ammunitions and the necessary instructions for their repair and maintenance."[26]

A number of economic integration programs paralleled the establishment of the hemispheric security system. They include the Multilateral Treaty for Free Commerce and the Central American Association of Free Trade in 1960, the Alliance for Progress in 1961, the Andean Pact in 1969, and the Caribbean Economic Community (CARICOM) in 1974. These integration efforts helped to engender a sense of common interests among Latin American countries. In the same vein, the Organization of American States (OAS) also played an important political role during this period to the extent that it succeeded in coordinating divergent national projects at critical moments for the region, as was seen during the discussion of the Cuban issue that concluded with the expulsion of Cuba from the OAS.

But the level of modernization expected by the Latin American armies was never achieved. The United States undertook a modest transfer of secondhand weapons used during World War II to Latin America, which coincided with some sales by Great Britain to the navies of the subcontinent.[27]

By the early 1960s, pan-American military relations acquired a clear political orientation centered on the ideological indoctrination of military personnel. Primary importance was given to overall training, with a special emphasis on the ideological indoctrination of officers and troops. One U.S. military officer in 1961 identified advantageous cultural traits: "In spite of Soviet efforts to attract Latin America towards international communism, there still exists in this continent strong elements which promote democracy. Such elements can be said to be the following: (i) the individualism of Latin Americans and their aversion to regimentation; (ii) their political idealism and democratic conviction; (iii) the Roman Catholic Church; and (iv) *the military forces.*"[28]

Accordingly, the character of pan-American military relations was progressively reoriented away from concern with hemispheric military security and toward the internal political security of the countries of the region. As part of the new emphasis on neutralizing domestic security threats, the United States promoted civic-military action projects, starting with Guatemala in 1960.[29] The programs were designed to engage the military in the solution of those problems that created conditions for the growth of anti-U.S. movements in the continent.

Once regional military objectives were replaced by political ones, programs of transfer and professional training varied accordingly. As a result, the MAPs began to assume new connotations. According to US sources,

> [U.S.] efforts with regards to military aid will be geared, on the one hand, to the development, among the Latin American military forces, of small, mobile units, capable of rapid action; and, on the other, to the provision of strategic air support and defense naval forces conveniently equipped with those modern items required to successfully face the increasing revolutionary threat. . . . At the same time, civic actions have contributed to internal security by depriving insurgent groups from shelters in remote areas, and by improving the possibilities of the security forces to obtain intelligence information.[30]

The new importance accorded by the United States to matters of internal security was seen in the evolution of military and police aid starting in the late 1960s.[31]

The failure of these civic-military operations, coupled with the increasing challenge posed by guerrilla forces in almost all Latin American countries, provoked yet another shift in Inter-American military relations, this time back toward a political commitment. The following analysis of that situation illustrates the issue: "Increasing Cuban subversion and Soviet penetration in the hemisphere during the last years have required a political and military response in order to ensure the safety of the United States and of the hemisphere in general. Whereas the political reaction has involved a collective and unified action on the part of the majority of the nations of the hemisphere, the military response has been for the most part unilateral."[32]

It was for these reasons that the United States began to pressure, unsuccessfully, Latin American governments to create an inter-American military force. This proposal has been the most divisive hemispheric issue, and contributed to the breakdown of the inter-American military system.

Because relations among Latin American armed forces were more political than military, political, not military, concerns predominated in the interaction among the various armies and governments in the inter-American military system. This fragmentation of continental military concerns affected hemispheric relations as evidenced in two important events. The first of these took place in 1968, when Argentina proposed the creation of an inter-American security force. That proposal, presented by General Alejandro Lanusse, commander-in-chief of the Argentine armed forces, was defeated by a wide margin; it was supported only by some military regimes, such as Argentina, Brazil, El Salvador, Honduras, Nicaragua, and Paraguay. The United States abstained.[33] The second event that suggested the fragmentation of common continental military perspectives took place during the Tenth Conference of Commanders in Chief of the American Armies, held in Caracas from September 3 to 7, 1973. At this conference, Peruvian General Edgardo Mercado Jarrín unequivocally challenged the inter-American security system:

> The Peruvian Army, in accordance with the guidelines of foreign policy in our government, and moved by a position of dispassionate reflection and constructive criticism devoid of any antagonism, considers that the so-called "Inter-American military system" was created and conceived to serve a specific set of interests. Consequently, it is compelled to question the said system, serenely and objectively, until its structure and purpose are redefined in such a way that it meets the true interests and improvement of the Latin American armies.[34]

The political orientation given to the program by the United States heralded the program's own downfall. The shift in U.S.–Latin American military relations from an emphasis on the military aspects per se to an almost exclusively political interest frustrated the expectations of modernization held by the Latin American armed forces. And as each country's armed forces defined and worked toward their individual agendas, any possibility of military unity on the continent died out. The armed forces of the region were left floating in a fluid system of alliances, the nature of which depended on the political orientation of the participating governments, or of the top military staff, in the case of military regimes.

The hemispheric security system failed, chiefly, because it was *instrumental* to the security interests of the United States. The system was increasingly decoupled from regional interests. The United States, following an autistic approach to this issue,[35] often used the ITRA and the OAS as mediums to implement its own interest in the Latin American region. This situation has been the case for the last decade.

In fact, the U.S. policy in the region, especially in Central America, was to use the conflict for demonstration purposes vis-à-vis the USSR. According to Secretary of Defense Caspar Weinberger, U.S. deterrence has to meet four main tests: survivability, credibility, clarity, and safety.[36] Those conditions were tested in Grenada, as well as in the U.S. approach to Cuba and to the Sandinistas in Nicaragua. Because the United States had to deal from Weinberger's perspective with the USSR from a position of "strength and the promise of greater relative strength,"[37] these hemispheric issues were a good excuse to increase U.S. leverage and challenge the USSR's position in the region.

Furthermore, considering that hemispheric security was instrumental for U.S. international purposes, real and common security concerns were neglected. Thus, it was possible to replace them with U.S. *political-ideological* concerns on regional stability. As most U.S. policymakers shared the widespread notion that U.S. security "would not be affected if Latin America were, say, to sink to the bottom of the sea,"[38] U.S.–Latin American bilateral military relations were reoriented to take political as well as ideological affinities into account. This was the case with U.S.-Argentine military relations during the Falkland/Malvinas crisis, which produced one of the most dramatic failures of the U.S. approach to hemispheric issues.

Finally, the hemispheric security system has failed because hemispheric security relations have been much more important in *political* terms than in strategic ones. U.S. concern about regional instability has led the United States to view Latin American military establishments as political proxies responsible for containing undesirable social and political change in the area. This policy, condemned to failure, was observed in Central America and the Caribbean in the 1920s and was repeated in Vietnam in the 1960s and 1970s. The net effect of this policy has been not the alignment of Latin American armed forces with the United States but an increase in the autonomous positioning of these forces in the inter-national military arena. As a result, internationalization of local conflicts and the wider presence of extraregional military actors in the hemisphere have increased—precisely the opposite effect desired by the United States.

The U.S. damage control response to this failure has been a new interest to develop bilateral professional relations with its Latin American counterparts. Thus, the U.S. South Command (USSOUTHCOM) chief, General John Galvin, stated that during 1987 bilateral military operations were programed to be doubled.[39]

Nevertheless, here too, the very same concept of hemispheric security follows a nonmilitary path. It has been extended to include police issues like drug traffic. This elevation for strategic purposes of nonmilitary issues such as drug traffic and illegal migration explains the interest of a U.S. representative at the Twenty-seventh Conference of American Armies in November 1987 in Argentina to develop a military hemispheric organization to tackle the drug issue.[40] This proposal was rejected by all Latin American armies.

Accordingly, not only has confusion resulted because of the combined political and military roles of U.S. officials—a distinctive trait of U.S. hemispheric security policy—but also because U.S. military officers are competing with U.S. diplomats in the region. The confusion of these roles will create new and additional problems in hemispheric relations. U.S. policy coherence toward Latin American will decrease and military autonomy in hemispheric affairs will increase. This is an obvious contradiction to statements made in Washington to Latin American military officers by the undersecretary of state for hemispheric affairs when he reaffirmed the professional role of military personnel and criticized their political involvement.[41]

All in all, the total sum of bilateral military relations will not produce a hemispheric security order. The latter should be explored from different angles to determine if it is possible to develop common security interests among all parties involved. These common interests would be the only possible cohesive element to catalyze military collaboration in the hemisphere. For the United States it is crucial that it decide whether to be integrated into this new order, thereby overcoming its traditional bias toward these issues.

New Military Developments

The hemispheric security situation changed dramatically in the 1970s and the 1980s. Militarily, the ITRA was no longer a viable mechanism to secure the defense of the continent against extracontinental threats. Regional and subregional integration experiments failed,[42] and the OAS proved unable to solve tensions among its members, as demonstrated by the Peruvian-Ecuadorian border conflict of 1981 and the Falkland/Malvinas war between Argentina and the United Kingdom in 1982.

Simultaneously in the early 1970s, the level of regional political, economic, and military leverage enjoyed by the United States steadily declined.[43] The post–Vietnam War breakdown in the United States on a domestic consensus for foreign policy and economic competition from Japan and Europe weakened the ability of the United States to develop and maintain regional initiatives within the hemisphere. This inability of the United States to produce "common goods" in the security field fragmented the previous system of shared incentives, which created an archipelago of national positioning in the Latin American regional and global security structures. That the United states chose to support the United Kingdom during the Falkland/Malvinas war was the final straw for Latin American expectations for a common hemispheric defense.

In response to the breakdown of perceived shared interests, Latin American countries replaced the OAS with a regional organization and initiatives that excluded the United States. The Latin American Economic System (LAES) was designed to address regional economic problems independent of the United States. Actually, LAES has been designed to protect its members against the actions of U.S. multinationals.[44] The formation of the Contadora and Esquipulas groups are additional examples. However, these new forms of Latin American cooperation do not have enough standing yet to constitute a forum for collective action in security issues when national interests might be subordinated to those of the region as a whole.

The ITRA and bilateral MAPs have proved ineffectual, as the Falklands/ Malvinas war illustrates. Increased nationalism in some countries or U.S. disapproval of human rights abuses in other strategic countries such as Argentina, Chile, and Brazil during the Carter administration, all contributed to the adoption of more independent security policies by Latin American countries. At the same time the hemispheric security system was disintegrating, relations among South American countries were reorganized. Old disputes for hegemony resurfaced, nationalism was brought to life again, and new occasions for intraregional competition emerged.

Two defense mechanisms developed as a response to this new situation: bilateral alliances, tailored to fit the changing political traits of various regimes; and a significant increase in military capability of each individual country. The militarization of various countries is evident by an increase in military budgets and arms purchases abroad, larger military establishments, and the growth of local military industries as shown in Table 2.1. These trends have been fueled by the Falkland/Malvinas conflict. The arms buildup in the region has been aggravated as a consequence of Argentina's military defeat. Military budgets of Latin American countries have maintained a high ceiling since then. After the war, Argentina expended huge financial resources in spite of its return to civilian government in 1983 and the austerity measures introduced by the new democratic government.[45] Similar policies expanding and upgrading military hardware for their respective armed forces can also be observed in other military establishments in the continent.

TABLE 2.1
Militarization in Latin America, 1975-1985

	Military Expenditures (billions of US$[a])	Armed Forces[a] (thousands of personnel)	Arms Imports (thousands of US$[b])	Arms Exports (millions of US$[b])
1975	8.6	1,297	1,015	156
1976	9.8	1,328	1,568	310
1977	10.5	1,438	1,627	146
1978	10.2	1,478	2,417	143
1979	10.1	1,491	2,429	158
1980	10.8	1,561	2,166	175
1981	11.0	1,617	3,034	218
1982	13.7	1,687	3,201	418
1983	12.3	1,746	2,530	190
1984	12.7	1,798	3,321	590
1985	12.5	1,894	1,665	75

[a]Constant 1984 figures.
[b]Constant 1983 figures.

Source: Arms Control and Disarmament Agency, *World Military Expenditures and Arms Transfers*, Washington, D.C.: U.S. Government Printing Office, 1987 and 1988.

The Anglo-Argentine conflict forced a recognition by Latin American military circles that regional military agreements were now obsolete. The Brazilian Minister of Aeronautics Delio Jardim de Mattos declared that the very term "traditional allies is a mere rhetorical fiction devoid of any practical significance, particularly when it is associated with nations that belong to different worlds. . . . [W]ith very few exceptions, all alliances demand evenness of forces."[46] The war also revealed the considerable degree of competence attained by the armed forces of the continent; their relative disadvantage stemmed mainly from their technological inferiority. Great Britain's victory, backed by NATO's most modern and sophisticated technology and North America's communications systems, was overwhelming. It was impossible for the Argentine air force to compensate for the British technological advantage of nuclear submarines and land operations capability and especially their communications equipment, which made possible sophisticated nocturnal sorties. The Brazilians have responded to this security lag by modernizing their entire navy. The navy possesses 36 battleships, but Brazilian admirals consider it inferior given Brazil's economic status in comparison with other world powers. At present, the navy has only 1 aircraft carrier, 8 submarines—of which only 3 are modern—and no advanced destroyers. The Brazilian navy minister's statement that his country would need a fleet ten times as powerful in order to feel safe can be considered an example of these initial reactions to the Falklands/Malvinas war.

Another important effect of that conflict was the nuclearization of the continent. The presence of British nuclear submarines in Latin American territorial waters was a flagrant violation of the Treaty of Tlatelolco, especially considering that the United Kingdom signed two additional protocols that emphasized its support for the denuclearization of the area. If one of Great Britain's ships had been damaged, there would have been a serious radiation hazard in the South Atlantic. Argentina's response to Great Britain's treaty violation was articulated by the president of the Argentine National Atomic Energy Commission, Vice-Admiral Carlos Castro Madero: "Argentina should feel free in the future to develop a nuclear submarine without impairing any of the commitments already acquired . . . [and] it will also preserve the right to develop what euphemistically has come to be called 'non-probscribed nuclear activities.'"[47]

Actually, in statements made in 1987, the Brazilian military announced its intention to develop a nuclear-powered navy. This information was followed by the official announcement by President José Sarney that Brazil had developed its own technology for enriching uranium at 3 percent, enough to produce fuel for the Angra I nuclear plant. Because Brazil has one of the most important world reserves of uranium, it could be one of the most important producers of enriched uranium, which will be processed in the new plant of Ipero in the state of São Paulo.[48] The suspension of the obligations mandated by the multilateral treaties, coupled with the advances already achieved by Argentina, Brazil, and Chile in this regard—the former two countries supported by the USSR and West Germany, respectively—points toward a slow but certain nuclearization of the continent. In the same vein, the new acquisition strategies of the armed forces of the continent imply large financial outlays for modern communication technologies. For example, the Brazilian government recently commissioned Canada to construct a communication satellite.

This pressure for modern equipment acquisition for conventional, nuclear, and communication purposes will impinge on the armed forces in an unpredictable way. The historical relations among their various branches will change consequently. The traditional budgetary and political preeminence of the army over the rest of the armed forces (which originated in the antiguerrilla and policing functions it assumed during the 1960s and 1970s) will be weakened as the air force and navy seek greater effectiveness in the event of an armed conflict. The navy will be developed for power projection purposes. And the military's political functions may also be reorganized with important domestic consequences. A good example of the current questioning of the leading role of the armies in public affairs is the criticism to which the Argentine army has been subjected by the other branches of the armed forces.

In addition to these new developments and crucial changes as a consequence of the breakdown of the hemispheric security system, Latin America has recently seen the emergence of traditional interstate and extracontinental tensions as well as new tensions arising from changes in the world military structure. These emerging difficulties will be discussed next.

New Security Regimes in Latin America

The diversity of conflict formation structures and conflict management approaches explains why the current international security positioning of Latin American countries is so diverse. This heterogeneity is relatively new since there existed a regional security framework from the post–World War II period up to the seventies that satisfied common security needs, as viewed by the military. Nevertheless, the breakdown of the hemispheric security system led to the military developments previously described. Fragmentation of security interests in the hemisphere and changes in local defense structures could reinforce the inconvenience and impossibility of a new inter-American security arrangement. In contrast, however, one could argue for the convenience of and explore the possibility for new security regimes.

The diversity of conflict formations in the hemisphere, the crisis of the previous hemispheric security system, and the increasingly diverse and independent security positioning of Latin American countries in the international military arena explain the lack of a functioning security regime.[49] These structural aspects are blocking the emergence of one security system that is able to contain all tensions and rivalries and integrate all the state in the region.

Previously I described how peaceful settlement of conflicts and tensions is possible only, if on the one hand, ruling elites abandon fundamentalism and replace it with a pragmatic approach to the settlement of conflicts.[50] Peace can become a reality in Latin America only through a long process of educating military and political elites in the hemisphere by reaffirming the importance of a pragmatic approach to both internal and international conflicts. A continuing education program in theories and concepts that

		NORTH/SOUTH RELATIONS	
		Cooperation	Conflict
INTRA-REGIONAL RELATIONS	Cooperation	Specific security regimes	Regional global security regime
	Conflict	Alignment	Internationalization of conflicts

FIGURE 2.3 Cooperative and Conflicting Hemispheric Security Regimes

illustrate the feasibility of peaceful coexistence and cooperation is one of the most important prerequisites to establishing lasting peace in the hemisphere.

On the other hand, regional security will result if specific security regimes are developed that tackle the diversity of conflict formation in the hemisphere in a fresh way. These security regimes will be difficult to develop because unequal expectations exist between the security interests of the United States in the region and those of Latin American countries (Figure 2.3). Cooperative security regimes with common incentives are not easy to develop and sustain.

Because of the diversity of conflict formation and security positioning in Latin America, few options are left for hemispheric security regimes. On the one hand, total alignment of the region behind the United States in its East-West confrontation would stimulate and create new conflicts in the area. On the other hand, the development of a single and comprehensive security regime—if possible—would imply the preeminence of U.S. interests, reproducing instabilities and confrontations. Finally, the lack of any security system at all would imply the potential danger of internationalization of conflicts in the region. The only way to solve this dilemma is to find specific security regimes that have the potentiality to attract the parties involved because they possess incentives for mutual cooperation. Accordingly, suggestions to abandon regional security networks in order to prevent an increasing fragmentation of regional security could be prevented.[51]

The search of new security regimes is urgent because common security at the global level requires the development of regional security structures.[52] In the Latin American case, the U.S. presence in the region cannot be ignored. On the contrary, it should be transformed into a positive presence, aiding the development of a common global security. For this reason, the participation of the United States in hemispheric security regimes genuinely responding to common shared interests could be an additional reinforcement for global security.

Usually, hemispheric security regimes, being globally or issue-oriented, embrace all security dimensions included in the national defense systems of individual countries. To overcome this obstacle, specific security regimes could be developed according to *particular dimensions of security*. These could include all aspects of national defense, that is, aerial, naval, and territorial. In each of these dimensions one can imagine specific security regimes.

One crucial hemispheric strategic regime could be developed in the naval area. The incentive for cooperation for all the parties in the region stems from the fact that all are interested in free naval transit in the Atlantic and Pacific oceans. Nevertheless, this free transit through sea lines of communication (SLC) should have some restrictions in order to be supported by all Latin American states, that is, the nuclear disarmament of those ships in transit in the area. Even though this restriction could be difficult for the United States to accept, it could have the additional incentive that it be applied in equal terms to the USSR. Considering the distance of Soviet ships and submarines from their bases, this restriction would relatively favor the United States. Nuclear waste in the area of SLCs should also be forbidden. Finally, no naval offensive bases either belonging to the United States or the USSR nor any other military power should be accepted in Latin America.

This naval hemispheric regime should be able to enforce its policies. Accordingly, consultation and verification mechanisms and institutions should be developed to work out alternatives. A joint naval command for verification and control at the hemispheric level would be highly useful.

From this perspective, naval hemispheric cooperation as expressed in the UNITAS exercises should emphasize antisubmarine warfare preparation and readiness, instead of disembarkment exercises for marines. Similarly, aerial operations could be linked to these exercises, giving substance to hemispheric security relations among the air forces in the region.

Another specific security regime could be developed in the aerial field. In addition to the support of naval control and verification procedures, this regime could include the development of a joint agency for the peaceful use of space, using all the facilities provided by President

Ronald Reagan's national space strategy and Congress' space policy legislation.[53]

This security regime should prohibit the installation in Latin American continental and insular territories of strategic launching sites, as well as the existence of terrestrial facilities for military uses of space. It could be also used to perform control and verification functions in extensive continental areas usually under sovereignty claims by Latin American states. The control and verification role could also be used by an aerial security regime to protect the Latin American exclusive economic zone. Even though the United States has been reluctant to accept this common Latin American position,[54] it could be an incentive for the United States to join this regime as it would provide effective security in the hemisphere.

Finally, a third specific security regime could be a territorial one. The incentive for all parties concerned would be the existence of a conflict control regime that would protect the continent from internal military confrontations and the hemisphere from the internationalization of the very same conflicts. To achieve these purposes a Latin American commission for peaceful management of disputes should be supported and could be created even in the context of the OAS or of the LAES.

In addition to this diplomatic initiative, a specific military policy should be developed. Like the specific security regimes, the territorial regime should emphasize the defensive aspect of local military power. A positive U.S. policy toward the Latin American military could emphasize a new professionalization process concentrating training as well as arms transfers around defensive doctrines and weapons.

Notwithstanding these arguments for hemispheric security, the most important issues in the continent in the territorial field for the United States are drug traffic and terrorism. From a Latin American perspective, these issues could be handled by police institutions instead of military ones. In order not to repeat the errors of previous decades of hemispheric military relations it should be necessary to emphasize the fact that these problems do not have a military nature similar to those mentioned above. The former are conflicts derived from state power projections. The latter are produced by local social and economic conditions as well as by the absence of political compromises. To deal with them from a military perspective could be counterproductive, stimulating the problem instead of providing a real solution.

The same could be said regarding the U.S. approach to low-intensity conflicts.[55] In this case, U.S. policy uses surrogate military forces in a given area to maintain credibility and presence without directly involving U.S. troops in these operations. This kind of hemispheric military relationship degrades any regional security system because it fuses political aims with military operations, subverting the latter into unequal, second-class joint ventures. This lopsidedness has been traditionally observed in U.S.–Latin American military relations. The use of military forces—surrogates or not—as well as the use of covert actions in the area, should be overcome to permit the emergence of real and shared military and security interests. A regional security system could only be developed if all parties involved renounce the use of military force against each other to solve political problems. This democratic conviction, so widely disseminated in the United States, should also be reflected in U.S. military policymaking in order to democratize regional military relations.

The usual response to the use of Latin America as a "buffer zone," not involving it in the East-West confrontation, is the argument that U.S. withdrawal from its traditional political-military roles in the region would create a power vacuum that would be an irrestible attraction for the USSR. Therefore, the United States should not withdraw from the area; on the contrary, it should strengthen its position in the region. A power vacuum could be a magnet for the internationalization of conflict, but it could also be a repellent. "As long as all the major outside actors stay out, or at the fringes," this power vacuum will be transformed into a power repellent. "It is the intrusion of one that may attract the rivals."[56] U.S.–Latin American cooperation to transform the hemisphere into a "power repellent" region could be the product of a set of military and security policies that would make the area able to absorb and moderate East-West tensions with nonaligned military actors. This alternative could have the potential to create enough incentives for all parties involved— including the United States—to develop specific security regimes that are able to generate and sustain a new, peaceful military hemispheric order.

Notes

1. A useful historical analysis of hemispheric relations can be found in Edwin Lieuwen, *U.S. Policy in Latin America* (New York: Praeger Publishers, 1965), 10.

2. On "international regimes," see Robert O. Keohane, *After Hegemony. Cooperation and Discord in World Political Economy* (Princeton: Princeton University Press, 1984).

3. On the economic policies of authoritarian regimes, see Alejandro Foxley, *Latin American Experiments in Neo-Conservative Economics* (Berkeley: University of California Press, 1984).

4. On the nature and function of the Latin American state, see Norbert Lechner, ed., *Estado y Política en América Latina* (Mexico: Siglo XXI, 1981).

5. On this subject, see Miriam Muñiz, "Aspectos básicos de la fase imperialista en la dominación colonial sobre Puerto Rico" (Basic Aspects of the Imperialist Phase in the Colonial Domination of Puerto Rico) (San Juan, n.d., Mimeographed).

6. On the subject of the Islas Malvinas (Falkland Islands), see Oscar Cardoso, Ricardo Kirschbaum, and Eduardo van der Kooj, *Malvinas. La Trama Secreta* (Malvinas. The Secret Plot) (Buenos Aires: Sudamericana/Planeta, 1983).

7. For an analysis of Latin American interstate conflicts, see John Child, "Geopolitical Thinking in Latin America," *Latin American Research Review,* no. 2, (1979); Michael Morris and Victor Millan, *Controlling Latin American Conflicts, Ten Approaches* (Boulder, Colo.: Westview Press, 1983); John Child, "South American Geopolitical Thinking and Antarctica" (Paper presented to the panel on International Law and Polar Politics, 26th Annual Convention of the International Studies Association, Washington, D.C., March 7, 1985).

8. See Amilcar Herrera et al., *Armamentismo e o Brasil* (Armaments and Brazil) (Rio de Janeiro: Editora Brasiliense, 1985).

9. See Richard Fagen and Olga Pellicier, eds., *The Future of Central America* (Stanford, Calif.: Stanford University Press, 1983); and Wolf Grabendorff, Heinrich-W. Krunwiede, and Jöng Todt, *Political Change in Central America* (Boulder, Colo.: Westview Press, 1984).

10. On this aspect of the Central American conflict, see Fernando Morán, "El papel de Europa en Centroamérica: Un enfoque socialista español" (The Role of Europe in Central America: A Spanish Socialist Approach), in *Nuevas Formas de Cooperación Europa-Centroamérica* (New Forms of European-Central American Cooperation) (San Jose, Costa Rica: Facultad Latinoamericana de Ciencias Sociales (FLACSO)–Centro de Investigaciones Europes-Latinoamericanas (IRELA), Ministry of Information and Communication, 1985).

11. For an analysis of the orientations of U.S. foreign policy see Stanley Hoffman, *Primacy of World Order* (New York: McGraw-Hill, 1978). On Soviet interests in the region, see Augusto Varas, "Soviet-Latin American Relations Under United States Hegemony," in Augusto Varas, ed., *Soviet–Latin American Relations in the 1980s* (Boulder, Colo.: Westview Press, 1987).

12. On this aspect, see Augusto Varas, *Militarization and the International Arms Race in Latin America* (Boulder, Colo.: Westview Press, 1985).

13. See Antonio Cavalla, *Geopolítica y Seguridad Nacional en América* (Mexico: Universidad Nacional Autónoma de México (UNAM) 1979); John Child, "Geopolitical Thinking in Latin America; Augusto Varas, "Acumulación financiera y gobiernos militares de derecha en América Latina," in Carlos Portales, ed., *América Latina y el Nuevo Orden Económico Internacional.* (Mexico: Fondo de Cultura Económica, 1983). For an analysis of political conceptualizations, see Jorge Chateau, "Características principales del pensamiento geopolítico chileno: análisis; de dos libros," *Documento de Trabajo* (Santiago: FLACSO, 1977). A critique is found in Comandante Juan de Zavala, "Valor actual de la geopolítica," *Ejército,* June 1955. This Spanish official maintained that "geopolitical analysis became obsessed with geographical considerations to the point that they failed to consider other factors or causes. For a different type of critique, see José Medina E., "Presentaciones y planteos," *Papeles de Sociología,* Biblioteca de Ensayos Sociológicos, Instituto de Investigaciones Sociales (Mexico: UNAM, 1953).

14. See the critical analysis made by F. A. Sondermann, "The Concept of National Interest," *Orbis* (Spring 1977), 121–138.

15. The preceding quotes are drawn from Child, "South American Geopolitical Thinking."
16. See Frank D. McCann, "Brazilian Foreign Relations in the Twentieth Century," in *Brazil in the International System: The Rise of a Middle Power,* ed. Wayne A. Selcher (Boulder, Colo.: Westview Press, 1981).
17. On the process of transition to democracy in Latin America, see Augusto Varas, *Transición a la Democracia, América Latina y Chile* (Transition to Democracy, Latin America and Chile) (Santiago: ACHIP-Ainavillo, 1985).
18. For an analysis of the relations between the two countries, see Riordan Roett and Scott D. Tollefson, eds., "Brazil's Status as an Intermediate Power," *SAIS* (Washington, D.C., 1985).
19. In this respect see my *Militarization and the International Arms Race.*
20. General George S. Brown, chairman of the Joint Chiefs of Staff, *United States Military Posture for FY 1979,* (Washington, D.C.: U.S. Government Printing Office, 1978).
21. See John Child, *Unequal Alliance: The Inter-American Military System, 1938–1978* (Boulder, Colo.: Westview Press, 1980).
22. See Inter-American Conference for the Consolidation of Peace, "Inter-American Reciprocal Assistance Treaty" (Rio de Janeiro, 1947), p. 4.
23. Lieutenant Colonel D. A. Raymond, "Reflections on Mutual Defense Assistance Program," *Military Review* 35, no. 5 (August 1955):31–49. On May 22, 1947 President Truman signed Public Law No. 75 authorizing military aid for Greece and Turkey. In 1949, the 81st Congress formalized the Program of Mutual Assistance and Defense. The Mutual Security Act, which was to be in operation between 1953 and 1961, was established soon after, as well as the Foreign Assistance Act of 1961, established under the Kennedy administration. The latter act expired in 1980.
24. See Major T. Wyckoff, "South America's Strategic Position," *Military Review* 36 (July 1956), 26.
25. Lieutenant Colonel R. Salinas, "La Posición Estratégica de Chile en la defensa del Continente," *Memorial del Ejército de Chile,* July-October, 1947, 123.
26. General J. del Carmen Marín, "El Perú y la defensa hemisférica," *Revista Militaria del Perú,* June 1965. Conference presented at the Center for Higher Military Studies on the occasion of a visit of students of the National War College of the United States.
27. For an analysis of the transference of arms to Latin America during the postwar period, see John L. Sutton and Geoffrey Kemp, "Arms to Developing Countries, 1945–1965," *Adelphi Papers* (October 1966); D. Wood, "Armed Forces in Central and South America," *Adelphi Papers* (April 1967); and Gertrude E. Heare, "Trends in Latin American Military Expenditures, 1940–1970," U.S. Department of State, December, 1971.
28. J. B. McConaughy, "Latin America: A Soviet Objective," *Military Review* 41 (October 1961), 13. Emphasis added.
29. For a characterization of these programs, see Lieutenant Colonel H. F. Walterhouse (Retired), "The Good Uniformed Neighbor," *Military Review* 45 (February 1965) 11–19; and Major C. Smith, Jr., "Civic-Military Actions in Central America," *Military Review* 49 (January 1969), 76–84.

30. General R. W. Porter, "Looking to Latin America," *Military Review* 48 (June 1968), p. 22.

31. For a recent analysis of U.S.–Latin American military relations see Lars Schoultz, *National Security and United States Policy Toward Latin America* (Princeton: Princeton University Press, 1987).

32. Lieutenant Colonel H. R. Aaron, "The Inter-American Military Forces," *Military Review* 45 (June 1965), 38.

33. General Alejandro Lanusse, "El perfeccionamiento del sistema militar interamericano," *Revista de la Escuela Superior de Guerra* (September-December 1968); Lieutenant Colonel L. A. Leoni, "La seguridad en América," *Revista de la Escuela Superior de Guerra* (March-April 1968).

34. General Edgardo Mercado Jarrín, "Reflexiones sobre la seguridad y el desarrollo en América Latina," *Estrategia* 24 (September-October, 1973), 39–40.

35. On strategic autism, see Dieter Senghaas, *Rüstung und Militarismus* (Frankfurt: Suhrkamp Verlag, 1972).

36. Casper Weinberger, "U.S. Defense Strategy," *Foreign Affairs* (Spring 1986):677.

37. Ibid., 697.

38. Lars Schoultz, *National Security and United States Policy Toward Latin America*, 310.

39. "U.S. Will Increase Latin War Games," *New York Times*, February 22, 1987.

40. *Ambito Financiero* (Buenos Aires), November 22, 1987.

41. "Discurso del Secretario de Estado Adjunto Elliot Abrams en el Colegio Interamericano de Defensa" (Washington, D.C., June 13, 1986. Texto oficial Servicio de Cultura y Prensa, Embajada de los Estados Unidos de América (Santiago, Chile).

42. An analysis of the main limitations of various experiences of integration in Latin America is found in Germánico Salgado, "El Mercado Regional Latinoamericano: El Proyecto y las Realidades," *Revista de la CEPAL*, April 1979.

43. See Mark Falcoff's contribution, Chapter 3, in this volume.

44. In this respect see Luis Maira, *El Fin de la Hegemonía Norteamericana* (Lima: DESCO, 1982).

45. See Stockholm International Peace Research Institute (SIPRI), *World Armaments and Disarmament, Yearbook 1987* (Cambridge: Oxford University Press, 1987).

46. Quoted in Augusto Varas, "Democratization, Peace and Security in Latin America," *Alternatives*, no. 4 (1985):619.

47. Ibid.

48. See "Uranium Enriched by Brazil," *International Herald Tribune*, September 7, 1987, 3.

49. We define "regime" following Stephen Krasner, ed., *International Regimes* (Ithaca, N.Y.: Cornell University Press, 1983) as a "set of implicit or explicit principles, norms, rules and decision-making procedures around which actors' expectations converge in a given area of international relations. Principles are beliefs of fact, causation, and rectitude. Norms are standards of behaviour defined

in terms of rights and obligations. Rules are specific prescriptions or proscriptions for action. Decision-making procedures are prevailing practices for making and implementing collective choice." Quoted in Robert O. Keohane, *After Hegemony. Cooperation and Discord in World Political Economy* (Princeton: Princeton University Press, 1984), 57.

50. On realism and pragmatism in politics, see Franz Hinkelammert, "El realismo en política como arte de lo posible" (Realism in Politics as the Art of the Possible), *Contribuciones* (Santiago: FLACSO, 1984); and Angel Flisfisch, "Hacia un realismo político distinto" (Toward a Different Kind of Political Realism), *Working Paper* (Santiago: FLACSO, 1984).

51. As proposed by Falcoff in Chapter 3 of this volume.

52. See United Nations, "Report of the Independent Commission on Disarmament and Security," A/CN.10/38 (United Nations, 1983). This report has been known as the "Palme Report."

53. See Marcia S. Smith, "Space Policy and Funding: NASA and Civilian Space Programs Updated 07/01/85," *Congressional Research Service Issue Brief,* IB82118 (Washington, D.C., 1985).

54. On U.S. policy toward this issue, see Department of State, "Current Development in the U.S. Oceans Policy," *Department of State Bulletin,* September 1986.

55. See Lilia Bermúdez and Raúl Benítez, chapter 6 of this volume.

56. See Stanley Hoffmann, *Dead Ends* (Cambridge, Mass.: Ballinger Publishing Co., 1983), 134.

3

Military and Strategic Issues in Latin America

Mark Falcoff

The military question—that is, what role the armed forces will play in society—is arguably the oldest and most enduring issue in Latin American history. It has implications not merely for the political order but for the economic system and the network of international alliances to which Latin American states are a party. To define an ideal pattern of civil-military relations is, in fact, the most all-inclusive political statement any Latin American can make. That is why, even now in the late 1980s, when economic issues seem so much more pressing, that publicists and politicians continue to devote so much of their time to the subject. Their concern is shared, of course, by all those foreign powers who exercise, or hope to exercise, influence within the region. This chapter analyzes the present situation and suggests where the evolving circumstances may take the Western Hemisphere in the future.

The Role of the Military in Society

In the narrowest political terms, Latin America has entered a long cycle of demilitarization. Since 1979 alone, six nations—Ecuador, Peru, Honduras, El Salvador, Argentina, and Uruguay—have witnessed a return to civilian government. Two more, Guatemala and Brazil, are in the process of so doing; in two more, Chile and Paraguay, strong personalistic elements suggest that the regimes may not outlive their leaders. Some countries with virtually no tradition of civilian rule, Venezuela and the Dominican Republic, have managed to sustain it for 20 years or more; and one, Mexico—with a very indifferent record—has not had a military government, properly speaking, since 1930 nor a president of military provenance since 1946.

Unfortunately, in many cases this situation owes far less to the strength of civilian institutions than to wounds self-inflicted by the armed forces themselves during long periods of de facto rule. In Peru, for example, it was gross economic mismanagement and a sudden flood of due bills, not love of democracy, that persuaded the generals to call elections in 1979. In Argentina, nothing short of humiliation on the field of battle was sufficient to break the military's determination to remain in power. It is also true, however, that the international environment for military governments is far less congenial than it once was. The cloud of indifference behind which they could conduct business as usual in Western Europe and the United States has been penetrated by human rights organizations, the media, churches, and political parties. Many Latin American soldiers, whatever their private preferences, are now convinced that their corporate interests are best served by allowing civilians to rule. As long as certain minimal requirements are met, this is likely to remain the case.

Meeting those requirements may, of course, be easier for some countries than for others. They include the preservation of public order, relative parity of weaponry with those countries to which military establishment compares itself, and the perpetuation and enhancement of such pre-rogatives as salaries, housing, commissary privileges, and foreign travel. In addition, in some countries the military is accustomed to playing a very large role in the economy, and the deficits of public sector enterprises cannot be cut without injuring the welfare of many flag officers, both active and retired. Finally, governments must show "respect for the honor of the armed forces," an omnibus term that, however vague, has concrete meaning in specific times and places. It may mean giving soldiers the right to vote in national elections, allowing the service chiefs to participate in the deliberations of the national cabinet, conceding direction of key government agencies to serving general officers, resisting political pres-sures to abolish conscription, or minimizing the scope and impact of investigations of previous military governments.

Even in the best of times, in no Latin American country can the military be considered nonpolitical. For one thing, it is often the only really well-organized political community, with a clear-cut sense of mission and an unambiguous pattern of authority. For another, in some countries the armed forces have a near monopoly on skills essential for development, particularly in the fields of civil engineering, atomic power, and communications. For still another, civilian politicians themselves have not been above encouraging soldiers to speak their minds, sometimes quite sharply, in cabinet councils or in the media. Almost all populist movements in fact have assiduously courted the military and attempted to turn it to essentially partisan purposes: Juan Perón in Argentina,

Salvador Allende in Chile, and Getúlio Vargas and Joao Goulart in Brazil. In sum, the Anglo-Saxon model of civil-military relations is not merely foreign to the Latin American experience, but also, one must candidly admit, to Latin American tastes.

If this much is typical in periods of relative normality, what can be expected in times of economic and social crisis? In the past, the civilian political order in Latin America generally succumbed to the first strong wind. As of the late 1980s that is less likely. In countries like Argentina, the memory of military misrule is simply too recent and too painful; in El Salvador and Honduras, too much depends upon the goodwill of the U.S. Congress; and in Mexico, the local political system still retains the resources to deal with major shocks. In Chile and Brazil, economic crisis probably tends to move things, willy-nilly, as much toward civilian rule as away from it. A remilitarization of politics in Peru or Bolivia is still possible, but if accomplished along traditional lines, only at very considerable cost, both in domestic and in international spheres.

The classic military regime, which seeks to restore order by draconian means, working hand in glove with local conservative interests, has roots too deep in Latin American history to be written off altogether. It is far less likely now, however, than two new variations. The first of these might be called "military populist" or "Nasserist." Because such a government existed in Peru between 1968 and 1979, it is quite possible to anticipate its principal characteristics. First, its ostensible purpose is not to restore order or to defend traditional values but to transform the society, reordering social hierarchies in a more egalitarian fashion. For this purpose it tends to expropriate major landowners and industrialists and to create new social organizations whose professed purpose is to represent the poor and the dispossessed. Second, although hostile to historical foreign interests, particularly oil and mining companies, it is open to new investment willing to operate according to more stringent rules. Third, it pursues an independent foreign policy, diversifying its dependencies and taking an active part in the Nonaligned Movement, the Group of 77, the Latin American Economic System, and other caucuses associated with the New International Economic Order. Fourth, it places military officers at the head of virtually every ministry and government agency, unlike the "classic" regime, which is in effect a coalition of generals and conservative politicians.

If the Peruvian experience is any indication, this kind of regime will not abolish the distinctions between rich and poor, much less after the ranking of the state in the hierarchy of developed and developing nations. It will succeed in bankrupting traditional elites and replacing them with new business groups, drawn from close relations or silent partners of serving officers. Moreover, precisely because such governments are military in the most thoroughgoing sense of the term, they devote a large share of their budgetary resources to the purchase of sophisticated and extremely costly weaponry. Finally, when they have exhausted all of the resources of the local economy, expropriated what enterprises they can, and worn out their welcome with fly-by-night bankers, unscrupulous international businessmen, and multilateral lending agencies, they will finally return the government to the hapless civilians.

The fact that Peru is so manifestly worse off in 1988 than in 1968 by no means suggests that the experiment there will not be repeated in other countries, for the advantages such regimes afford are simply too numerous to be ignored. By using nationalism, they bridge the historical gap between civilian and military communities; by expropriating the wealthy and major foreign interests, they preempt the left and even co-opt many of its leaders; by aligning with the nonaligned—which is to say, by distancing themselves from the United States—they are guaranteed an automatic thumping majority at the United Nations. The fact that such regimes allow their leaders to advance personal and corporate interests even more effectively than the more traditional "right-wing" military government does nothing, of course, to detract from their appeal.

The other variation is already present in Cuba and Nicaragua, two countries not normally thought to have military governments at all. Consider, however, the fact that they are ruled by uniformed dictators of service rank, who preside over a "revolutionized" armed forces several times the size of the institution it has replaced. If they differ from the Nasserist model, it is only in degree. They generally have many more men (and sometimes women) under arms; they tend to break down the barriers between the armed forces and the civilian population by creating militias and reserve formations that extend military experience to the very boundaries of society; and they normally devote the largest share of resources to the acquisition of arms. Unlike the Nasserist regime, the Cuban-Nicaraguan model projects a military presence outward, either in the form of overseas expeditions (as in Africa) or the training of cadres from other countries and the transshipment of arms to them. As they are openly allied to the Soviet Union, they have a direct pipeline to the one thing that country is in a position to offer them—military aid—and on a scale far greater than anything the United States has ever been in a position to offer. Finally, because such regimes operate within a Leninist framework of political organization, they need not fear the consequences of economic mismanagement, corruption, or growing popular discontent: They are there to stay.

Alignment, Nonalignment, Realignment:
Strategic Issues

Since 1947 all of the Spanish-speaking nations of the hemisphere and Brazil have been linked to the United States in a functional military alliance known as the Rio Treaty. Although that charter and the institutions it created are still in place, the utility of both—at least for the United States—has steadily eroded over the past twenty-five years. Two states, Cuba and Nicaragua, have virtually or formally withdrawn from the alliance and enlisted in its Soviet analogue. Several others—Venezuela, Panama, Colombia, Argentina, and Brazil—have become observers or full members of the Nonaligned Movement. Perhaps the only really stalwart members that remain are military regimes in Guatemala, Chile, and Paraguay. This suggests that if democracy is, as most interested observers hope, the wave of the future in Latin America, there will be a decline of U.S. influence in military- and security-related matters.

In the event of an outright attack upon a Latin American nation by some outside power, the country affected and the United States could still probably marshal some sort of unified response within the framework of the Rio Treaty, although one could not be certain that it would go much beyond a platonic resolution of solidarity. Unfortunately, the inter-American alliance is not likely to face so conveniently clear-cut a decision. Rather, it must now confront aggression from within the region, or even more seriously, local aggression in collusion with some outside power. The Rio Treaty apparently anticipated such eventualities: Article 6 requires a collective response not merely in cases of foreign invasion but in "any other fact or situation that might endanger the peace and security of America." Unfortunately, today there is no consensus among signatories on what that "fact" or "situation" might be, and such consensus is frankly not in prospect.

Two factors have conspired to create this state of affairs. First, the United States is no longer the only, or in some cases the principal, supplier of advanced weaponry to the Latin American nations. It is difficult to exaggerate the importance of this fact, because it was precisely the U.S. quasi monopoly of modern arms that led all Latin American armies, even one as residually hostile as that of Argentina, to press their governments to sign the Rio Treaty in 1947. Today the situation is vastly different: By value, the largest supplier of weaponry to the region is the Soviet Union, followed by France, Italy, the United Kingdom, and then the United States.[1] To some degree, the loss of hegemony was inevitable, as European countries recovered from World War II and, within the context of the NATO alliance, developed their own arms industries. It also, however, reflects a voluntary withdrawal from certain markets by the United States in a desire not to be regarded as an accomplice to regimes that systematically violated human rights. Although the actual impact of that policy on its intended objective remains a matter of controversy, undoubtedly one effect was to open new Latin American markets to European suppliers formerly unable to compete with the United States on economic grounds alone. Inevitable, too, has been the growth of an indigenous arms industry in Argentina and Brazil as part of a conscious policy to remove national security from the vagaries of policy in Western Europe and the United States and, not incidentally, to develop new lines of export and new sources of foreign exchange.

The second factor in the decline of U.S. influence is of equal importance. Most Latin American countries today have succeeded in greatly diversifying their economic dependence, so that although the United States is still the principal source of credit and financial services, it is decreasingly so in other fields: direct investment, manufactured goods, and new technology. There is, in short, no solid, unambiguous economic underpinning to the inter-American alliance, and one is not likely to develop in the future. At this point all the differences over Latin American policy between the two major parties in the United States turn upon politicomilitary issues: arms sales to El Salvador, aid to the contras in Nicaragua, and human rights everywhere. There is no constituency for a new Alliance for Progress, and even the Reagan administration's extremely modest Caribbean Basin Initiative may fail to negotiate its way past multiple congressional obstacles.

How are these two factors likely to influence the Latin American diplomatic and strategic environment? One possible outcome would be a generalized withdrawal from the Rio Treaty and its replacement by a purely Latin American security organization. This is actually a very old idea[2] that periodically resurfaces whenever the existing system is perceived to be overtaxed by U.S. national interests. (The most recent example was the wave of recrimination that followed the Argentine war with Great Britain in 1982.) Such an eventuality presupposes, however, a demonstrated community of Latin American interest, which the countries have so far been unable to demonstrate in such organizations as the Andean Pact and the Latin American Economic System. It would also require the allocation of new Latin American resources to defense, particularly naval defense, which for many countries—including some quite important ones like Mexico—can for the present be comfortably left to the U.S. taxpayer. Moreover, to mount a new system would require overcoming the considerable inertia that sustains the old. The Inter-American Defense Board,[3] like all other international organizations, generates its own imperatives, clear enough to those who benefit from them, if often invisible to others.

Another option—the one the United States fears most—would be the entry of several Latin American countries into a military alliance with the Soviet Union. Of course, this has already happened in Cuba and seems well on its way in Nicaragua. Other Latin American governments, however, can consider this option seriously only if they are prepared to overturn all the established institutions of society and mount the full apparatus of a totalitarian state. Short of that, a purely commercial relationship with the Soviet Union, such as Argentina's, does not seem to have very far-reaching security implications. Arms sales alone, even on a massive scale, as the case of Peru demonstrates, do not guarantee a country's strategic realignment.

A third option would be genuine nonalignment. This is a real possibility for the larger Latin American countries, whose links to the outside world are sufficiently complex to balance and counterbalance pressures and influences along either an East-West or North-South axis. Perhaps the classic example is Brazil, which manages to be both "West" and "South," depending upon the issue. There are strong trends in this direction, though, in Venezuela, Colombia, Argentina, and Mexico. Although in theory such a policy should position a country to derive maximum advantage from so-called superpower rivalries and the purported po-lycentrism of the international system, it could be argued that nonalign-ment really does little more than enhance the self-esteem of a country's foreign policy establishment. Certainly, it could only improve one's bargaining position if one of the two major world powers believed that a country could be won over to alignment, whereas the whole point of the exercise is to maintain some form of equidistance. Moreover, non-alignment has become so common that it has lost its menacing aspect, at least for the United States, except where it is really a euphemism for realignment with the Soviets, as in the case of Cuba or Nicaragua.

Two other options are not really options at all, merely eventualities. One is the breakdown of public order in one or more countries as the result of acute economic and social crisis. Although nowadays this admittedly apocalyptic scenario is being retailed a bit more often than the facts probably justify, in some countries it is far less fantastic than some people imagine. Here, the security threat would not be a hostile government, but the lack of any kind of enforceable authority. Instead, such a country would be converted into a safe haven for transnational terrorism and subversive operations under Soviet, Cuban, Libyan, or Palestine Liberation Organization (PLO) agents. Unfortunately, Bolivia seems poised to fall into just such a morass. In this case all five countries that share its borders would have ample reason for alarm. What is worse, because the local government would bear no responsibility for such a state of affairs, there would be no diplomatic mechanism by which other countries could effectively respond.

The most likely outcome is a combination of all of these. There will be no new departures in security policy for the Latin American nations: They will have other things on their minds and leave the United States to handle the most extreme situations. There will be no open support for the United States, however—not even verbal support—no matter what those situations are. In spite of continued formal alignment with Washington, most Latin American actors will increasingly strive for a posture of nonalignment. Although constricted by commitments to non-intervention made in another era and under entirely different circum-stances, the United States will increasingly go it alone, determining which problems deserve serious response and which must be written off as outside U.S. geographic and logistic capabilities. Although this is not, admittedly, a very pleasant prospect for the United States, in time it may be evident that it is not very appealing for the Latin American countries either. For once the latter have, in effect, opted out of the inter-American system, they will find it impossible to conjure up the kinds of issues capable of getting serious policy attention in Washington, much less coaxing it into something approaching a satisfactory response.

Notes

1. U.S. Department of State, Arms Control and Disarmament Agency, *World Military Expenditures, 1978–82* (Washington, D.C.: U.S. Government Printing Office, 1984), Table 3.

2. Arthur P. Whitaker, *The Western Hemisphere Idea: Its Rise and Decline* (Ithaca, N.Y.: Cornell University Press, 1954).

3. The Inter-American Defense Board is a consortium of flag officers rep-resenting all the Rio Treaty signatories whose mission is joint strategic planning.

4

Understanding U.S. Policy Toward Latin America

Margaret Daly Hayes

To craft a policy toward Latin America, it is first necessary to understand U.S. interests in Latin America. For that, it is necessary to know the constraints of the policymaking process. Too many administrations, academicians, and amateur policymakers have had a policy first and then have tried to match U.S. and Latin American interests in the region to their policy. It is not surprising that the policies have failed or fallen short of expectations.

To complicate the process, there is a reluctance among scholars and the public to confront the notion of a U.S. interest in Latin America, other world regions, or in specific sets of events. The U.S. public is often more comfortable reacting to world events than working to shape them. As Henry Kissinger (1973) wrote in his 1967 essay "An Inquiry into the American National Interest,"

> Americans have historically shied away from addressing the essence of our national interest and the premises of our foreign policy. . . . A mature conception of our interests in the world . . . takes into account widespread interest in the "need" for stability and peaceful change. It would deal with two fundamental questions: "What is it in our interest to prevent?" and "What would we seek to accomplish?"

This chapter is an effort to explore the requirements of a more goal-oriented policy in Latin America than the United States has had recently and to explain the limits and constraints on the choices inherent in that policy in other words, what we might seek to accomplish and what we might seek to prevent. Although the proposed policy framework is applicable to the whole hemisphere, the specific focus of discussion is Central America. The presentation is divided into three sections: a definition of U.S. interests in Latin America, a discussion of current policies and their relations to specific U.S. interests, and finally, a discussion of U.S. attitudes and actions related to the Contadora peace process in Central America.

A Definition of U.S. Interests in Latin America

In my own work I have sought to develop a formulation of the interests the United States has in Latin America that encompass the broader concept of national interest that Kissinger described. A definition of U.S. interests in Latin America must encompass political, economic, and security considerations, in addition to the narrower concept of military security usually adopted (see Hayes 1983; 1984). The formulation is intended to capture what U.S. policy might be; the values it might reflect; and what it must be, given the constraints of the U.S. political process. It is a definition of U.S. interests defined from a U.S. point of view, not of policies that others might want to elicit from the United States. I believe that my definition describes fairly accurately the fundamental components of interest that drive our Latin American policy: "It is in the United States' national interest that there exist in the Western Hemisphere, friendly, prosperous states with stable responsible governments that permit the free movement of goods and services throughout the region; that respect the political integrity of their neighbours; and that offer no support to the United States global political rivals" (see Hayes 1982; 1983; 1984).

Of course, not all policy flows from these premises. The policy process is not deductive. Nevertheless, when put to an empirical test, I believe the basic elements of the definition are upheld. In the following section, I discuss the formulation point by point.

U.S. Interest in Government Responsibility and System Stability

It is in the national interest of the United States that the nations of the hemisphere have stable political systems and responsible governments. U.S. government attention focuses principally on East-West issues, on U.S. relations with its allies in Europe and Japan, and on major problem areas like the Middle East. Frequently in the past, and less so in the present, Latin America receives high-level attention only when it is rent by crisis. Despite a desire by regional specialists within the government and without to see greater and more sophisticated consideration given to routine Western Hemisphere issues, this is not likely to obtain in the foreseeable future. This is a lamentable fact that many would like to correct. Its consequence is that U.S.–Latin American relations in general are managed with limited resources and certain constraints on the U.S. government's policy flexibility.

Political instability anywhere in the world is of concern to the United States for a variety of reasons. Because of U.S. global commitments, instability in the regions proximate to U.S. borders, particularly when that instability has ideological overtones, is especially worrisome to the U.S. government. Instability in the hemisphere has a direct impact in the United States. Recent instability in the hemisphere has resulted in massive migrations of Latin American populations to the United States. Such migrations are difficult to manage and to absorb. Moreover, they drain some of the best human resources from developing countries, compromising the future growth prospects of those countries. Finally, managing crises and instabilities in this hemisphere requires a great deal of decisionmaker time in the United States, and there is a limited amount of high-level time that has been, that is presently, or that will likely be devoted in the future to the Western Hemisphere.[1]

For all of these reasons it is in the interest of the United States that Latin American countries be able to conduct their own affairs and to cope with and to accommodate change so that the United States is not called upon to deal with regional events on a crisis basis. Countries that can cope with or accommodate change are more likely to be more politically stable and more responsible in their dealings with their domestic political problems.

In the past, in part because of the limited interest in the region, the United States has focused almost exclusively on the stability of regional governments, forgetting that stability may be a temporary thing if governments do not serve the needs of their societies in some minimal way. Increasingly, governments have come to be judged by what they have accomplished for their societies. Governments must be responsible and responsive to their societies. Responsible government in this sense means a government that respects human rights, plans for the political and economic well-being of the population, and responds to the demands of a variety of groups. Many Latin American governments can be found wanting in this essential attention to the needs and desires of their populations. More and more, political thinking in the United States recognizes that these failures of government responsibility have contributed to the endemic political instability of the region.

Stability as it is used here does not mean status quo, right-wing dictatorships; rather it means effective, efficient, responsive governments that are able to cope with the demands of their own populations. It also means political systems that can conduct elections and absorb changes of political leadership through constitutional means and not

just by a coup or revolution. By stability, I also mean political systems
and practices that serve to incorporate all elements of society into the
political process—in effect, "good government."

U.S. Interest in Friendly Relations in the Americas

It is in the national interest of the United States that relations among
the nations of the hemisphere and with the United States be friendly.
Friendly relations mean cordial relations that facilitate accomplishing
mutual goals. They presume a level of confidence and trust among
leaders. Having friendly relations does not mean, however, that there
are no differences between countries. Too often it is assumed that the
United States demands that its Latin American neighbors acquiesce to
U.S. desires. This is not the case, nor should it be. The United States
has friendly relations with its allies Europe and Japan and yet has
important differences with those countries as well. Having friendly
relations means keeping differences in perspective.

Friendly relations need have nothing to do with alignment or nonalignment. Factors other than mere labels define the quality of relations
between nations. Having friendly relations does mean avoiding name
calling. It means using normal diplomatic channels to accomplish the
business of a bilateral relationship; purposely irritating uses of high
rhetoric should be avoided. High rhetoric characterizes the poor relationships that exist between the United States and Cuba, Nicaragua,
and, from time to time, other countries of the region. Latin American
politicians sometimes fail to appreciate how their use of rhetoric in
asserting their national independence from the dominant regional power
complicates the quality of U.S.–Latin American relations.

U.S. Interest in Regional Economic Prosperity

For countries of the Western Hemisphere to prosper is in'the national
interest of the United States. Though barely conscious of it, the U.S.
public generally wishes prosperity and well-being for its neighbors. U.S.
assistance programs are supported in Congress because of a sense of
responsibility for assisting the poor of other nations.

Regional economic prosperity is a key interest of the United States.
Clearly, the region's poverty and deprivation are a shocking human
tragedy that cannot be ignored; that poverty and income inequality have
direct consequences for the United States.

Although the United States often benefits from the presence of migrant
workers in the U.S. labor market, large-scale, uncontrolled and illegal
migrations from Central America and the Caribbean region are increas-

ingly difficult for the United States to deal with (see Pastor 1985 for a review of Caribbean migration to the United States). From time to time taxpayer backlash threatens against such migrants. The political factors that cause migrations complicate U.S. domestic and foreign policy.

Furthermore, Latin America's economic recession of the early 1980s resulted in hundreds of thousands of lost income dollars and employment in the United States as purchases from Mexico, Brazil, and other large market countries were cut back. More urgently, regional poverty and income inequality have created fertile ground for the development of political instability, for exploitation by hostile ideologues, and for the emergence of militant opposition groups. In this regard, bad governments generally do not solve economic problems well. Thus, the question of economic prosperity goes hand in glove with the question of political stability and responsible government. The less responsible the government, the greater the prospects for political instability in the developing country, and the less will be done to ameliorate economic problems. A vicious cycle ensues.

I should stress, however, that prosperity does not mean economic activity dominated by U.S. multinational corporations. Latin American governments long ago learned to regulate and control foreign investors for their own purposes.[2] Nor does economic prosperity mean just growth measured by an expanding gross domestic product. It also means distribution of the benefits of growth across the populations and the involvement of that population in the development process. Stable economic growth requires not only access to external markets and sources of hard currency, but also broad-based domestic consumption.

Fundamental changes in the domestic economic policies of Latin American countries must be undertaken in order to end the cyclical and structural causes of the severe economic problems that they face. In the past, the United States has regarded issues of economic management to be the responsibility and concern of national governments. Because of the direct effects that Latin America's economic management and mismanagement have on the U.S. economy, the U.S. government now is pressing economic reform and adjustment aggressively.

In seeking to stimulate greater prosperity in Latin America, policy-makers have become much more conscious of (1) the limits of foreign assistance; (2) the regional requirements for investment capital to fuel the engine of economic growth; (3) the roles of governments and multilateral institutions in providing complementary funding; and finally (4) the need to coordinate development programs across institutions. These realizations have come in the United States at a time when mainstream economists in Latin America and in multilateral lending institutions also have recognized the limits of import substituting industrialization. All parties have now begun to look for ways to develop export markets and to encourage foreign capital investment in their respective economies.

The world economic situation in the mid-1980s does not promise an easy flow of new capital to the developing world. The policy community is concerned that neither the multilateral lending institutions, the private commercial banks, nor private entrepreneurs have the capital needed to restart growth in Latin America.[3] Moreover, a very large share of the domestic capital of the region is languishing in European and North American bank accounts. These Latin American funds must be recaptured and channelled to productive use at home.

U.S. Interest in the Free Movement
of Goods and Services

In describing U.S. security interests in the Caribbean Basin, U.S. government spokesmen and academicians like to exhibit a large map of the region with fat arrows pointing out U.S. strategic military and commercial sea lanes (sea lines of communication, or SLCs). These sea lanes are vital to the United States in the event of global conflict and must be defended. However, even the most pessimistic of future conflict scenarios grants low probability to sustained global conflict.

A much more immediate requirement for U.S. security in the region is regional prosperity and growth. Prosperity must be associated with increased commerce throughout the hemisphere. The economies of the Caribbean Basin countries and of many of the South American countries are too small to support diversity of economic activity necessary to achieve prosperity and competitiveness in the world. Even the larger economies of Mexico, Brazil, and Argentina must export today as an integral part of efforts to recover economic development momentum.

The United States is itself more export-oriented today in the late 1980s than ever before. U.S. citizens are beginning to understand what it means to be in an interdependent world. The ability of the United States to export depends on the prosperity of the economies of its neighbors. Their ability to import from the United States depends on their ability to sell to that country.

U.S. goods will move through the Caribbean to its major markets in Europe, Japan, and elsewhere despite changes in the world economic environment. However, it is more difficult to ensure the commerce of other small and less developed nations of the region. The key is enhanced trade relations.

The United States supports an open market even when strong pressures exist for protection in some industries. But more importantly, in the

Western Hemisphere, and especially in Central America and the Caribbean Basin, open markets and a division of productive labor are needed if the countries of the region are to realize economies of scale on which to create viable industries.

In Central America, the Contadora countries recognize that the economic integration that occurred during the heyday of the Central American Common Market must be renewed. The Eastern Caribbean countries are becoming much more conscious of the need for an integrated and common economic policy in their region. U.S. programs like the Caribbean Basin Initiative with its one-way, duty-free entry policy, or the National Bipartisan Commission on Central America (Kissinger commission) recommendations for stimulating private sector initiative and economic growth are all intended to increase regional productivity. The Central American and Caribbean economies are reacting positively to the incentives. One hopes that this will contribute to prosperity and political stability.

U.S. Interest in Respect
for Political Integrity of Borders

On a more political level, it is in the national interest of the United States that the countries of the region respect each other's sovereignty and the political integrity of each other's borders. For the most part, Latin American countries have managed disagreements over border definitions and other classic international disputes peacefully and well. The record for managing subversion is less clear.

Latin American tradition is one of nonintervention in the affairs of its neighbors as interfering in the domestic affairs of one's neighbors is simply not respectable national behavior. In more practical terms, interference by one nation in the affairs of another creates instability and uncertainty as it fosters a sense of threat and lack of confidence in the predictability and reliability of the words and behavior of one's neighbors. When governments and political institutions are threatened, all other efforts to pursue desirable social and economic goals are undercut except for the desire to survive. Moreover, fragile political institutions are not well-equipped to manage such interference. Repression, political and economic instability, and policy failure are a few of the consequences of hostile interference across borders.

From the U.S. perspective, Latin America's broad tolerance for cross-border movements of political organizers of the left is sometimes viewed as excessive. U.S. concerns are justified to the extent that regional instability affects U.S. domestic and foreign affairs. The effects are often quite direct. When there is instability in the region, the United States is called upon to take sides. The example of El Salvador is illustrative. At the height of the recent Salvadoran crisis, representatives of the center, the right, and the left all came to the United States, particularly to Congress, but also to universities, churches, and towns, seeking to establish and exploit constituencies. The U.S. public was ineluctably drawn into and made part of the domestic conflict in El Salvador. The country's domestic political contest and U.S. foreign policy became intertwined and confused in the minds of the public and policymakers alike. Activists on all sides of the political spectrum failed to comprehend that very real limits of U.S. policy existed—both what the United States would support and what it would tolerate.

It does not suit the U.S. political system to have foreign political disputes fought out on the floor of the U.S. Congress, in university classrooms, church pulpits, or town meetings. There is very little that the United States as a nation can do to resolve the domestic political problems of other countries. As Henry Kissinger argued in the essay previously cited, "The United States is no longer in a position to operate programs globally; it has to encourage them. It can no longer impose its preferred solution, it must seek to evoke it. . . . [The role of the United States is] to contribute to a structure that will foster the initiative of others . . . to encourage and not stifle a sense of local responsibility" (Kissinger 1973).

The political problems of Latin American countries must be resolved by the people of those countries themselves. Nevertheless, the United States is drawn into the political instability of the region when the political institutions of those countries are threatened. For these reasons it is in the interest of the United States and in the interest of every country of the region that those institutions be strengthened.

U.S. Interest in the Political Alignment
of Its Neighbors

Finally, it is in the national interest of the United States that the countries of the region not provide support for or align themselves with U.S. global political rivals. This, of course, is the key to current problems with Cuba and Nicaragua in the hemisphere.

As a global power, the global power balance is of vital interest to the United States. In this sense, it supports the world status quo. I use that term as it was used by political realists like Hans J. Morgenthau, for whom the status quo referred to the distribution of power among nations at any given moment in time. But, I hasten to add, as Morgenthau himself added, the status quo does not refer to the distribution of power within nations; that is to say, the political make-up of individual nations, other things being equal, does not need to concern the United States (see Morgenthau 1973). But the political support and alliances that nations might establish with its major rivals, especially hostile rivals, is important and vitally so.

In the context of the global power balance, and from the U.S. perspective, Latin America is a part of East-West competition. A cornerstone of U.S. policy toward the hemisphere has always been that the ideological balance shall not shift against it, and in recent times, against the Western bloc. It is useful to reflect on John F. Kennedy's pronouncements in this regard after the 1962 missile crisis. The public record states that Kennedy's understanding of the "agreement" reached with the Soviet Union was that the Soviet Union would withdraw its missiles from Cuba in exchange for a U.S. commitment not to threaten Cuba. The United States in turn would understand that Cuba would not interfere in the politics of the countries of the region. That is, Cuba would not seek to export its revolution or to aid "brothers in revolution" in the Western Hemisphere.

Of course, most of these understandings were not joined by either the Soviets or the Cubans; neither was eager to limit its future options in that way. Nevertheless, the principles established in Kennedy's statements—U.S. acceptance of a Marxist Cuba and Cuban nonintervention outside its borders—have remained a cornerstone of U.S. policy toward the region. Most critics of recent policy in Central America have failed to appreciate the singularity and consistency with which those principles have persisted and have guided the formulation of attitudes at the highest levels of the U.S. government and in the public at large.

A second anecdote of the Kennedy period underscores this posture and also illustrates the dilemma the United States confronts in dealing with ideology in the hemisphere. The anecdote concerns Kennedy's reflection on possible U.S. policy positions following the death of the dictator Rafael Trujillo in the Dominican Republic. Arthur M. Schlesinger, Jr., reported in his book on the Kennedy period, *A Thousand Days*, the discussions among Kennedy's inner staff on what might emerge in the untested political system of the Dominican Republic following Trujillo's death. Kennedy noted, "There are three possibilities . . . in descending order of preference: a decent democratic regime, a continuation of the Trujillo regime, or a Castro regime. We ought to aim at the first, but we really can't renounce the second until we are sure that we can avoid the third" (Schlesinger, 1968).

The issue here for U.S. foreign policy is foremost one of alignment. Internal political dynamics are secondary in the U.S. assessment of other countries' attitudes toward its global political rivals; foreign policy is the element on which a country is judged most strictly. In this respect, it is conceivable that a Spanish (social democratic) or even a Yugoslav (independent Communist) model might prevail in the hemisphere. However, it is difficult to envisage a Communist government that does not have an aggressive, pro-Soviet foreign policy. Certainly, past experience provides little encouragement for such expectations. The current situation in Central America and the Caribbean is instructive. The Reagan administration has argued that the Nicaraguan government has supported guerrillas in El Salvador and that Cuban and Soviet advisers in turn are supporting the Nicaraguan government. Elsewhere, in Grenada, in spite of Maurice Bishop's desire for a warming of relations with the opposition, it ultimately disposed of him to have its way. Even while Bishop was asking for more lenience on the part of the United States, Grenada was voting in the United Nations in support of the Soviet invasion of Afghanistan, an issue on which only the hardest-line Soviet bloc countries cast their votes with the Soviet Union. Papers of the Bishop government now show that Bishop was also committed to a Marxist-Leninist regime for Grenada (see Valenta and Ellison 1986). In 1979 the United States and many other countries wished the Nicaraguan Sandinistas well in their efforts to bring a better quality of life in Nicaragua. As the Sandinistas have moved more and more purposively toward Cuba, the Soviet Union, and its Eastern bloc allies, U.S. government policy and U.S. public opinion have turned increasingly against the Nicaraguan regime.

Conclusion

To be successful, U.S. policies toward Latin America must build upon and be consistent with U.S. interests in the region. These policies must be feasible within the limits established by public interest and tolerance, and they must also find a positive response in the societies toward which they are directed. U.S. policy must recognize the interests, attitudes, and aspirations of Latin American countries and encourage responses that are commensurate with U.S. interests and aspirations.

U.S. policies and initiatives toward Latin America have often been practiced in an on-again, off-again fashion. Sometimes initiatives have been exercised on behalf of special interests, but, more often, policy actions have reflected a too narrow set of political goals for the region that have focused on the absence of outside (extrahemispheric) intervention. In the more complex world of the late 1980s and beyond, U.S. interests in and goals for Latin America must be broader. U.S. interests in the region must include economic and political security, respect for human rights, good government, and freedom from physical and ideological aggression. These interests are not inconsistent with the interests of Latin American countries; how effectively the United States and Latin America work to achieve these goals is the key to the quality of the future relationship.

Notes

1. This idea is developed in greater detail in Hayes 1982.

2. Latin American governments have been so successful in regulating the activities of multinationals that the region has ceased to be an especially desirable place for investment. See Council of the Americas 1984.

3. The Inter-American Development Bank estimated that Latin America will require approximately U.S. $47 billion in new money in the 1984–1989 period if it is to achieve a sustainable recovery and rate of growth of 5 percent per year (see Inter-American Development Bank 1984).

References

Council of the Americas. 1984. "Debt, Economic Crisis and United States Corporations in Latin America." Mimeograph.

Hayes, Margaret Daly. 1982. "United States Security Interests in Central America in Global Perspective." In *Central America: the International Dimensions of the Crisis*, edited by Richard Feinberg. New York: Holmes and Meier.

_____. 1983. "Promoting U.S. Security Interests in Central America." Lead consultant's presentation to the National Bipartisan Commission on Central America (September).

_____. 1983. "Regional Perspectives on the Situation in Central America." Manuscript prepared for the Council on Foreign Relations Central America Study Group (November).

_____. 1984. *Latin America and the U.S. National Interest: A Basis for U.S. Foreign Policy*. Boulder, Colo.: Westview Press.

Kissinger, Henry A. 1973. "On the National Interest." In *American Foreign Policy* (expanded edition). New York: W. W. Norton and Co., Inc.

Morgenthau, Hans J. 1973. *Politics Among Nations: The Struggle for Power and Peace*. 5th ed. New York: Alfred A. Knopf.

Pastor, Robert. 1984. "Migration and Development in the Caribbean: The Policy Challenge." Paper prepared for Conference on Migration and Development in the Caribbean, September 1984, at School of Public Affairs, University of Maryland.

Report of the National Bipartisan Commission on Central America. 1984. Washington, D.C.: U.S. Government Printing Office.

Schlesinger, Arthur M., Jr. 1968. *A Thousand Days*. Boston: Houghton Mifflin.

Summers, Jr., Harry G. 1982. *On Strategy: A Critical Analysis of the Vietnam War*. New York: Dell Publishing Co.

U.S. Congress. Senate. Committee on Foreign Relations. 1984. *Hearings on the Report of the National Bipartisan Commission on Central America.* 98th Cong. 2d sess. Washington, D.C.: U.S. Government Printing Office.

Valenta, Jiri, and Herbert J. Ellison, eds. 1986. *Grenada and Soviet/Cuban Policy: Internal Crisis and U.S./OECS Intervention.* Boulder, Colo.: Westview Press.

PART TWO

Regional Security Issues

5

U.S. Caribbean Policy and Regional Militarization

Jorge Rodríguez Beruff

Most analysts on Caribbean affairs would agree that a major revision of U.S. regional policy occurred in the eventful year of 1979, a revision that represented a break with many aspects of foreign policy during the period following the Dominican invasion of 1965. Likewise, numerous commentaries have placed great emphasis on the dominant role that military instruments of external policy—from military aid and training to outright invasion—seem to play in the new regional policy. For the first six years in which the new Caribbean policy has been put in effect, one can attempt, with greater historical depth, to characterize this new policy and assess what it has achieved, what its implications are for contemporary politics in the region, and what tendencies and contradictions can be identified.

Although the main focus of this chapter will be the military aspects of post-1979 U.S. regional policy,[1] my analysis will be partial in nature because military measures are organically related to nonmilitary (economic, diplomatic, political, and ideological) aspects of external policy, though not necessarily in a harmonious manner. I will make only summary reference to nonmilitary aspects. In addition, Caribbean policy, despite its specific features, has been conditioned by the global redefinition of foreign policy during the two Reagan administrations (the so-called second cold war) and particularly by overall policy toward neocolonial or dependent societies. More immediately, changes in Caribbean policy have also been related to developments in Central America. An explanation of the logic of Caribbean policy and of its military aspects must take this broader framework into account. My analysis, however, will stress specific regional developments.

My main argument is that the revision of Caribbean policy, apart from the broader global and Central American events that intervened in its articulation, was based on the following evaluation of specifically regional developments:

1. the region had entered in the late seventies into a profound and prolonged economic, social, and political crisis;
2. this crisis could not be overcome by short-term economic measures but rather demanded a long-term capitalist restructuring of the Caribbean economies to stabilize the region;
3. the main threat to U.S. interests in the region were emerging popular movements[2] with diverse levels of strength, forms of organization, and ideological orientation in the different countries that could potentially articulate, and in some cases were actually implementing, viable strategies to deal with the crisis. These movements were perceived as further weakening U.S. regional power;
4. Cuba was using the thaw in relations with Washington and the new regional conjuncture to gradually overcome its isolation and establish political, diplomatic, assistance, and cultural links with other countries;
5. a serious erosion had occurred in the traditional instruments of U.S. power in the region, particularly those relating to military presence and influence, while new regional actors had appeared, lessening U.S. capabilities to influence regional developments and contain the emerging political forces;
6. the situation required an alliance with the most conservative neocolonial forces within the Caribbean, the strengthening of the state apparatus (particularly its police and military forces), the reconstruction of U.S. instruments of power in all spheres but particularly the links with the local military structures and the capability for direct military intervention *before* a longer term economic strategy could be articulated and implemented;
7. given the relative weakness and lack of maturity of popular movements in the Caribbean vis-à-vis Central America (shown during the electoral processes of the early eighties and in the post–Grenada invasion period), the task of pacifying the region could meet with greater immediate success and provide a convenient environment for a U.S.-imposed solution in that region than was possible in Central America.

The prominence of military measures (direct military presence, military intervention, aid, training, arms sales, intelligence, strengthening of the police forces, and so forth) within the new U.S. regional policy has promoted a process of militarization of Caribbean societies with far-reaching implications. By militarization I mean (1) the growing diversion of economic resources, internal or external, from social to military expenditures; (2) the expansion of state security forces; (3) the enhanced political weight of the military in articulating state policy; (4) the penetration of traditionally civil spheres of state bureaucracy (for example, the police, customs, immigration, and so on) by the military, or their organization along military lines; (5) a growing trend to resort to force as a means of buttressing the dominant position of the ruling classes; (6) the revision of the legal framework to respond to the military's interest or outlook (state security legislation); and (7) the promotion of military forms of organization and values in civil society. All of these dimensions may not be present in specific countries, but they do represent general trends in the Caribbean taken as a whole.

This process has been set in motion with the active support of the conservative political forces that have risen to power throughout most of the countries due to their fragile base of social support. One of the most notable aspects of this process has been the rapid growth of the small, or heretofore nonexistent, military establishments in the Eastern Caribbean. The United States has also promoted the growth and the internal weight of the military in countries such as the Dominican Republic, Jamaica, and Haiti, and has produced a dramatic increase in U.S. military activities in Puerto Rico. Cuba has not escaped this process of regional militarization due to a greater concern for security, having launched a costly program of military expansion, which has diverted resources from economic development.

The Late 1970s: Emergence of Popular Movements and Erosion of U.S. Power

It could be argued that a U.S.-Caribbean policy—in the sense of a distinct strategy based on an evaluation of specific interests and trends in the region—is a relatively recent development, if we take into consideration the post–World War II period. I would like to suggest that the Carter administration was the first to recognize the need of formulating a coherent regional strategy. This need was derived from three central concerns: (1) the urgent question of how to deal with the emergence of popular mass movements and progressive or reformist regimes throughout the Caribbean and Central American region; (2) the equally pressing and related issue of redefining and modernizing the traditional forms of the U.S. presence in the region (particularly in the military sphere) in the context of the post-Vietnam military and political crisis; and (3) the perceived urgency of overcoming the also traditional "Cuba-centered" view of the Caribbean that was considered an obstacle to developing effective policies geared to the new regional situation.

In short, the main problem facing the Carter administration was twofold: how to neutralize or integrate, through negotiation or pressure, the popular movements and thus to bring the process of change in the Caribbean under control and to channel this process in directions that were not antagonistic to U.S. interests. At the same time the administration wanted to generally reduce the direct U.S. military presence and traditional forms of U.S. military influence.[3] The latter was deemed necessary not only for economic reasons but also because of the ideological persuasion (generally derived from the Vietnam defeat) that military means were ineffective in containing revolutionary movements and provoked long-term contradictions that further radicalized popular struggles.[4]

The paramount importance that Carter attached to the Caribbean was reflected in his April 1977 speech to the OAS delineating his policy toward Latin America. Three of the most important points (support for the Central American Common Market, solution of the Panama Canal status, and improvement of U.S.-Cuba relations) dealt with regional problems. He also stressed "flexible" bilateral relations based on respect for the "individuality" and national sovereignty of each country. This position can be understood as an implicit acceptance of ideological and political pluralism in the region.[5] This emphasis on the Caribbean was also reflected in high-level visits to the English-speaking Caribbean, an expansion of the diplomatic presence in the Eastern Caribbean, and a sharp concern for developments in the Dominican Republic and Jamaica. As we know, this initial policy was clearly abandoned in 1979 when it was felt that regional developments were getting out of hand, and a wave of conservative revivalism was threatening to electorally engulf "soft" reformism in favor of a harder line that placed greater emphasis on military instruments of power and served as a convenient transition to the Caribbean Basin policy of the Reagan administration.

Despite the obvious differences between the first two years of Carter's administration and the first two years of Reagan's, I believe that major elements of continuity exist: (1) the shared conviction of the need for a distinct regional policy (though less clear in the case of Reagan due to the Caribbean Basin conception); (2) the main concern with developing an effective means to contain the main antagonist (defined as popular and progressive movements and regimes) and to bring the process of change in the Caribbean under U.S. control (which is what is really involved in Reagan's cold war rhetoric on the Soviet threat); and (3) the overall reshaping of U.S. instruments of foreign policy to adapt them to the new regional situation.

Understanding the Policy Shift

The shift in U.S. Caribbean policy in the mid to late seventies can be more clearly identified if we briefly consider the evolution of previous policy. During the late forties and fifties, regional policy was an extension of a hemispheric, that is, Latin American, strategy based on cold war tenets that prescribed the preferential promotion of friendly authoritarian regimes with the support of the exporters to ensure political stability. In this sense, the logic for supporting Manuel Odría in Peru was the same as that for supporting Anastasio Somoza in Nicaragua, Fulgenao Batista in Cuba, François Duvalier in Haiti, and Rafael Trujillo in the Dominican Republic. The clientelization of national armed forces through the structure of USSOUTHCOM became an efficient means of ensuring regional power. Perceived threats to U.S. interests in the region, as in Guatemala and Guyana, were expediently dealt with through "low-intensity" ad hoc measures (CIA intervention) without bringing into question major policy tenets.

The Cuban revolution provoked a major revision of U.S.–Latin American policy represented by the reformism combined with countersubversion of the brief Alliance for Progress period. The possibility of armed revolution in Latin America seemed a more imminent threat than revolutionary developments in the Caribbean. Thus, Caribbean policy became mainly an anti-Cuban policy while Latin American policy, by and large, developed as a negative image of prevalent Cuban revolutionary conceptions regarding Latin America. The strategy for the Caribbean was subsumed within this broader policy and conditioned by it. The slogan of "no more Cubas" of the Kennedy and Johnson administrations applied equally to Bolivia, Guatemala, or Jamaica.[6] The assassination of Trujillo fit in well with the policy of preventive reformism applied throughout Latin America.

The main factor underlying the lack of particular concern with the Caribbean (apart from Cuba) was its relative stability and the apparent weakness of revolutionary movements in the region, particularly after the Dominican invasion of 1965. By then, any direct military threat to U.S. security had been removed by the Kennedy-Khrushchev agreements of 1963 while the left forces (reformist or revolutionary) suffered successive setbacks in most of the countries.

The Dominican intervention firmly installed in power Joaquín Balaguer, a shrewd conservative politician who ruthlessly crushed the popular leadership that had emerged during the revolution. The United States appeared determined to remove by force any national revolutionary movement in the region as expressed in the significant title of a contemporary article of John Plank: "The Caribbean: Intervention, When and How."[7] The previous year, Cheddi Jagan had been toppled in Guyana and replaced with Forbes Burnham. The first wave of guerrilla warfare in Central America (for example, in Guatemala) was effectively routed near the end of the 1960s. This trend reoccurred throughout Latin America, and a counterrevolutionary military alliance, Consejo de Defensa

Centroamericano (CONDECA), was sponsored in Central America to
prevent future insurgency. Many countries in the region were still under
British colonial control, and Britain was steering them toward an apparently orderly transition to independence. In Haiti, the installation of
the new president-for-life, Jean Claude Duvalier, had proceeded smoothly
and facilitated a greater U.S. penetration of the security forces.

The only disturbing developments, apart from the Constitutionalist
Revolution in the Dominican Republic and the Jagan regime in Guyana,
were the Panama riots of 1964 (which eventually led to General Omar
Torrijos's rise to power) and the Black Power civil-military rebellion of
1970 in Trinidad. The Third World rhetoric of the Burnham regime was
a minor irritant that could be tolerated as long as it kept Jagan's People's
Political party (PPP) and other left forces in check.

By the mid-seventies this situation began to change. The serious
economic recession of 1974 to 1975 visibly affected all countries in the
region. Foreign investment and tourism declined while energy costs
rapidly rose, producing economic contraction and reducing real incomes
of large segments of the population.[8] The recession also meant a
substantial increase in unemployment even in countries such as Puerto
Rico. Its net effect was the heightening of social contradictions and the
revitalization of progressive forces in most countries of the region. In
those countries where reformist forces were in power (Jamaica, Trinidad,
and Guyana), the recession radicalized government policies in the direction
of state ownership, income redistribution, and control of foreign capital
(with different emphasis according to the country) to cushion the effect
on the masses of the crisis. In other countries, the power of the traditional
ruling class was eroded as popular opposition gained momentum. Even
the apparently stable government of Balaguer lost the elections to the
Partido Revolucionario Dominicano (PRD).

This began to occur at a very low point in U.S. global and regional
power. The Vietnam War had severely weakened the United States
economically and militarily. As Zbigniew Brzezinski aptly noted, "The
mounting U.S. engagement in the war in Vietnam . . . significantly
reduced American freedom of action, prompted severe strains in the
U.S. economy and society, absorbed much of the U.S. defense budget
and weakened the U.S. international position."[9] The Vietnam War had
led to an internal crisis of legitimacy of the U.S. military establishment
and of external military policy that, together with pressing economic
considerations, demanded the abandonment of the "global intervention-
ism" of the Kennedy, Johnson, and early Nixon administrations and the
pursuit of a policy of retrenchment and cuts in military spending. This
was combined with the broader crisis of legitimacy provoked by Watergate.
In face of a weak and reluctant executive, it fell upon Congress to

delineate new limits on military policy through budgetary constraints and legislation.

The post-Vietnam crisis also weakened the United States in Latin America. The United States could not devote substantial amounts of aid to stabilize the regional economies while it was forced to reduce its military presence and aid. That is why new regional actors (mainly the alleged "middle powers," Mexico and Venezuela, and European social democracy) appeared to gain autonomy.

Accomplishing the Policy Shift

Since the late sixties, the United States began a process of reduction of its considerable regional infrastructure of bases and installations. The Chaguaramas naval base in Trinidad was transferred to the Williams government in 1968.[10] In Puerto Rico, a large number of minor army installations were phased out, culminating, in 1973, in the closure of the large Strategic Air Command (SAC) airfield (Ramey Field). A broad movement mobilized under the leadership of independence groups, also forced the navy to reluctantly relinquish its training ground in Culebra. Even the main army installation in San Juan, Fort Buchanan, was phased down in preparations for eventual closure. Military activities tended to concentrate in the naval base of Roosevelt Roads.[11] In 1979, the small military installation (St. Lucy) in the island of Barbados was also abandoned. The other important military installation in the region, Guantánamo, was clearly of little strategic value due to its vulnerability. Finally, the Torrijos-Carter agreements of 1977 committed the United States to gradually dismantling its numerous bases in Panama.

On the other hand, congressional action and budgetary constraints considerably limited traditional instruments of military influence over and support of regional military establishments and police forces. These instruments consisted of military aid, training and arms sales, and assistance and training of police forces.[12]

If we examine the figures of military and police aid until the 1970s (see Table 5.1), several elements stand out: (1) only a small number of countries (Dominican Republic, Haiti, Jamaica, Panama and Guyana), which were also the larger, received assistance; (2) a very large proportion of the aid and training devoted to the insular Caribbean went to the security forces of the Dominican Republic; (3) due to their colonial status or lack of military forces, the Eastern Caribbean states Belize and Surinam were not incorporated into the U.S. network of aid and training; and (4) links with the Trinidad and Guyana security forces were not par- ticularly strong. The new military policy has meant that *all* countries in the Caribbean, with the single exception of Cuba and the remaining

TABLE 5.1
Military Aid to Caribbean Countries, 1946-1976 (thousands of current US$)

	MAP	FMS Credits	Surplus Arms	IMET	Economic Support Fund	Total
Dominican Republic	21,700	1,300	3,900	9,100	209,200	245,400
Haiti	2,400	—	200	900	47,700	51,200
Jamaica	1,100	—	a	a	—	1,100
Panama	4,300	500	1,800	3,500	27,000	37,100
Trinidad-Tobago	—	—	—	—	29,700	29,700
Total	29,700	1,800	5,900	13,500	313,600	364,500

aLess than $50,000.

Notes: MAP: Military Assistance Program; FMS: Foreign Military Sales; IMET: International Military Education and Training Program; Economic Support Fund: Security-related emergency assistance.

Source: Michael Klare, "Abasteciendo represión," *Cuadernos Semestrales*, no. 4 (Centro de Investigación y Docencia en Economía, Second Semester, 1978), p. 113.

TABLE 5.2
Training of Military Personnel of Caribbean Countries, 1950-1976

	Personnel Trained
Dominican Republic	3,945
Haiti	593
Jamaica	11
Panama	4,389
Total	8,938

Source: Michael Klare, "Abasteciendo represión," Cuadernos Semestrales, no. 4 (Centro de Investigación y Docencia en Economía, Second Semester, 1978), p. 117.

French colonies, have been incorporated in aid and training programs (see Table 5.2).

An important complement to military assistance and training was the Agency for International Development (AID) Public Safety Program, which trained over 450 police officers of 4 countries in the region (Dominican Republic, Guyana, Jamaica, and Panama) and provided resident advisers to regional police forces (see Table 5.3). The program was abolished by Congress in 1974.

The Nixon administration tried to offset the reduction in military and police assistance by vigorously promoting arms sales. However, this expedient could hardly provide the political influence that traditional mechanisms had ensured, particularly in a region where many countries had small or no military structures and limited resources to purchase weapons. In addition, Great Britain still retained in the early seventies the status of monopoly supplier to countries such as Guyana (93 percent) and Trinidad (100 percent).[13] In any case, the Carter administration reversed the Nixon policy of promoting arms sales to underdeveloped countries, including those of the Caribbean.

By 1979, assistance to police forces under the AID Public Safety Program had entirely ceased and military aid had been reduced to a trickle. (Assistance to police forces subsequently had to be channeled under a drug control program of the Drug Enforcement Administration.) In that year, excluding Panama, only three countries (Barbados, Haiti, and the Dominican Republic) received some form of assistance. Of this small amount of aid, almost three-fourths was destined for the Dominican Republic (see Table 5.4).

TABLE 5.3
Agency for International Development Public Safety Program in the Caribbean

	Year of Initiation	Total Expenditure (millions of US$)	Personnel Trained in U.S.	Public Safety Advisors 1968	1972
Dominican Republic	1962	4.2	204	15	3
Guyana	1966	1.3	53	2	---
Jamaica	1967	0.8	92	2	1
Panama	1959	2.2	202	3	3
Total		8.5	551	22	7

Source: North American Congress on Latin America, *U.S. Military and Police Operations in the Third World*, n.d., pp. 10, 22; and Michael Klare, "Abasteciendo represión," *Cuadernos Semestrales*, no. 4 (Centro de Investigación y Docencia en Economía, Second Semester, 1978), p. 103.

TABLE 5.4

U.S. Military Aid to Caribbean Countries, 1979 (thousands of US$)

	FMS	ESF	MAP	IMET	Total	Per Capita
Barbados	---	---	---	6	6	.02
Haiti	200	---	---	175	375	.06
Dominican Republic	500	---	7	477	984	.17
Panama	1,000	---	4	1,000	1,399	.74

Notes: FMS: Foreign Military Sales; ESF: Economic Support Fund; MAP: Military Assistance Program; IMET: International Military Education and Training Program.

Source: U.S. Department of Defense, Congressional Presentation, Security Assistance Programs, 1982.

The decline in the U.S. military presence and influence was not a source of concern as long as other instruments of policy (ideological, political, economic, and covert) sufficed to control regional developments. It should be remembered that these had appeared sufficient in dealing with the Torrijos regime (the Canal treaties and consequent aid arrangements), in blunting Michael Manley's initial radicalism (International Monetary Fund [IMF] pressures and destabilization), and in arranging an orderly transition of power to Antonio Guzmán and the conservative wing of the PRD in the Dominican Republic.

During the years 1979 and 1980, a series of events in the region brought into sharp relief the erosion of U.S. power. Clearly, the two most dramatic were the New Jewel Movement ascent to power in Grenada (March 13, 1979) and the Sandinista victory in Nicaragua (July 19, 1979). These were not isolated occurrences but part of a pattern that indicated the ascent to power of new political forces. In that same year, the conservative government of Patrick John in Dominica was removed and replaced by the Committee of National Salvation, which included left figures. The St. Lucia Labour party won a resounding electoral victory against John Compton on the basis of a progressive program. The People's National party (PNP) government in Jamaica appeared to be steering a left course by reinstating D. K. Duncan in the leadership and denouncing the IMF agreements. In El Salvador, the armed struggle was beginning to gain momentum. The Arron government in Surinam was toppled in 1980 by a discontented military, which initially included left officers. Finally, the massive emigration of Haitians indicated the precariousness of the Duvalier regime while, more generally, the increased flow of Caribbean migrants focused U.S. attention on Caribbean developments.

In addition, these developments appeared favorable to the broadening of relations between Cuba and the other countries in the region, thus undermining the U.S. policy of isolation.[14] Cuba had been able to establish relations with Jamaica, Nicaragua, Grenada, Surinam, in addition to its links with Guyana. Belize also indicated its willingness to establish links while the issue of relations with Cuba became hotly debated in the Eastern Caribbean. The United States could hardly impose a policy of no-relations while seeking to improve relations with Cuba itself.

It was in this political context that the new regional policy, including its military aspects, began to be articulated by Carter in 1979, and subsequently by Reagan.

From Carter to Reagan:
The Formulation of the New Military Policy

The shift in military policy toward the Caribbean must be located in the second half of 1979, when the original foreign policy premises of the Carter administration were revised. As has been noted, the revision of foreign policy was not limited to the Caribbean but rather formed part of a new orientation toward revolutionary processes in the under-developed world in general and was conditioned by events (such as the Soviet involvement in Afghanistan) that went beyond the region.[15] However, the main concern at that time was related to developments in two regions: the Caribbean and Central America, and the Middle East. For all practical purposes, the geopolitical and cold war ideological orientation of the new right began to inform foreign policy even before Reagan's electoral victory. On this basis, a new consensus emerged among U.S. ruling groups who believed that trends in those two regions were unfavorable to U.S. interests and required a more aggressive response.[16]

The adjustments made in regional policy were explained by Robert Pastor, staff member of the National Security Council responsible for Latin American and Caribbean policy in the Carter administration:

> Changes in the region and the world in 1979 and 1980 made the Carter administration more sensitive to traditional military concerns. The coup in Grenada in March 1979, and the collapse of the Somoza dynasty in July brought new leaders to power, who tended to see Castro's Cuba as the answer . . . and the U.S. as the problem. . . . Simultaneously an economic decline in the region and a more aggressive Cuban posture—exemplified by the obstrusive role played by the Cuban Ambassador in

the 1980 Jamaican elections—further unsettled the region. This instability naturally was viewed in the U.S. in the context of more ominous international developments—the invasion of Afghanistan, hostages in Iran, uncertainty in the Persian Gulf, and Soviet threats against Poland. The U.S. cooled the relationship [with Grenada] and sought to expand aid to Grenada's neighbors as a signal that only democracy would be rewarded in the region. In the security area, a task force was established in Key West to coordinate naval exercises in the region, and there was a modest increase in security aid. Economic assistance also continued to increase, as did the numbers and quality of official personnel stationed in the area.[17]

The artificial crisis created by the presence of a "Soviet brigade" in Cuba, September 1979, served to legitimate the new orientation toward the region. In the following month, simultaneous announcements were made of an increase in economic aid for the Caribbean and the creation of a Caribbean Joint Task Force in Key West. Subsequently, intense military activity began with an increase in military maneuvers and numerous visits by high level Pentagon officials to the region in order to offer military aid and seek access to new bases.

Toward the end of 1979, Admiral Harry Train, commander of the Atlantic Fleet, visited Venezuela and other countries to discuss regional security. In a 1980 visit to the Dominican Republic, Major General Robert L. Scheitzer offered "all types of military aid to combat communism." A later visit by Admiral Train to the same country provoked street disturbances. U.S. attempts to obtain additional military bases in Haiti and the Dominican Republic were revealed in the framework of these visits.

Even though the overall picture of military assistance for the Caribbean (without taking into account Central America) was not dramatically altered between 1979 and 1980, we can note a growing interest in the Eastern Caribbean. By 1980 and 1981, a sharp increase occurred in all types of security assistance, particularly marked in those countries considered strategically important, such as Barbados (and others of the Eastern Caribbean) and Jamaica.

These initial military measures were coupled with blatant interference in the electoral processes in the English-speaking Caribbean. In Jamaica, St. Lucia, St. Vincent, Antigua, and Dominica, the United States openly and successfully supported conservative neocolonial political forces, thus creating a favorable environment for its regional military buildup (and, eventually, grounds for the invasion of Grenada). George Odlum, a progressive Lucian leader who was one of the political casualties of this period, has described the process in the following terms:

I think they moved very purposefully in every election in the Caribbean after the St. Lucia election. The St. Vincent election, the Dominica election, the Antigua election, and the greatest of all the Jamaica election. In all these elections, American money influenced the course of the elections. . . . The Americans see it in purely strategic terms and they would move to halt any nationalist movement which looked as if it might be fair material for propelling Cuban influence in the Caribbean area. Secondly they thought . . . that we had a solid base in the working class of this country. This coming hard on the heels of the emergence of Maurice Bishop in Grenada, and the possibilities of other groups operating in other parts of the Caribbean, they saw a type of domino theory behind it all.[18]

With the Reagan administration, revision of U.S. foreign policy accelerated, and the goals to be pursued in the region were clearly delineated. The order of priorities established by Thomas Enders (former assistant secretary of state for inter-American affairs) in his June 1981 address was significant. Of the four points relating to the new regional policy, only the third point referred to economic aspects. The first and second emphasized the need for military assistance and preventive measures in "threatened countries." The fourth point committed the United States to an increase of military pressures against Cuba.[19] This emphasis on military aspects of external policy has been a central feature of policy documents and official pronouncements of the Reagan administration. For example, although Reagan did not mention military measures in his 1982 address on the Caribbean Basin Initiative, he did underscore that its leitmotiv was security considerations.[20]

The main lines of the new military policy toward the Caribbean— in this case, including Central America—are contained in an important study of the Strategic Studies Institute of the U.S. Army War College. This study was concluded on October 26, 1981, several months before Reagan's Caribbean Basin Initiative speech. It was ordered in December 1980 by the U.S. Army Office for Operations and Plans in coordination with USSOUTHCOM. Among other things the study directive mentioned that "emerging nationalism, increased radicalization, Cuban activism, and expanding Soviet interest in the region pose direct challenges to U.S. security interests." The study directive requested the institute to "identify, assess, and recommend alternative uses of military resources as part of a coordinated and comprehensive policy response to secure U.S. strategic interest in the region. . . . The study will emphasize the development of military alternatives designed to reduce the occurrence of destabilizing events. . . ."[21]

The final document was a comprehensive evaluation of the regional situation, including a country-by-country analysis and recommendations in all policy areas. Some of the economic proposals (for example, an increase in economic aid and commercial concessions) were later incorporated in the Caribbean Basin Initiative package. Among the recommendations on military policy specifically relating to the Caribbean, the following proposals stand out:

- Promote the capabilities and professionalism of friendly regional military forces and their self-confidence in handling both external and internal threats.
- Promote collective security arrangements, interoperability and common military doctrine with regional military establishments. . . .
- Establish a network of military-to-military relationships which can (1) gain for the United States an understanding of the current position and future direction of the various Caribbean militaries and leadership elites; (2) foster increased access to decisional elites in order to enhance U.S. influence; and (3) serve as a bridge between regional military elites in order to encourage intraregional cooperation and the peaceful solution of conflicting interest. . . .
- Increase the overall size of the security assistance effort.
- In the Insular Caribbean, provide assistance for maritime security, navigation safety, and for law-and-order forces: police, constabulary, and Coast Guard forces. . . .
- Increase International Military Education and Training program (IMET) spending for the region. . . .
- Expand the role of the U.S. Coast Guard. . . .[22]

The study also advocated a reorganization of the U.S. direct military presence in the region with particular emphasis on the role of the "military diplomat" (that is, advisers) and the strengthening of US-SOUTHCOM. A policy of "indirect confrontation" with Cuba was discussed but conclusions regarding Cuban policy cannot be found in the document due to extensive deletions of relevant parts.

Another important and heavily deleted document reflecting the new military policy was a review of war plans against Cuba begun on March 1979 (significantly coinciding with the Grenada revolution) by the Atlantic Command and concluded in August 1981. This review was obviously necessary if an intervention in Grenada, and a possible confrontation with Cuba, was being considered. The plan considered as an option in a general war situation massive air strikes and naval actions against a "sample" of 41 targets designed to neutralize Cuban air and naval capabilities. According to the document, this option was considered "acceptable, but not optimal." A "defensive-deterrent" option (distinct from a status quo but not defined in the parts made public) was apparently preferred, because "the primary Cuban strategic objective in a general war between NATO and Warsaw Pact may be their ultimate survival and independence."[23]

This military planning was accompanied by an increasingly aggressive rhetoric aimed at Cuba, threatening to make that country "pay the cost" of the revolutionary upsurge in the region. Even an apparently "rea-sonable" proposal advanced by Edward Gonzalez of the Rand Corpo-ration—of compellling the "Findlandization" of Cuba through indirect confrontation—had ominous implications, as it is difficult to envisage that design outside the context of an all-out war.[24]

In November 1983, David Ronfeldt advanced a coherent case for the new regional military policy being implemented by the Reagan admin-istration in a Rand study entitled *Geopolitics, Security and U.S. Strategy in the Caribbean Basin.* It reproduced many of the arguments and recommendations of the 1981 document of the Strategic Studies Institute. Some of Rondfeldt's arguments, however, are worth noting.

He stressed that, although it might be necessary to resort to force in "extreme situations," military policy should be mainly "preventive and anticipatory." This preventive policy must be implemented in the context of an alliance with internal political forces interested in a policy of "collective hegemony." "Collective security cannot be based simply on opposition to extremists; it must rest on modest centrist forces (including the militaries) as natural U.S. allies. The United States is the only power that can foster and shield a strong political center in the area. However, the center is now partly defined by Social Democratic and Christian Democratic forces that look to Western Europe. A major U.S. effort is needed to cultivate these political elites."[25]

Among the military measures he proposed were the following: (1) the revision of the command structure, the strengthening of USSOUTH-COM, and the consideration of a possible "North America security zone" that would embrace Canada, the United States, Central America, and the Caribbean; (2) the consolidation of U.S. military presence in Panama and Puerto Rico ("the potential for instability in Panama and Puerto Rico argues for keeping bases in both"); (3) the increase in aid and training to regional militaries ("U.S. assistance should emphasize military leadership training and organizational development"); and (4) the de-velopment of a "coalitional (or collective) approach" to regional security. The latter could even become a vehicle for a multilateral intervention in Central America. "The ultimate expression might be a regional peacekeeping mechanism that, perhaps in the event of disintegrating El Salvador, could conduct a politico-military interposition. . . ."[26]

It should be noted that in the documents mentioned and in other expressions of official U.S. policy, the new regional military policy was not conceived as a short-term expedient to confront the immediate "threat" of Grenada but rather as a long-term revision of external policy necessary to reconstruct regional hegemony. Although some aspects of regional policy have been abandoned following the Grenada invasion (for example, massive military maneuvers), the promotion of the militaries in the region has continued unabated as exemplified in the 1986 military aid package that included a request for over $35 million in the Military Assistance Program (MAP) and $400,000 in IMET funds for the Eastern Caribbean, in addition to $66 million in security-related Economic Support Fund (ESF) resources.[27]

The New Regional Military Policy and the Militarization of Caribbean Societies

As has been noted, the redefinition of military policy toward the Caribbean began in mid-1979 under the Carter administration. The first measures taken were the creation of the Caribbean Joint Task Force in Key West; a significant hardening of the U.S. attitude toward Cuba; the greater importance attached to maneuvers in Puerto Rico and Guantánamo, such as Solid Shield 80 and Readex 80; a higher level of military activity in traditional bastions such as Puerto Rico; and an upward revision of levels of military assistance, particularly to Eastern Caribbean countries such as Barbados. However, it was the Reagan administration that forcefully pursued a policy of increasing the direct military presence of the United States in the region and the promotion and coordination of the regional security forces.

In order to review the actual implementation of policy, it is useful to distinguish between the command structure and direct presence of the regular U.S. armed forces in the region, on the one hand, and the promotion—through assistance, coordination, training, and arms sales—of the regional military and security forces, on the other.

The revision of military policy toward the Caribbean initially found expression in a series of large-scale military maneuvers that virtually transformed the region into a war games scenario. These massive exercises, which took place during the period 1981 to 1984, had the purpose of bringing military pressure to bear on Cuba (for example, Operation Safepass in 1982); preparing and planning an invasion of Grenada (Ocean Venture 1981 and 1982, and Universal Trek 1-83); and generally increasing the level of training of U.S. forces, particularly of components of the rapid deployment force. The intensity of the exercises was unprecedented in postwar history. Ocean Venture 1981, for example, included 120,000 troops, 240 ships, and 1,000 airplanes. In Ocean Venture 1984, B-52 planes flew nonstop from their California bases to carry out bombing exercises.[28]

An indication of the Grenada focus of these maneuvers has been the tendency prevailing since 1984 toward a reduction of the scale of the exercises. Recent exercises have mainly been smaller scale events designed to train the security forces of the Eastern Caribbean to develop what the U.S. military calls "coalition warfare" capabilities—acting together with regular U.S. forces in auxiliary roles. The exercise Exotic Palm held in September 1985, for example, involved 500 Caribbean effectives drawn from the newly created special service units and coast guard of St. Lucia, St. Kitts-Nevis, Dominica, and Grenada and the "defence forces" of Antigua, Barbados, and Jamaica, together with U.S. and British regular military forces.[29] The purpose of the exercise was, significantly, an invasion of an island modeled after the Grenada operation. In November 1986, the operation Upward Key was carried out in Antigua with 100 U.S. effectives and Antigua's special service unit and defence force.[30] The impact of these "modest" war games in small islands with little previous experience with military structures and strong civilist traditions should not be underestimated.

Another important dimension of the shift in military policy has been the redefinition of the regional command and base structure of the regular U.S. armed forces.

In the late seventies, responsibility for the Central American Caribbean region was divided between USSOUTHCOM, located in Panama, which dealt with the land portions of Central America, and the Antilles Defense Command, located in the Roosevelt Roads Naval Base in Puerto Rico, which included the Caribbean Sea and the insular Caribbean. This last command was in turn subordinated to the U.S. Atlantic Command (LANTCOM) in Norfolk, Virginia. The Caribbean and Central American region was thus divided between the army and the navy. The existing command structure was apparently weak and considered ineffective to confront regional developments.

The first indication of the revision of the command structure was the creation of the Caribbean Joint Task Force in Key West. This new structure was assigned responsibility regarding planning and intelligence vis-à-vis Cuba. In 1981, the Antilles Defense Command was transferred from Puerto Rico to Key West apparently giving this unit the subordinated command functions Roosevelt Roads had previously played. On the other hand, USSOUTHCOM was significantly phased down in the context of the Panama Canal treaties of 1977, and its eventual closure and transfer of its functions to the continental United States was being actively considered. The concern with the weakness of SOUTHCOM was expressed in no uncertain terms in the 1981 study of the Strategic

Studies Institute. "A credible and effective U.S. military presence requires a Command that is adequately staffed and properly trained. Today SOUTHCOM is neither. . . . While the study team did not undertake a detailed analysis of staffing requirements, it is common fare in Washington and in Panama that SOUTHCOM's small staff is insufficient to deal effectively with the many and complex political-military issues which it must confront."[31]

The question of the regional command structure generated a sharp debate within the U.S. military and foreign policy establishment. An important current of opinion favored placing the entire Caribbean Basin region (understood as Central America and the Caribbean) under a strengthened USSOUTHCOM, in order to make the command structure coherent with prevalent geostrategic conceptions. Even the possibility of placing Cuba under the Continental United States Command (CONUS) and creating a "North America security zone" was entertained. However, the outcome of this debate has been the confirmation of the traditional division of labor between a stronger USSOUTHCOM and a reformed LANTCOM (to which the Key West unit has been added). Puerto Rico apparently no longer plays important regional command functions but rather has been assigned the role of logistic and air support and strategic rearguard in operations such as the Grenada invasion. The latter was entirely under the direct control of the Norfolk, Virginia, LANTCOM.[32]

The strengthening and clarification of the command structure has paralleled the expansion of the regional U.S. infrastructure of bases and installations. The process in Central America is well known. It has mainly consisted in upgrading the military presence in Panama and attempting to postpone the application of the military provisions of the Panama Canal treaties while simultaneously building an alternative network of airfields, intelligence installations, a regional military training center, and other facilities in Honduras.[33] Installations that could no longer be kept in Panama, such as the School of the Americas, have been transferred to the United States or Puerto Rico, rather than dismantling them. In fact, the School of the Americas has been significantly expanded in its new location at Fort Benning, Georgia, with an increased flow of students from the Caribbean and Central America. The number of students from the Caribbean has more than doubled compared to 1980 (see Table 5.5).

A similar process has occurred in the Caribbean with a significantly higher level of military activities in Puerto Rico and the development of subregional bases of operation in the Eastern Caribbean, mainly in Barbados and Antigua. The former played the role, together with Puerto Rico, of a staging point for the Grenada invasion, while in Antigua the existing base structure has been expanded and a regional training center

TABLE 5.5

Students from Caribbean Countries Trained Under the International Military
Education and Training Programs (selected years)

	1979	1980	1983	Estimated 1984	Proposed 1985
Bahamas	---	---	---	---	10
Barbados	1	13	a	a	a
Belize	---	---	19	49	49
Eastern Caribbean[b]	---	---	62	136	120
Guyana	---	---	10	27	27
Haiti	17	11	32	51	53
Jamaica	---	---	73	98	124
Dominican Republic	113	51	157	200	200
Panama	187	204	304	269	346
Surinam	67	195	---	17	26
Trinidad-Tobago	---	---	---	---	10
Total	385	474	657	847	965

[a]Included in Eastern Caribbean.
[b]Includes Antigua, Barbados, Dominica, St. Lucia, St. Vincent, Grenada,
St. Kitts-Nevis, Anguilla, British Virgin Islands, Montserrat.

Source: U.S. Department of Defense, *Congressional Presentation, Security
Assistance Programs*, 1982 and 1985.

(possibly similar to that in Honduras) is being built at a cost of $11
million.

The reorientation in U.S. foreign policy toward the Caribbean produced
an immediate increase in military activities in Puerto Rico. In 1979, for
example, the regionalization of National Guard functions began, when
units were sent to the Dominican Republic to carry out rescue efforts
in the wake of Hurricanes David and Federico. Military maneuvers
increased in intensity, and the attitude of the navy notably hardened in
the face of opposition to its practices on the Puerto Rican island of
Vieques. The geopolitical mindset that became dominant with the Reagan
administration served to emphasize the strategic military importance
assigned to Puerto Rico as an Eastern Caribbean enclave, and to accelerate
and increase its integration into military policy toward the region. United
Nations Ambassador Jeane Kirkpatrick brazenly expressed the attitude
of the U.S. government by saying that Puerto Rico was not a domestic

or international question, but rather a geopolitical bastion, strategic-military and nonnegotiable.[34] The strategic importance of Puerto Rico was also emphasized in a subsequent analysis of the Grenada invasion. "[Deletion] The [deletion] importance of the airfield facility at Naval Station, Roosevelt Roads, PR [Puerto Rico] was vividly demonstrated particularly in view of the present instability in the Caribbean region. [Deletion] airfields may not be readily available for similar future op-erations elsewhere. Access to Roosevelt Roads remains a [deletion] requirement."[35]

The changes that have taken place in the military and security functions of Puerto Rico in the Caribbean encompass the following aspects:

1. An increase in the presence and activities of the regular U.S. armed forces and readjustments in command structures in order to improve their capability for direct intervention, culminating in the use of Puerto Rico in crucial aspects of the invasion of Grenada.

2. Higher levels of recruitment of Puerto Ricans for all branches of the regular U.S. armed forces, thereby increasing the presence of Spanish-speaking military effectives that could be utilized in the region.

3. A strengthening and regionalization of the role of the Puerto Rican National Guard by integrating into it activities of aid and training of military forces from Central America and the Caribbean, and increasing its training as an auxiliary force for possible external use.

4. Regionalization of the forces of the Puerto Rican police as an intermediary in training activities, technical assistance, and intel-ligence through Interpol [International Police Organization] and use of Puerto Rico by the FBI [Federal Bureau of Investigation] for training police forces from the Caribbean and Central America.[36]

This more intensive military use of Puerto Rico has resulted in considerably higher levels of U.S. military expenditures in that country (see Table 5.6).

The U.S. military buildup has had the effect of increasing Cuban military preparations in all fields. This trend has been particularly marked since 1981 when arms shipments from the Soviet Union sharply increased, which has led to a significantly higher level of military expenditures (see Table 5.7). Though I do not have post–Grenada invasion figures, the actual confrontation of Cuban personnel (with about 40 deaths and over 50 wounded) and U.S. forces must have sharpened that country's concern for security.

The level of assistance and training to regional military and police forces has grown explosively since the late seventies. Total military

TABLE 5.6
Military and Security Expenditures of the United States and Puerto Rico, 1979-1983[a] (millions of US$)

	1979	1980	1981	1982	1983
U.S. military agencies					
Veterans Administration	54.7	72.0	77.3	86.0	95.3
Defense Department	101.2	74.7	152.1	142.7	174.7
Veterans benefits	202.4	223.3	230.5	274.1	279.9
Justice Department[b] (includes the FBI)	11.7	9.6	8.1	22.0	13.8
Aid to Puerto Rican agencies					
Civil Defense	.8	9.9	2.5	na	na
Police	1.3	5.4	1.9	na	na
National Guard[c]	na	72.5	72.5	72.5	72.5
Total		467.7	544.9		

aThese figures apparently do not include military purchases of materials and equipment exported to the United States from industries in Puerto Rico. In 1983 one industry alone sold $52.6 million to the Pentagon.

bOnly a part of the expenditures is used to finance the FBI. Because I do not have this figure, I have included the total expenditures. This has the effect of inflating the security expenditure totals.

cThe official budget of the National Guard is around $5 million, of which less than $2 million is U.S. assistance. Nevertheless, this body received an additional $70 million in assistance in 1983, according to the deposition of its commander before the Puerto Rican legislature. These monies do not pass through the Department of the Treasury and are not reflected in official documents. The figures for 1980 to 1982 are estimates based on that information.

na: Not available.

Source: Puerto Rican Government (Planning Council), *Balanza de Pagos*, 1981, Tables 10 and 14; and Puerto Rican Government (Planning Council), *Económico al Gobernador*, 1982-1983, vol. I, Tables 18 and 19.

TABLE 5.7
Cuban Military Expenditures (millions of US$, constant price figures; percentage of government expenditure, 1978-1983)

1974	1975	1976	1977	1978	1979	1980	1981	1982	1983
386	(446)	na	957	1,028	1,103	1,053	976	1,017	1,178
				8.6%	8.9%	8.5%	7.5%	9.4%	11.2%

na: Not available.

Note: Percentages are average annual increases. Figure in parentheses is an estimate.

Source: For constant price figures, Stockholm International Peace Research Institute (SIPRI), SIPRI Yearbook 1984, London: Taylor and Francis, 1984, p. 118. For 1978-1981 percentages, Economía y Desarrollo, January-February 1982, Table 15; 1982, Granma, October 10, 1982; 1983, Latin America Regional Report RC-83-01, January 21, 1983. Cited in SIPRI, SIPRI Yearbook 1984, London: Taylor and Francis, 1984, p. 98.

TABLE 5.8
Security Assistance to Caribbean Countries (selected years, thousands of US$)[a]

	1979	1980	1985	1986 Requested
Bahamas	---	---	50	50
Barbados	6	58	b	b
Belize	---	---	4,600	5,100
Eastern Caribbean[c]	---	4,000	25,300	45,400
Guyana	---	---	50	50
Haiti	---	1,127	5,750	130
Jamaica	---	---	72,250	78,280
Dominican Republic	984	3,450	53,750	60,800
Panama	1,399	291	40,000	59,100
Surinam	---	26	80	50
Trinidad-Tobago	---	---	50	50
Total	2,728	8,952	204,880	249,010

[a]Includes Military Assistance Program, International Military Education and Training Program, Foreign Military Sales, and Economic Support Fund.
[b]Included in Eastern Caribbean.
[c]Antigua, Barbados, Dominica, Grenada, St. Lucia, St. Vincent, and St. Kitts-Nevis.

Source: Department of Defense, *Congressional Presentation, Security Assistance Program*, 1982 and 1985; and Langhorne A. Motley, "Aid and U.S. Interests in Latin America and the Caribbean," *Caribbean Today*, vol. 2, no. 2, p. 26.

assistance to countries in the region has increased from $8 million to about $250 million in the requested budget for 1986 (see Table 5.8). Particularly sharp increases have occurred in the cases of Jamaica, Panama, and the Eastern Caribbean. A similar process has taken place with the number of Caribbean military officers trained under IMET. This expansion of military training to consistently high levels during the mid-eighties will mean that most of the officers in the Caribbean will undergo some form of U.S. training. For example, 318 Jamaican officers have been trained in the period 1983 to 1985. The creation of a new training center in Antigua will ensure that also middle and lower ranking military and police effectives are incorporated in this process.

TABLE 5.9
Commercial Exports to the Caribbean Licensed Under the Arms Export Control
Act (thousands of current US$)

	1979	1985 Estimated	Percentage Increase
Antigua	5	20	100.00
Bahamas	21	200	852.38
Barbados	26	20	-23.08
Belize	55	220	3,900.00
Bermuda	52	200	284.62
British Virgin Islands	---	25	100.00
Cayman Islands	151	5	-96.69
Dominica	---	---	---
Dominican Republic	196	1,500	665.31
Grenada	7	1	85.71
Guadeloupe	1	10	900.00
Guyana	5	600	11,900.00
Haiti	17	300	1,664.71
Jamaica	87	550	532.18
Martinique	2	3	50.00
Netherland Antilles	242	400	65.29
Panama	828	3,000	262.32
St. Christ Anguilla	1	---	-100.00
St. Lucia	4	4	0.00
Surinam	11	30	172.73
Trinidad-Tobago	61	500	719.67
Total	1,772	7,585	328.22

Source: U.S. Department of Defense, *Congressional Presentation,* 1982 and 1985, pp. 549 and 540.

Arms sales have followed the same trend as military assistance and training. Commercial sales to the Caribbean have increased from $1.7 million in 1979 to $7.6 million in 1985. Sales to the Bahamas, Belize, the Dominican Republic, Guadaloupe, Guyana, Haiti, Jamaica, and Trinidad-Tobago have increased at an extremely rapid pace (see Table 5.9).

Although reliable figures for military expenditures in the Caribbean region are difficult to obtain, it would be safe to assume, particularly taking commercial arms sales as an indicator, that the military budgets of most countries have tended to grow. This has been clearly the case of Trinidad-Tobago, which has significantly expanded its military establishment. Then a portion of increased U.S. aid funds, such as the resources transferred under the Economic Support Fund, are being absorbed by the military.

The overall regional trend has been toward a "Dominicanization" of the Caribbean militaries, that is, the reproduction of the model of clientelization and subordination of the armed forces of the Dominican Republic in the entire region.

Of particular importance has been the impact of U.S. military policy in the English-speaking Caribbean because it has promoted a process of militarization in countries with small or nonexistent military structures. This process was begun in the pre–Grenada invasion period through training of Jamaican, Dominican, and Barbadian effectives in Puerto Rico and the promotion of an anti-Grenada military pact among Eastern Caribbean states in 1982.

During the period 1982 to 1984, it seemed that the United States was moving toward the formation of a regional defense force based in Barbados. However, the marginal importance attached to the Caribbean multinational force during the Grenada invasion (included in the invasion plan almost as a political afterthought) indicated the lack of U.S. interest in this arrangement. These defense forces, called the Caribbean Peace-keeping Force (CPF), mainly performed postinvasion police functions. Cost considerations (estimated at about $100 million) also seem to have played a role. "Initially the role and the composition of the CPF was not clear. During preliminary and final planning the control of the CPF was not coordinated with the CJTF [Caribbean Joint Task Force], . . . and created early confusion on the planning for inserting the CPF. Once missions and locations were assigned and liaison effected, the hard problems dissolved. . . ."[37]

The United States has chosen instead to build up the national military, police, and coast guard forces through bilateral assistance while coordinating these forces in what is now called a regional security system. In those Eastern Caribbean countries where no military forces existed, 80-personnel special service units have been created within the existing police forces and trained in countersubversive tactics by 100 Green Beret advisers. Special service units have been established in Dominica, St. Lucia, Grenada, and St. Kitts-Nevis. The United States has also sought and obtained, Canadian and British support in training Eastern Caribbean police forces.[38]

The Caribbean: A New Pax Americana?

Caribbean policy has been presented as a glowing success of Reagan's foreign policy, in contrast to the evident stalemate in Central America, and as an example of what "determination" can achieve. The militarization of the region, the Grenada invasion, and the buttressing of a constellation of conservative, pro-U.S. governments seem to have stemmed the tide of popular movements that began in the mid-seventies. The Grenada invasion, particularly, led to an upsurge of modern jingoism and self-congratulation in the Reagan administration. More recently, the apparently smooth departure of Duvalier and the installation of a *Duvalierista* military junta in Haiti seemed to indicate that the United States is still in full control of the situation.

This, however, may only be superficially true as actual trends indicate that the new regional policy may have only postponed necessary changes toward democracy, self-determination, and social justice in the region. The incapacity of the Haitian military to contain popular democratic demands through repression was evidenced in the fall of the original junta. The cry "down with the Leopards" voiced by Haitian masses indicates the new contradictions created by the process of militarization. In the Dominican Republic, the governing PRD has suffered a significant erosion of popular support in the aftermath of the bloody repression (90 killed) of the April 1983 popular protests. Support for the Seaga regime in Jamaica is at its lowest since the 1980 elections, and conservative Eastern Caribbean leaders such as Eugenia Charles are confronting similar political difficulties.

The erosion of democratic rights and the militarization of Caribbean societies has generated increasing internal opposition, while the growing diversion of economic resources to a bloated military establishment will hardly contribute to an overcoming of the prolonged economic and social crisis of the region. That is why the conservative neocolonial leaders promoted to power by the Carter and Reagan administrations are clamoring for results—hitherto meager—in the economic aspects of the Caribbean Basin Initiative.

Seen from this perspective, the United States may have increasingly to resort to military regimes in the future (as it has done in Haiti), leading to a further erosion of democracy in the region and deepening the crisis of legitimacy of regional states.

Notes

1. In this paper I define region as the insular Caribbean as distinct from the concept of the Caribbean Basin. For historical reasons, I also include Belize, Guyana, Surinam, and Panama as part of the Caribbean. I agree, however, with the broader conception of the Caribbean espoused by Xavier Gorostiaga in his writings. See, for example, "Centroamérica y el Caribe: Geopolítica de la crisis regional," CIDE, *Cuadernos Semestrales*, no. 15 (First Semester, 1984), pp. 65–92.

2. I recognize both the need to define this concept with rigor and the difficulties inherent in such a definition due to the region's diversity. However, I wish to make clear that I am not referring only to "left" party formations but also diverse forms of popular political organization (trade unions, cooperatives, churches, communal groups, and so forth) that articulated the interests of subordinated classes and have tended to coalesce behind programs of social change that express, to use Gorostiaga's expression, the "logic of the majorities."

3. Haiti seems to have been an exception, as the Jean Claude Duvalier government promoted a greater collaboration with the U.S. military. There, countersubversive units, such as the Leopards, were promoted during the seventies.

4. Such a situation occurred in Panama, where a direct military presence had galvanized the opposition forces, and also in the Southern Cone, where fascist military regimes had risen to power with extremely narrow bases of support.

5. See DESCO, *Informativo Político*, no. 55 (Lima, April 1977):8–9. Also Wolf Grabendorff, "Das interamerikanische Verhältnis seit dem Amstritt Carters," *Aus politik und zeit geschichte*, (August 20, 1977):29–38, and Bernd Greiner, "Konturen der Aussenpolitik Präsident Carters," *Blätter für deutsche und internationale Politik* (August 1977):948–969. For an apologetic "inside" view of Carter's policy see Robert Pastor, "U.S. Policy Toward the Caribbean" in *Latin America and the Caribbean Contemporary Record*, Jack Hopkins, ed., vol. 1 (New York and London: Holmes and Meier, 1983), pp. 78–89.

6. For an interesting analysis of the formulation of U.S.–Latin America policy in the Kennedy and Johnson periods, see F. Parkinson, *Latin America, the Cold War and the World Powers: 1945–1973* (Beverly Hills and London: Sage Publications, 1974).

7. *Foreign Affairs* 44, no. 1 (October 1965):36–48.

8. The effects of the recession were not the same for all. Cuba, because of its socialist economy and links with the socialist countries, and Puerto Rico and Trinidad—for different reasons—did not experience as grave a crisis as other countries. In Puerto Rico, a dramatic increase in U.S. transfer payments to individuals (food stamps) prevented the economic downturn from becoming a social and political crisis. Trinidad's oil resources played a similar role for that country. But Puerto Rico and Trinidad were affected by the recession.

9. Zbigniew Brzezinski, "How the Cold War was Played," *Foreign Affairs* 51, no. 1 (October 1972):195.

10. It should be noted that the United States had vehemently opposed the closure of the base, demanded by nationalist forces, in the early 1960s. By the late sixties, however, it was felt that the base was no longer vital.

11. John Enders, *La presencia militar norteamericana en Puerto Rico*, Proyecto Carbeño de Justicia y Paz (Río Piedras, 1980); and Jorge Rodríguez, "El aparato militar norteamericano en Puerto Rico," *Casa de las Américas* (November-December, 1980), pp. 7–25.

12. Military aid to Latin America dropped from $82 million in 1966 to $21.4 million in 1969. Likewise, Military Assistance and Advisory Group (MAAG)

personnel were reduced from 791 in 1969 to 498 in 1970. In 1967, the Conte-Long and Symington amendments introduced limitations in transfers and sales of arms. The Foreign Military Sales Act placed a limit of $75 million in arms sales to Latin America, which was in force until 1971. A year later, exports of arms to military dictatorships "hindering human rights" were curbed. The ceiling for arms was eventually raised by Nixon, but aid and training never recovered its high level of the 1960s. Finally, the Foreign Assistance Act of 1974 abolished the Public Safety Program, under which the police forces of the Dominican Republic, Guyana, Jamaica, and Panama had been trained. See Michael Klare, "Abasteciendo represión," CIDE, *Cuadernos Semestrales*, no. 4 (Second Semester, 1978), 99–111; and Stephen S. Kaplan, "U.S. Arms Transfers to Latin America, 1945–1974," *International Studies Quarterly* 19, no. 4 (December 1975):399–431.

13. Jan Oberg, "Arms Trade with the Third World as an Aspect of Imperialism," *Journal of Peace Research* 12, no. 3 (1975), 218; and Michael Klare, "La Política della Vendita delle Armi degli Stati Uniti in America Latina," *Russell Tribunal II Document*, (Rome: January 1976), pp. 2–3.

14. It should be remembered that the meeting of the Nonaligned Movement held in La Habana in 1979, with the participation of several Caribbean heads of state, and the subsequent presidency of that movement by Fidel Castro became a source of sharp concern to the Carter government as it was considered to enhance Cuban influence in the Third World and the Caribbean.

15. The changes in Central American policy during this period are discussed in Antonio Cavalla Rojas, "U.S. Military Strategy in Central America: From Carter to Reagan," *Contemporary Marxism*, no. 3 (n.d.):114–130.

16. For an interesting analysis of the role of the Committee on the Present Danger in the neoconservative ideological offensive, see Jerry W. Saunders, *Peddlers of Crisis* (Boston: South End Press, 1983). A 1980 document of the CPD stated, "in the Caribbean . . . the Soviet Union has been steadily improving its position. Soviet planes, submarines, and combat troops [have been] based in Cuba, and military assistance has been given from Cuba to revolutionary movements in Nicaragua, El Salvador, and other countries in the area. A potential is being built up from which the Soviet Union can threaten our Atlantic sea lanes, our communications with Central and South America, and the territory of the United States itself." Cited in Saunders, pp. 278–279.

17. Robert Pastor, "US Policy Towards the Caribbean" in Jack Hopkins, ed., *Latin America and the Caribbean Contemporary Record*, vol. 1 (New York and London: Holmes and Meier, 1983), p. 85.

18. D. Sinclair DaBreo, *Of Men and Politics, the Agony of St. Lucia* (St. Lucia: Commonwealth Publishers, 1981), pp. 194–195.

19. "Discurso de Thomas Enders ante el Consejo de las Américas," June 3, 1981, INFO Service.

20. "I wouldn't propose it if I were not convinced that it is vital to the security interests of this hemisphere." *New York Times*, February 25, 1962, p. A14.

21. Strategic Studies Institute, U.S. Army War College, Carlisle Barracks, *The Role of the U.S. Military: Caribbean Basin*, ACN 80049, Final Report (October 26, 1980), summary and ch. 4.

22. Ibid.

23. Strategic Studies Institute, U.S. Army War College, Carlisle Barracks, *Non-Nato Contributions to Coalition Warfare*, Final Report (February 23, 1981), appendix G.

24. Edward Gonzalez, *A Strategy for Dealing with Cuba in the 1980s*, (Santa Barbara: Rand Corporation, September 1982).

25. David Rondfeldt, *Geopolitics, Security and U.S. Strategy in the Caribbean Basin*, (Santa Monica: Rand Corporation, November 1983), p. v.

26. Ibid., pp. xii, passim. Another contemporary study that proposes closer military links with the region is Curtis S. Morris, Jr., Lieutenant Colonel, USAF, *The United States-Caribbean Basin Connection: A Perspective on Regional Military-to-Military Relationships* (Washington, D.C.: Center for Hemispheric Studies, American Enterprise Institute for Public Policy Research, August 1983).

27. House of Representatives Committee on Foreign Affairs, Subcommittee on Western Hemisphere Affairs, *Review of Proposed Economic and Security Assistance Requests for Latin America and the Caribbean, Hearings and Markup*, March 5 and 19, 1985.

28. For a more extensive discussion of these maneuvers see Jorge Rodríguez Beruff, "Puerto Rico y la militarización del Caribe: 1979-1984," CIDE, *Cuadernos Semestrales*, no. 15 (First Semester, 1984), pp. 224–255. Also National Action and Research on the Military Industrial Complex (NARMIC), *The Central American War: A Guide to the U.S. Military Buildup* (Philadelphia: American Friends Service Committee, 1983), p. 7.

29. Humberto García, "Intervención, seguridad regional y militarización en el Caribe, 1979–1986," *Revista di Ciencias Sociales*, 518–519; also Joseph B. Treaster, "Caribbean War Games: Not Everyone is Delighted," *New York Times*, September 16, 1985, p. 2. I am greatly indebted to García's work, particularly his painstaking analysis of Eastern Caribbean developments.

30. García, p. 555.

31. Strategic Studies Institute, *The Role of the U.S. Military: Caribbean Basin*, ch. 4; see also Strategic Studies Institute, *Non-Nato Contributions to Coalition Warfare*, p. G-9. This latter document states that the "creation of an Inter-American Canal Defense Force need not eliminate SOUTHCOM which could be reoriented to have more comprehensive capabilities such as Caribbean defense."

32. For an excellent discussion of the regional command structure see Humberto García, "Intervención en el Caribe," pp. 7–16; also John A. Fesmire, "United States Military Command Relationships in Latin America: Could They Be Better?" (Individual study project, U.S. Army War College, May 6, 1982); Ronfeldt, "Geopolitics, Security, and U.S. Strategy," passim.

33. See Raul Leis, "El Comando Sur, poder hostil," *Nueva Sociedad*, no. 81, 77–88.

34. *Pensamiento Crítico*, June-July 1981, p. 6.

35. Commander in Chief of the Atlantic Command (CINCLANT), *Operation Urgent Fury Report, October 25–November 2, 1983* (Norfolk, Virginia: Atlantic Command, February 6, 1984), p. 6.

36. I have discussed the militarization of Puerto Rico in greater detail in "Puerto Rico y la militarización del Caribe: 1979–1984," CIDE, *Cuadernos Semestrales*, no. 15 (First Semester, 1984), pp. 217–234.

37. CINCLANT, *Operation Urgent Fury Report*, p. I-2.

38. For a detailed analysis of military policy toward the Eastern Caribbean refer to Humberto García, "Intervención en el Caribe," passim. Also Dion Philips, "Caribbean Militarization: A Response to the Crisis," *Contemporary Marxism*, no. 10 (n.d.):92–109; and Bernard Diederich, "The End of West Indian Innocence, Arming the Police," *Caribbean Review* 13, no. 2 (Spring 1984):10–13.

6

Freedom Fighters and Low-Intensity Warfare Against Nicaragua

Lilia Bermúdez and Raúl Benítez

The support that the U.S. government has been giving to the contras in Nicaragua is one of the components of the doctrine of low-intensity warfare (LIW). The central objective of this doctrine is to avoid, as much as possible, the direct involvement of U.S. combat troops in any foreign country or to reduce the costs of an invasion, should one prove necessary. This doctrine points to a substantial change in the policy implemented by the first Reagan administration, which was dedicated to the search for an exclusively military solution to the Central American situation. During the first four years of Ronald Reagan's presidency, intense preparations were made to ensure the creation of the necessary operational, logistic, and training conditions for an invasion of U.S. troops. The inability to obtain a supposedly rapid military victory against the Salvadorian FMLN-FDR (Frente Farabundo Martí para la Liberación Nacional–Frente Democrático Revolucionario), as well as the political consolidation of the Sandinista government in Nicaragua, has forced U.S. policy-makers to the following conclusion: The costs of a direct military invasion would be extremely high because such an invasion would inevitably bog down.

This change in military strategy reflects a more pragmatic, but no less ideological, vision of conflict in the Third World. Noam Chomsky has expressed this situation with great acumen: "The fact that the Russians are not in Nicaragua is irrelevant, since here we are dealing with theology—not with reason—and in theology the facts are irrelevant."[1]

Since the beginning of the 1980s, U.S. think-tanks and military strategists have been reflecting on possible ways to handle low-intensity conflicts (LICs). Their ideas have been made public in articles, documents, and seminars and are now commonly used in the military's own literature where analysts have denounced the U.S. lack of preparation with respect to low-intensity conflicts.

Although the debate about these ideas has remained open, a series of definitions have already been pragmatically tested in zones of conflict. These elements underline the global nature of the new strategy and some of its objectives, which are oriented toward regaining U.S. hegemony at the global level.

Definitions of low-intensity conflict are abundant. We will quote only two of them, to show how they are mutually complementary.

> "Low-Intensity conflict" as used here, refers to the range of activities and operations on the lower end of the conflict spectrum involving the use of military or a variety of semi-military forces (both combat and noncombat) on the part of the intervening power to influence and compel the adversary to accept a particular political-military condition. Employment of force is a concept closely related, but broader in scope and in policy option. The employment of force is not exclusively concerned with combat, but includes a variety of methods and strategies in which military force or its perceived use can influence the environment and actions of other states without necessarily resorting to battle. It encompasses the threat of force (without employment or combat), the employment of force (without combat), and the use of force in combat. Employment of force and low-intensity conflict, as concepts, blend into one another. It is difficult to develop credibility for a policy for force employment without being prepared to commit forces to combat. A foreign state (or states) must be convinced that the state employing force is also prepared to use it in combat.[2]

A study prepared for the U.S. Army Training and Doctrine Command in July of 1983, which summarized the literature on low-intensity conflict, pointed out the following:

> Low-intensity warfare is the military recourse of nations and organizations to limited force or the threat of force to achieve political objectives without the full-scale commitment of resources and will that characterizes nationstate wars of survival or conquest. Typically, low-intensity conflict involves relatively small numbers of participants from all sides in relation to the importance of the political objectives at stake; these are always highly leveraged, usually asymmetrical, forms of political action. Low-intensity conflict (whether conducted by the U.S. or by others) can include coercive diplomacy, police functions, psychological operations, insurgency, guerrilla warfare, counterterror activities, and military/paramilitary deployment with limited goals. While the intensity may be low, the duration may be very long. Because unconventional tactics are often used, success in low-intensity

conflict is seldom that of conventional victory by force of arms; success often is measured only by avoidance of certain outcomes or by attitudinal changes in a target group. Low-intensity operations are not confined to overseas but may be necessary within the U.S. in response to civil disorder or terrorism.[3]

In general, the literature on LIW assumes that this type of conflict will be prevalent during the next few years and that by the 1990s, the most probable arenas for its use on the American continent will be Central America, Mexico, Colombia, Venezuela, and Puerto Rico. In the case of Puerto Rico, military analysts do not rule out the possiblity of a buildup to the level of conventional warfare.[4]

From the "theological" perspective that Chomsky mentions, the U.S. concept of LIW—within the context of its plan of confrontation with the Soviet Union in the Third World—has several objectives: (1) to stop popular movements from triumphing or fighting for the right of self-determination, national sovereignty, and nonalignment; and (2) the roll-back of governments already consolidated and in power. It is imperative that this second objective be obtained through legal measures, both at the national and international level. And, finally, (3) implementation of an antiterrorist struggle, the terrorism supposedly fomented by pro-Soviet governments.

To a greater or lesser extent—and without *any proof* of the need for it—all three objectives have been applied or implicated against the Nicaraguan government. The Sandinista government has been accused of being Communist, of providing armaments to the Salvadorian FMLN, and, finally, of fomenting terrorist groups.

The need to obtain an internal consensus for LIW has obliged the U.S. government to the more frequent use of misinformation as an instrument of ideological warfare, as "the American public should not be predisposed to support any form of low-intensity operations which have the appearance of 'foreign interventions,' especially those that are dirtied with the label of 'covert operations.'"[5]

For this reason,

with the introduction of the doctrine of LIC, the White House thought that it had finally found the correct posture. The name itself is soothing. By placing emphasis on the limited nature of the combat, this doctrine suggests that the United States will continue to involve itself in Third World conflicts. Even more, by emphasizing the dangers of terrorism, this doctrine can be presented as a policy of reply, as a prudent and legitimate reaction to the violence, instability, anti-Americanism and aggression fomented by the Soviets.[6]

Rollback of the Nicaraguan Government
and Low-Intensity Conflict

At the theoretical-doctrinal level, the use of LIW is directly related to the reinstatement of an offensive posture, in itself the second principle of warfare:

> This principle could be better entitled the principle of the intitiative, for its essence has to do with maintaining initiative and freedom of action on the battlefield. The simplest way to accomplish this is through both the strategic and tactical offensive, by carrying the war to the enemy and destroying his army to break his will to resist. This is the way the United States fought the Mexican War, the Spanish-American War and the two world wars.[7]

By adopting this position, U.S. policymakers dispense with burdensome doctrines like containment, elaborated by George Kennan at the beginning of the cold war. This doctrine proposed a defensive strategy that tolerated the existence of Communist regimes and stopped direct interventions in certain conflicts that might have inclined the balance toward the West (for example, the Hungarian uprising in 1957 and the Cuban missile crisis of 1962). "Thus, U.S. national policy dictated that, in any conflict with the Soviet Union or its surrogates, the United States would not pursue the strategic offensive (rollback or liberation) but would, instead, pursue the strategic defensive (containment)."[8]

This kind of doctrine must have a national consensus that allows it to transcend the use of clandestine or covert support, thereby legitimizing its application internationally. The consensus is usually based on the legitimacy and political and military credibility of the groups being supported. Vietnam is a good example: "American military intervention in support of a governing elite or political system that does not have some minimum level of internal support is likely to erode any existing public support. This does not necessarily mean that such intervention is doomed to failure. Rather, it means that American intervention must be a balanced political-military one, primarily concerned with the reinforcement and legitimation of the existing system."[9]

In a literal sense, this need for legitimacy is easily observed in the case of the Salvadoran president, the Christian Democrat Napoleon Duarte, and in the document entitled "Washington's Point of View," which was made public to the U.S. press and served as the basis for discussion in the meeting in Panama held in September of 1985, where all the Central American ambassadors met with Assistant Secretary for Inter-American Affairs Elliott Abrams. The document states, "We have finally gotten people to believe that El Salvador has become a reformist country and that the guerrillas do not represent the Salvadorean people. We must continue to cultivate this belief."

This principle is equally valid in the case of the Nicaraguan contras. The U.S. president himself has undertaken a publicity campaign that has reached extraordinary levels, whether the objective has been to obtain the support of Congress, either for "humanitarian" aid ($27 million voted in July of 1985), or open military support (from $75 to $100 million, with was solicited at the beginning of 1986).

The desired image change of the contras has required work within that organization itself. Great efforts have been taken to disguise its pro-Somoza origins and to obtain internal unity, principally with the promotion to top-level positions certain anti-Somoza civilian members such as Alfonso Robelo, Arturo Cruz, Adolfo Calero, and Edén Pastora. This last leader has been justly opposed to such an artifical unity because he is aware of the majority presence of former members of the National Guard within the Fuerza Democrática Nicaragüense (FDN or Nicaraguan Democratic Force), the largest of the anti-Sandinista organizations. Changes have also been implemented with respect to the behavior of this organization and its relations with the Nicaraguan people. For example, the highly publicized CIA manual gives the following advice:

> During patrols or other operations near or within towns, each guerrilla fighter should be *respectful and courteous* to all the people. All guerrillas should always move with great caution and be ready to fight at any moment, if necessary. But they should not consider that all the people are enemies nor should they treat people with suspicion or hostility. Even in war, it *is possible to smile, to laugh and to say hello to the people.* The real source of our revolutionary base, the true reason for which we fight, is our people. We should always be respectful of them, whenever the opportunity presents itself. . . . Guerrilla fighters should be very careful *not to become explicit agents of terror,* because this would result in a loss of popular support.[10]

The publicity measures were increased when it came to finding formulas for "humanizing" the war for the U.S. public. On August 20, 1985, the FDN announced the creation of a committee for the Red Cross, a human rights commission, an attorney general's office, and appeal and exception courts. With these measures, the intention was "to establish norms for the exchange of prisoners, guarantee medical attention for the wounded of both bands, create demilitarized zones, permit freedom of movement for paramedics and Red Cross aids and guarantee the protection of the civilian population."[11] The attorney general's office was to be in charge of judging war crimes committed by members of the FDN or any other breach of moral and behavior codes. Arturo Cruz announced its creation in October 1985.

This publicity campaign attempted to undermine the denunciations of systematic violation of human rights by the contras against the Nicaraguan population. These accusations have been made by different U.S. and international organizations, many of them of religious affiliation, as well as by the U.S. press.

On the other hand, one of the fundamental objectives of LIW is political, that is, the answers to the types of conflict that make up LIW cannot be exclusively military. They must incorporate other, nonmilitary elements into the war such as civic action, psychological operations, as well as economic measures:

> In low-intensity conflict, the initiative rests with those who can influence or exploit the process of change. That process must be influenced where and when it serves *our* national interests. This is a long-term process in which the political, economic and psychological options provide the best route to lasting success. . . . The basic difference between military operations in low-intensity conflict and the mid-to high-intensity levels is the nature of military success. At the mid-to high-intensity levels, military success is measured in terms of winning campaigns and battles. In low-intensity conflict, it is achieving U.S. national objectives without recourse to protracted combat. . . . In low-intensity conflict, nonmilitary factors play a far greater role at all levels from strategic to tactical. . . . Actions taken in the military arena cannot be separated from—and will have an effect on—the political, economic, psychological and social environments as well. . . . Conversely, not every condition will require a military effort.[12]

The CIA manual has also tried to synthesize these ideas. The first sentence of the preface says, "Guerrilla warfare is, essentially, a political war."[13] The introduction, which summarizes the seven chapters of the manual, emphasizes the importance of psychological operations (its principal objective): "The tactical effort of guerrilla warfare is directed toward the weaknesses of the enemy and towards the destruction of his military capacity to resist, and should be accompanied by a psychological effort to weaken and destroy his sociopolitical capacity as well. In guerrilla warfare—more than any other kind of military enterprise— psychological activities must go hand in hand with military activities, in order to achieve the desired objectives."[14]

If the objective is political and nonmilitary elements are introduced into the war, it is because this new doctrine emphasizes the need to win over the population by psychological warfare. In the Nicaraguan case, this implies the use of propaganda and the manipulation of public opinion, as well as improving the local image of the contras. In order to achieve this objective, radio stations have been installed in Honduras and Costa Rica and transmit in Nicaragua:

> This conception of guerrilla warfare as a political war converts the psychological operations into the factor which determines the results. Therefore, the target is the minds of the population; of the whole population: our troops, the enemy troops and the civilian population.[15]

> [Psychological warfare implies] hanging up our arms, and working side by side with them [the peasants] in their fields, in construction activities, in the harvest, in fishing, etc.[16]

Nevertheless, because the fundamental objective in Nicaragua of LIW is the destabilization of the Sandinista government, the CIA manual also encourages the practice of assassination of different leaders: "Carefully selected and planned targets may be *neutralized,* such as judges, police officials or State security officers, heads of the CDS [Comités de Defensa Sandinista, or Sandinista Defense Committees], etc."[17] All of the tactics described above have also gone hand-in-hand with the need to destroy the prestige of the Sandinista government by making it into an accomplice of international drug traffic and terrorism.

Within the framework of LIC, the concept of terrorism has changed; it has become a "strategic value tactic," used by "neo-nihilistic subnational groups" or by nation-states.[18] Seen from the vantage point of LIC, "a terrorist warfare, sponsored by sovereign states or organized political entities to achieve political objectives, is a threat to the United States, and is increasing at an alarming rate."[19]

Terrorism has fully emerged as the definitive weapon that can enable nations with inferior military forces to gain a degree of strategic equality with the world's major industrial powers. Terrorism is an alternative to the acquisition of nuclear weapons. It is also an alternative to developing large conventional forces. The key, and in some cases only, strategic weapon for these nations is terrorism. Terrorism, with its associated violence, offers the small and less powerful nations an option for influencing the policies and behavior of larger and more powerful nations."[20] Even though the U.S. counterterrorism campaign has been directed principally toward the Middle East, up until now, the only proposal for legislation to fight terrorism (presented to Congress September 27, 1985) has to do with Central America: the Law Enforcement Counterterrorism Assistance Program, with a budget of $54 million. The campaign to get this law through Congress began on July 2, 1985, with an unprecedented declaration by Ronald Reagan: "Iran, Libya,

Cuba, Nicaragua and North Korea form a Confederation of Terrorist States, led by degenerate, misadapted, crazy and squalid delinquents."[21]

Originally, terrorism was considered to be a form of nonmilitary combat that would yield to low-intensity conflict.[22] Currently, many believe that terrorism can make another country strategically equal, alongside the major industrial powers of the world. Such ideas are alarming because of the objective that they pursue: to provide the ideological justification for "surgical" military interventions against those states that supposedly foment terrorism. On the other hand, and as we previously mentioned, these ideas are used as tools to undermine the prestige of "enemy" governments. And what is even more alarming, they may serve as an argument in favor of a large-scale invasion: "It is not hard to imagine state-sponsored terrorism targeting U.S. forces conducting exercises in Honduras. Significant U.S. military casualties in Central America would be the catalyst for strong and swift public and congressional action to change U.S. foreign policy in the region."[23]

Finally, according to the doctrine of LIW in the military sense, this kind of warfare is fundamentally irregular. A country cannot solely employ conventional troops but must use troops specially trained in LIW, such as the Special Operations Forces (SOF), whose reactivation program in the United States began in 1982. Members of the SOF, especially the Green Berets, started arriving in Central America on training missions to the local armed forces in July 1983. "Although it has been a CIA operation, suspicions have been raised of covert Special Operations Forces assistance to the contras, and a revival of the Vietnam-era close cooperation between the CIA and the SOF."[24]

The public revelation of this collaboration between the CIA and the SOF was alleged in the last quarter of 1985, when a Mexican newspaper announced that Nicaraguan Contras and Afghan resistance fighters would be the first students of a new school opening in Boulder, Colorado. Called the Institute for International and Regional Studies, this new center has former Green Berets among its faculty, all under the direction of retired Colonel Alexander McColl.[25] According to a telephone conversation with McColl, the purpose of the school is to conduct "studies on externally supported terrorist activities."

In line with the foregoing allegations, the SOF, it would seem, are the privileged military instrument of LIW, because "Special Forces units are trained to organize and advise either resistance or host-government forces. . . . Although Special Forces units are best utilized as advisors to friendly government forces or to resistance forces, the units are also capable of conducting quick-response clandestine or overt operations in remote areas against lightly defended targets."[26]

The Constitution of the Contras Army

The Sandinista triumph of July 19, 1979, caused the complete disintegration of Anastasio Somoza's National Guard. A new army was created in Nicaragua, whose reorganization was based on the guerrilla columns constituted between 1978 and 1979 in order to defeat the dictatorship. This new army, known as Ejército Popular Sandinista (EPS), was officially recognized as the armed institution of the new Nicaraguan state in November of 1979.

The former dictator's defeated praetorian guard was dispersed, and its members sought refuge in Honduras while its leaders went into exile in the United States, principally in Miami. However, at the same time the revolutionary triumph in Nicaragua was underway.[27]

In the beginning, the leaders of the defeated National Guard were subject to enormous international isolation, due in part to the great sympathy enjoyed by the Sandinista movement during the insurrection and to the constant denunciations concerning the behavior of members of the guard in their relation to the Nicaraguan people. Even so, Somoza was able to ensure a "safe" refuge in Paraguay and to reorganize his army in Argentina. The late 1979 period was considered to have been the best of the Argentine military dictatorship because it had obtained a great victory against "communism" in Argentina. For this reason, during the Thirteenth Conference of American Armies held in Bogota, Colombia, from November 3 to 5 of 1979, the famous Viola Doctrine was proclaimed. This doctrine was based on the idea that once victory was obtained in one country, the same military strategy could be exported to other countries threatened by communism. This explains why the Argentines supported the coup d'état against Lidia Gueiler in 1980 in Bolivia in favor of General Luis García Meza. Argentina also sent the first team of military advisers to Honduras in order to begin attacks against Nicaragua. These measures were taken with the knowledge of Policarpo Paz García, Honduran chief of state.[28]

During 1980 and 1981, a triad was established against Nicaragua. The triad consisted of Argentine advisers, U.S. funds, and Nicaraguan soldiers, in addition to a territorial-logistic rearguard in Honduras. There was an effort made to incorporate the Honduran army into the triad, especially during the period when General Gustavo Alvarez Martínez was chief of the armed forces of Honduras (January 1982 to March 1984).

With the ascent of Ronald Reagan to the presidency of the United States in January of 1981, anti-Nicaraguan propaganda acquired official legitimacy because it was seen in the context of the East-West conflict. Also at this time, the CIA began discussing with the Argentine government the possibility of establishing training bases for counterrevolutionaries in Argentine territory, according to contra sources.[29] In fact, 1981 is considered to have been the year of the best-ever bilateral relations between Argentina and the United States. This spirit of goodwill was crowned by General Leopoldo Galtieri's visit to Washington, where he was received by top officials within the Reagan administration.[30]

One of the most important steps toward the consolidation of the administration's direct support for the contras was taken in March of 1981. The so-called Nicaraguan support of the Salvadoran guerrillas was discovered by intelligence committees of Congress. The revelation of this alleged support was used to legitimize the famous White Paper[31] that established that a transfer of arms was in the national interest of the United States.[32] In November 1981, the National Security Council elaborated a ten-point plan, signed by Reagan on December which made public U.S. support for the following use of force: "Work primarily through non-Americans to achieve the foregoing, [support the contras] but in some circumstances the CIA might [possibly using U.S. personnel] take unilateral paramilitary action against special Cuban targets."[33] This plan included $19 million in funding for the CIA to create a new force of 500 Contras.

Thus, December 1981, the contra army was founded with less than 1,000 members, separated into different groups, one of which was the Legión 15 de septiembre. The core of the army consisted of about 600 former national guardsmen who had taken refuge in Honduras. Its two main leaders were Enrique Bermúdez Varela (former military attaché of the Somoza government in Washington) and Arístides Sánchez (pro-Somoza landowner). The other groups that made up the contras were Ejército de Liberación Nacional (ELN, Army of National Liberation) and the Unión Democrática Nicaragüense" (UDN, Nicaraguan Democratic Union). The CIA's first important move was the creation of the Fuerza Democrática Nicaragüense (FDN, the Nicaraguan Democratic Force) in 1981, by means of the fusion of the Legión 15 de septiembre and the UDN. The ELN joined the FDN in 1982. During this same year the CIA assumed the operational direction of the contras and supported certain important organic changes in the new army due to the withdrawal of Argentine advisers because of the Falklands/Malvinas war, in which the United States gave its support to Great Britain.

In December 1982, the Political Directorate was created, formed by conservative Nicaraguan Contra leaders. The purpose of this organization was to give the contras a more moderate image to make it easier to obtain justification and approval for official U.S. aid.[34] This political-military reorganization culminated at the end of 1983, with the naming of Dr. Adolfo Calero Portocarrero (leader of the Conservative party and former manager of the Coca-Cola susidiary) as president of the directorate and commander in chief of the armed forces. According to contra sources, the organic evolution of this organization can be summed up as follows:

> In March of 1982, the forces of insurrection were able to make the first important blows against the Sandinista military infrastructure. . . . On December 7 [1982], less than two months after the October communiqué, a good-size group of Nicaraguans met in Fort Lauderdale, Florida, and designated the present National Directorate of the NDF [FDN; at this meeting Enrique Bermúdez was named commander in chief]. . . . At the end of 1983 the direction [of the FDN] was restructured and the new leadership was assigned a civic-military role. Dr. Adolfo Calero Portocarrero was named president of the directorate and Commander in Chief of the military forces.[35]

During 1982 and 1983, the contras organized their present internal structure based on patrols (destacamentos) of 20 members. Three patrols made up a group, with 60 members. These groups in turn were organized into work forces of 4 to 5 groups with approximately 260 to 325 members. Finally, 3 or 4 work forces made up a regional command, with 780 to 1,300 soldiers in each command. According to the contras, there were eight regional commands operating in a territory of 63,000 square kilometers in the provinces of Madriz, Nueva Segovia, Estelí, Jinotega, Matagalpa, Boaco Chontales, and in one-third of the provinces of Zelaya and Chinandega.[36] This information coincides with that given by the Nicaraguan government, which added that another regional command was created in 1985.[37]

Perceptions of the War Within the United States and Within Nicaragua

Until the end of 1982, the Reagan administration had no difficulty in managing the constitution of the contras and the covert support given to them. However, in November 1982, *Newsweek* uncovered the real dimensions of the U.S. government's involvement in Central America. The news coverage especially emphasized the activities underway to destabilize Nicaragua.[38]

The full extent of U.S. involvement in Latin America became more public: the active political role against the Sandinistas played by the U.S. ambassador, John Demitri Negroponte; the extent of the covert actions taken against the Nicaraguan economy. The similarities between the situation in Central America and the direct U.S. involvement in the Vietnam War were aired. Concurrently with the adverse media coverage, massive military maneuvers were begun. The majority of these maneuvers were based on the philosophy of direct intervention. It is important to note that not since 1981, when the Halcon Vista (Falcon View) maneuver took place, had important military exercises taken place; in February 1983, these maneuvers began again, with Ahuas Tara I (Big Pine I), and they received great notoriety.

Although we believe that the Central America conflict, especially the establishment of the anti-Nicaraguan army, must be understood within the context of LIC, the ideological dimension that the Reagan administration has given to the conflict has the flavor of a total liberation crusade. Reagan himself compared the contras to American revolutionaries, to the anti-fascist resistance in France, and to Simón Bolívar's liberation army. This obliges us to point out two distinct perceptions of the war against Nicaragua: (1) At the military level, it is low-intensity warfare, not strategic, and can be prolonged in time (and possibly in space, should the conflict become regionalized); and (2) at the political level, the war is totally relentless. These points can be confirmed by the constant allusions that Reagan and his administration make to the threats they perceive against the national security of the United States. For example, ever since Reagan began his second term as president[39] this ideological propaganda has been stepped up so as to avoid any red tape in obtaining aid for the contras: "They are our brothers, these freedom fighters, and we owe them our help. . . . They are the moral equivalent of the Founding Fathers and the brave men and women of the French Resistance. We cannot turn away from them. For the struggle here is not right versus left, but right versus wrong."[40]

At the same time that the contras have been strengthened, the Nicaraguan government has lost prestige within the United States. This situation has permitted the Reagan administration to seek even more ambitious goals with respect to the aid it has solicited for the contras, using official and private channels to reach its objective. In Table 6.1, which is based on official Nicaraguan sources, approximately $100 million is mentioned as official aid received by the contras. At the same time, the Nicaraguan government has claimed the contras have received $1,000 million in private aid,[41] although it is very difficult to verify this statistic.

To the distinction already made with respect to the military and ideological perceptions in the United States of the war against Nicaragua, we need to address the perceptions of the war in Nicaragua. First, although this war at the military level is considered by the United States to be one of LIC, for Nicaragua it is a total war of defense (by a total war we mean a war where the sum total of a nation's resources are dedicated to the war effort). This perception is substantiated by examining

TABLE 6.1
Official Aid Given by the United States to the Contras

	US$ Million	Classification
November 1981	19.95	Approved by the Security Council for the realization of covert activities
December 1982	30.00	
December 1983	24.00	Approved by the U.S. Congress
June 1985	27-32.00	Both the House of Representatives and the Senate approved humanitarian aid to the counterrevolution

Source: Nicaraguan Government, *La Derrota de la Contrarrevolución: Datos Básicos* 1981-1985 (Managua, 1986).

the increase in government defense expenditures: from 14.7 percent in 1981 to more than 50 percent in 1985,[42] and to the enormous growth of the People's Sandinist Army (PSA), made up of regular troops and militia.[43] Second, at the political-ideological level, the Reagan administration's crusade against communism within the context of the East-West conflict, has been met by a rebuttal that emphasizes nationalism, self-determination, and nonintervention. The latter form the basis for the justification of the Sandinista revolution as political and social necessities for that country. For these reasons, the defensive war in Nicaragua not only means the defense of the Sandinista regime, but also the defense of the nation as a whole. In this way, the ideological perception in the United States that the Sandinista movement represents a threat to U.S. security is for Nicaragua a threat to *its own* national security, as military combat is taking place within its territory.

The Results of Low-Intensity Warfare Against Nicaragua

The effect of the military aggression against Nicaragua must be evaluated in two respects, military and economic. At the military level, it is evident that the results are not those that the Reagan administration had expected, as the Sandinista regime has proven to be more solidly established than its critics thought. An analysis of war statistics show

TABLE 6.2

Number of Military Encounters Between the Sandinista Troops and
Counterrevolutionary Forces

	Number of Encounters
1981	15
1982	78
1983	600
1984	948
1985	1,637
Total	3,278

Source: Nicaraguan Government, *La Derrota de la Contrarrevolución: Datos Básicos* 1981-1985 (Managua, 1986).

that, in spite of an increase in the war in every sense, the regime has suffered no loss of support in the short term, but the Sandinistas were increasingly in trouble due to the long-term effort made by the population. On the contrary, the political polarization that has resulted from the inevitable defensive measures adopted (such as the state of national emergency decree, which began May 15, 1982)[44] has fortified the Sandinista movement within the country. In so doing, U.S. expectations of a consolidation of an "internal front" that could serve as a political bastion for the contras have diminished. Table 6.2, based on official Nicaraguan data,[45] shows the increase in war efforts.

All of the military actions were carried out covertly by the SOF of the U.S. Army. One area of action that took on special importance during 1984 and 1985, was the mining of Nicaraguan ports. The objective was to frighten foreign shipping companies so that they would cease to trade with Nicaragua and to destroy its almost nonexistent merchant marine fleet. Special commandos also were responsible for the attack on the fuel deposit located in Puerto Corinto in October 1983. This attack was realized with the aid of "piraña boats." The Argentine weekly magazine *Siete Días* stated that this last attack was the responsibility of the Brigade of Underwater Demolitions (BUD) operating from ships controlled by the CIA.

Nicaragua has suffered the most at the economic level, and it is there perhaps, that the Reagan administration has obtained its best results. The ailing Nicaraguan economy, hard hit by the earthquake of 1972 and by the civil war of 1978–1979, has not been able to recuperate, due to constant military pressure. If the results for the Reagan administration have been excellent at the economic level and marginal at the military level, just the opposite is true from Nicaragua's perspective: No one can deny its military success, but at the same time everyone recognizes the impossiblity of an economic recuperation as long as the war continues. This is an important point because at the strategic level, the Sandinistas aim for an increase in the welfare of the Nicaraguan people, an objective that has not been reached for obvious reasons.

We have not taken into consideration other effects of this low-intensity conflict. However, it is necessary to at least mention some of them, as they are in themselves of great regional importance. The warfare has geo-political implications, such as the effect on the Honduran society of the presence of two new armies in its territory—the contras and the U.S. Army, and the Nicaraguan conflict has had repercussions on the war in El Salvador with the possibility that both wars will have common solutions. Also, the flow of refugees and their rejection from most of the countries of the area has impacted the entire region.

Conclusion

Although the Reagan administration has not obtained the general consensus it needs for its military strategy (as significant sectors of the population and the Democratic opposition are very reticent about this policy), there is no doubt that the administration has made important advances, expecially in the U.S. Congress.

For example, in terms of our own research, we must stress the importance of the approval of $27 million in "humanitarian" aid for the contras. This victory opened the doors for a second petition for aid coming from the president; the second time, the call was for explicit military aid. However, the debate in Congress has dealt more with the military inefficiency of the contras than with the real issues: the legality and moral—or immoral—nature of such a proposal. A Reagan victory in this area would show internal support for the administration's project to recapture U.S. hegemony in the region through the use of force.

Recently, the people of Haiti and the Philippines have imposed their will by expelling two dictators who were undeniable allies of the U.S. government. In both cases, the Reagan administration was forced to abandon its former allies, so as not to permit a greater polarization within these two countries. By so doing, it sought to guarantee the maximum degree of political continuity in order to avoid the complete destruction of the preexisting political structures.

And in Chile, the U.S. government seems to be assuming a new position with respect to Chile's dictatorship, as is evidenced by U.S.

approval of the condemnation voted against Chile in the United Nations for violations of human rights.

Nevertheless, a shift in U.S. policy toward Nicaragua does not seem likely. If the U.S. government increases its aid to the contras and thereby increases its military deployment, the war will continue to escalate and will continue with no end in sight. The Nicaraguan government will have to increase its defense budget, and the popular militia will continue to defend the Sandinista movement, alongside the regular army.

Under some circumstances, the doctrine of low-intensity warfare does not rule out the possiblity of a direct invasion as a last resort: "If local forces are unsuccessful, the preparation of the conflict area should support contingency plans for the employment of U.S. forces if required."[46] The preparation of the Central American area in this sense is undeniable. Honduras has assumed a leading role, especially in the areas of infrastructure and logistics. As of March 1986, 11 military airports, several highways, one field hospital, and several military bases existed. Logistically, Honduras is preparing its own and Salvadoran military forces and has undertaken a series of land and sea exercises.

With respect to the large-scale application of low-intensity warfare against Nicaragua, we can offer the following conclusions: Low-intensity warfare, as practiced by the United States, does not represent a regional strategy, limited to some areas of the Third World; rather, it clearly represents part of a global strategy. U.S. military strategy has as its objective the recapturing of the offensive at all levels, from low-intensity warfare right up to Reagan's Strategic Defensive Initiative, or "Star Wars." The ideological justifications that have been used to gain support for the contras are similar to those used in other areas of the world where the Reagan administration has sought to rollback other political processes that go against its interests.

In order to obtain support for the contras and to justify that support ideologically, the Reagan administration has frequently used misinformation as one of the central elements of its propaganda campaign. This is evident if we consider the lack of real proof as to the supposed Nicaraguan aid to the Salvadoran rebels, the lack of evidence as to the involvement of the Sandinistas in drug trafficking or their support for terrorist groups, and so forth. Nevertheless, all of these claims form part of the daily Reagan denunciations of the Sandinistas.

The war in Nicaragua is artificial because it did not originate as a result of unresolved internal conflicts. Rather, an external actor, the U.S. government, sustains, directs, and foments the war through its support to the contras.

The escalation of the war is also artificial because it is the product of a foreign power that does not permit the existence of political and social regimes unresponsive to its interests. Therefore, the U.S. government has created an artificial army, built up its numbers, perfected its armament, trained it, invented a rearguard in another country, given it "humanitarian" aid, and has openly obtained military aid from international private sources.

The conflict will be prolonged because it is a war of intervention versus a war of defense. The intervening force, the U.S. government, at least at the ideological level, recognizes the need to avoid its own direct participation as much as possible and for this purpose uses an allied army—the contras—to try to obtain a military victory, which the facts show will be impossible. Nevertheless, the contras continue to be a long-range instrument for political destabilization because the Nicarguan government cannot give up its own defense without giving up political power.

The doctrine of low-intensity warfare and its application relegate to a backrow seat even the most elementary norms of international law.

In the process of escalation of the war, we cannot rule out the possibility of U.S. invasion as a last resort, especially in case the U.S. government should decide (for political or military reasons) to accelerate the outcome of the war. If this should happen, the options are numerous, from a massive direct invasion, to the bombing of strategic targets or the annihilation of the PSA, or just rendering it ineffective. One military strategist has stated, "The objective in the commitment of U.S. forces to a combat or combat support role is to effect a decisive change in the conflict. Other objectives are to preserve U.S. interests in serious jeopardy or to provide the time and space for indigenous forces to regain the tactical initiative and resume control of tactical operations." The same strategist continued, "The goal is to restrict the use of force and the level of [U.S.] commitment to the minimum level feasible. This implies short and decisive actions to obtain the maximum effect."[47]

Whatever the options may be for an invasion, the inevitable result would be its bogging down, due to the truly massive support that the Sandinista revolution enjoys. In this case, is the United States prepared for another military conflict such as that in Vietnam?

Notes

1. "La política estadounidense en Centroamérica," interview with Noam Chomsky, in Heinz Dieterich, *Centroamérica en la Prensa Estadounidense* (Mexico: Mex-Sur Editorial, 1985), p. 89.

2. Sam C. Sarkesian, "American Policy and Low-Intensity Conflict: An Overview," in Sam Sarkesian and William L. Scully, eds., *U.S. Policy and Low-*

Intensity Conflict. Potentials for Military Struggles in the 1980s. (New Brunswick and London: Transaction Books, pp. 2–3.

3. Robert M. Kupperman Associates, Inc., *Low-Intensity Conflict* (Prepared for U.S. Army Training and Doctrine Command), vol. I Main Report, Contract no. DABT 60-83-C-0002, July 30, 1983, p. 21.

4. Ibid, p. 5.

5. Ibid, p. 7.

6. Michael T. Klare, "Low-Intensity Conflict. The New U.S. Strategic Doctrine," *The Nation,* December 28, 1985. Translated into Spanish by Gregorio Selser, *El Día,* January 23–29, 1986. (The retranslation into English for this paper is ours.)

7. Colonel Harry G. Summers, Jr., U.S. Army, "Principles of War and Low-Intensity Conflict," *Military Review* 65, no. 2 (March 1985):46.

8. Ibid.

9. Sarkesian, "American Policy and Low-Intensity Conflict," pp. 7–8.

10. Central Intelligence Agency, *Psychological Operations in Guerrilla Warfare* (Washington, D.C., 1983), pp. 26–27. Italics added.

11. UPI-AP, wire news, August 20, 1985.

12. Major General Donald R. Morelli, and Major (Retired) Michael M. Ferguson, "Low-Intensity Conflict: An Operational Perspective," *Military Review* 64, no. 11 (November 1984):6 and 9. Italics added.

13. *Operaciones Psicolóquicas,* p. 5.

14. Ibid., p. 13.

15. Ibid., p. 5.

16. Ibid., p. 9.

17. Ibid., p. 33. Italics added.

18. Kupperman Associates, *Low-Intensity Conflict,* p. 15.

19. *Report of the DOD Commission on Beirut International Airport Terrorist Act, October 23, 1983,* (Washington, D.C.: U.S. Government Printing Office, December 20, 1983), p. 4.

20. Major Jeffrey W. Wright, "Terrorism: A Mode of Warfare," *Military Review* 64, no. 10 (October 1984):38–39.

21. Lilia Bermúdez, *Guerra de Baja Intensidad. Reagan Contra Centroamérica* (Mexico: Siglo XXI, 1987), p. 194.

22. Klare, "Low-Intensity Conflict."

23. Wright, "Terrorism: A Mode of Warfare," p. 43.

24. "America's Secret Soldiers: The Buildup of U.S. Special Operation Forces," *Defense Monitor* 14, no. 2 (1985), p. 14.

25. *El Día,* October 1, 1985. Agencia France Press (AFP) and Prensa Latina (PL) cables.

26. Howard D. Groves, "U.S. Capabilities for Military Intervention," in Sarkesian and Scully, *U.S. Policy and Low-Intensity Conflict,* p. 72.

27. Mario Alfaro Alvarado, *Así es Fuerza Democrática Nicaragüense* (This is the Nicaraguan Democratic Force) (Undated). This book is considered to be one of the most important political and ideological documents of the contras, along with *El Libro Azul y blanco* (The Blue and White Book). Since 1983, the contras have been editing a monthly magazine called *Comandos.* There is no doubt that

the best book written from the point of view of the contras and which offers an ideological justification for their existence is by Jaime Morales Carazo, *Mejor que Somoza Cualquier Cosa!* (Anything is Better than Somoza) (Mexico City: Editorial Continental, 1986). The author of this last book claims that the contras have 20,000 members.

28. Christopher Dickey, *With the Contras. A Reporter in the Wilds of Nicaragua* (New York: Simon & Schuster, 1985), pp. 104–105; see also Gregorio Selser, "La ayuda de los militares argentinos" (Aid from the Argentine Military), in *Honduras, República Alquilada* (Honduras, a Republic for Rent) (Mexico City: Mex-Sur, 1983), pp. 338–341. In this article, Selser presents a thorough analysis of the Viola Doctrine and explains how Argentine military advice has been exported to Latin America.

29. Edgar Chamorro made this information public. He was expelled from the NDF in November of 1984. *Washington Post*, December 17, 1984.

30. Christopher Dickey, *Within Contras*, pp. 104–105.

31. U.S. Department of State, *Communist Interference in El Salvador*, Special Report No. 80 (Washington, D.C., February 23, 1981).

32. Christopher Dickey, *With the Contras*, pp. 104–105.

33. Richard Alan White, *The Morass. United States Intervention in Central America* (New York: Harper & Row, 1984), p. 53; see also Center for National Security Studies, *Congressional Action to Date on U.S. Covert Operations Against Nicaragua*, (Washington, D.C., 1984); *Washington Post*, February 14, 1982.

34. Central American Historical Institute, "Who's Who in Nicaragua's Military Opposition," *IPDA* 3, no. 24 (Washington, D.C., July 23, 1984). Other important groups that make up the contras are the Miskitos, Sumos, and Ramas (MISURA)— the acronym is made up of the first two letters from the name of each group that lives on the Atlantic Coast of Nicaragua—and Democratic Revolutionary Alliance (DRA) (Alianza Revolucionaria Democrática-ARDE) founded by Eden Pastora.

35. Mario Alfaro Alvarado, *Así es Fuerza Democrática Nicaragüense*, pp. 2–5.

36. Ibid., pp. 5–10. The regional commands (RC) that make up the contras are (1) RC Nicarao (Madriz), (2) RC Segovia (Nueva Segovia), (3) RC Dirianguen (Jinotega Sur), (4) RC Rafael Herrera (Jinotega Norte), (5) RC Jorge Salazar (Matagalpa), (6) RC San Jacinto (Boaco), (7) RC José Dolores Estrada (Esteli), (8) RC Andrés Castro, and (9) RC Juan Castro (the zone of action of this last regional command is not specified). In addition, we must mention the existence of the Special Operations Commands (SOC) (Comandos de Operaciones Especiales), which are used for special attack operations, such as attacking military posts of the PSA (SOCs have operated in the province of Matagalpa).

37. Nicaraguan Government, *La Derrota de la Contrarrevolución: Datos Básicos 1981–1985* (Managua, 1986), p. 2

38. *Newsweek*, November 8, 1982.

39. Lilia Bermúdez and Raúl Benítez Manaut, "La segunda administración Reagan en América Central" (The Second Reagan Administration in Central America, in *Polémica*, No. 16 (San Jose, Costa Rica, January-March, 1985).

40. President Ronald Reagan, March 1, 1985, quoted in Christopher Dickey, *With the Contras*, p. 14.

41. Nicaraguan government, *La Derrota de la Contrarrevolución*, p. 7.

42. For the year 1981, see International Institute for Strategic Studies, *The Military Balance 1981–1982* (London, 1981). For 1985, see Ricardo Pino Robles, "Nicaragua: el déficit comercial y la economía nicaragüense" (Nicaragua: The Commercial Deficit and the Nicaraguan Economy), in *Boletín Económico Centroamericano* (Central American Economic Bulletin), February 5, 1986.

43. There is much controversy within the United States with respect to Soviet and Cuban military aid to Nicaragua. The Reagan administration has argued that Nicaragua is militarized to a degree that exceeds its defensive needs and therefore has broken the regional military balance. This idea is shared by important political and military sectors in Honduras and Costa Rica, which support U.S. aid to the contras against Nicaragua. The Nicaraguan government has said that its military buildup is solely in response to defensive measures and has backed up this claim by referring to the low technical level of its army, which is only equipped with light individual weapons. In addition, the Nicaraguan government has pointed out the virtual nonexistence of its air force, which would be the only force capable of effectively attacking another country, and added that the presence in Nicaragua of approximately 60 Soviet T-54 and T-55 tanks represents no threat to Nicaragua's neighbors because of the geographic conditions of the terrain. One aspect of the Nicaraguan military that has been fortified is antiaircraft weapons to protect cities and economic objectives against possible air attacks. On this subject, see Caribbean Basin Information Project, *On a Short Fuse: Militarization in Central America* (San Francisco, 1985); Council on Hemispheric Affairs, *The Military Balance in Central America, An Analysis and Critical Evaluation of Administration Claims* (Washington, D.C., March 1, 1985); U.S. Department of State, *The Jacobsen Report. Soviet Attitudes Towards, Aid to, and Contacts with Central American Revolutionaries* (Washington, D.C., 1984); and, Theodore Scwab and Harold D. Sims, "Cuba and Nicaragua: A Key Regional Relationship, 1979–1984," *Cuban Studies/Estudios Cubanos* 15, no. 2 (Summer 1985), p. 76.

44. A state of emergency was declared on May 15, 1982. Since then, this decree has been ratified and modified, according to the situation imposed by the war. The decree was modified during July and August 1984, during the electoral campaign. This permitted the free circulation of the population and restored certain fundamental rights—to organize demonstrations, to hold meetings, to strike, and to exercise freedom of expression. Restrictions were maintained in the area of military and security matters. Individual rights were once again suspended on October 15, 1985, due to the increase in the military campaigns against Nicaragua.

45. All of the statistical tables are taken from Nicaraguan government, *La Derrota de la Contrarrevolución*.

46. Morelli and Ferguson, "Low-Intensity Conflict," p. 12.

47. Ibid., p. 14.

7

South American Regional Security and the United States

Carlos Portales

The study of regional security in the Western Hemisphere must consider particular subregional contexts. Regional security issues in South America have been different from those in Central America and the Caribbean during the 1980s. In some Central American countries, social conflict has become civil war, which has caused or threatened to cause change in regimes. These internal sociopolitical conflicts, in turn, have led interstate relations to a point dangerously near war. Furthermore, because such disputes are linked to the global conflict, the region's security problems go beyond the area: The United States has become the leading actor in the development and settlement of the Central American conflicts.

In South America, in contrast, the structure of conflicts has been more diversified and less acute. Skirmishes have been handled in such a way that disputes have ended—or at least halted temporarily—in peaceful settlement or as unarmed discord. Although such conflicts have not been, in most cases, the main issue of South American countries' foreign policies, they influence the international relations of these countries and affect the allocation of defense budget resources.

The United States, viewing the settlement of the conflicts in the region critical for its own national security, has developed a policy of active involvement in Central America and the Caribbean. However, U.S. activity vis-à-vis South American disputes has been intermittent and varied. U.S. involvement has increased in times of crisis and decreased when the situation has calmed down. In relatively stable times the United States has focused on policies such as arms transfer and nuclear pro-

This paper is a revised and updated version of a document presented at the Inter-American Dialogue in November 1985.

liferation; but it has ultimately recognized the limitations of its influence in the region.

This setting is entirely different from that of the post–World War II period. The inter-American security system was clearly organized so as to be linked to global security through a multilateral political system and was reinforced by bilateral military agreements between the United States and Latin American countries. The inter-American security system was able to unify interests and rivalries among the countries under the aegis of the United States. This was made possible by the hegemonic nature of U.S. power during the cold war and by the relative political and military weakness of Latin American states.

The change from hemispheric defense to internal defense and development doctrine in the inter-American military system injected the notion of the East-West conflict into the assessment of internal conflicts of Latin American countries. This new content, influenced by U.S. military thinking, was incorporated by Latin American armed forces as a national security doctrine. Although this consensus inspired both doctrines and practices of the Latin American military, governments never accepted it as a basis for the collective security system, as demonstrated by the failure of the attempts to establish a permanent Inter-American Security Force.[1] The postwar regional security system was eroded by later transformations in it: the relative decline of U.S. hegemony, the emergence of some states in Latin America, the loss of the U.S. monopoly over ties with Latin American military establishments, and the strengthening of the armed forces, particularly in South America.

The differences of interests between the United States and Latin American nations—which had been put aside during the cold war—reappeared during the sixties and seventies.[2] The development of the armed forces, particularly in South American countries, no longer satisfied exclusively inter-American security goals; the diffusion of world power and the proliferation of military supply centers allowed independent interests to take shape. Though a clash of security interests with the United States did not occur, governments and military establishments attained increasing autonomy in defining which security issues they would respond to. This was especially evident with the incorporation of new generations of weaponry for external security: The purchase of jets since the late 1960s and later of missiles, warships, and more modern weapons systems openly contradicted the U.S. policy of restricting the introduction of new generations of arms into the region.[3]

If one assumes that the system established during the postwar period is not suitable to regulate security relations among the countries of the hemisphere—though some of their institutions may continue to have formal legal validity—and if one assumes that Latin American realities lead to a distinction of the territorial boundaries within which these problems should be addressed, one could raise the following questions:

1. How should the *security areas* in the hemisphere be defined? Is it possible to delineate a specific area in the South American region?
2. Is there a common set of problems for South American countries? What are the main security *issues* and their current status?
3. What are the *likely trends* in the main South American security problems? How could policies be developed that contribute to establishing a security system emphasizing the *shared interests* of South American countries? And, finally, how is it possible to make those shared interests compatible with those of the United States?

This chapter attempts to contribute to answering these questions from a South American perspective.

The South American Area

In this section, I shall attempt to clarify the definition of regional security in the South American subcontinent.

1. The weakening of the inter-American military system did not have homogeneous effects on all of Latin America; there was a tendency for U.S. security concerns to focus on the Caribbean. From the end of the 1960s to the end of the 1970s, there was a deterioration of military links between the United States and Latin America. Human rights violations in countries ruled by the armed forces were one cause of this deterioration. It affected bilateral military relations essential to the system[4] and led to a weakening of ties with several countries of the zone, especially in South America. However, the negotiating process with Panama that led to the signing of a new treaty, the policy of rapprochement with Cuba and its subsequent deterioration, the search for new ways to protect sources of oil supply in the area—Mexico and Venezuela— and especially, the Sandinista revolution in Nicaragua and the civil war in El Salvador made the Caribbean and Central American area a security "hot spot."

The concept of the Caribbean Basin as a geopolitical unit that encompasses the Caribbean Islands, Central America, Colombia, Venezuela, Guyana, and Surinam was formalized in November 1981, when the U.S. Forces Caribbean Command was organized. It is a single command that comprises various forces responsible for waters and islands of the Caribbean, Gulf of Mexico, and parts of the Pacific Ocean bordering Central America.[5]

The security interests of the United States in this area include preventing the emergence of governments that could provide bases for U.S. enemies to operate in an effort to limit the free access of the United States to the region and establishing ties to facilitate military activities associated with overall U.S. defense goals. The United States was concerned about the penetration of the Soviet fleet, supported by bases in Cuba, in the Caribbean, which has trade and navy sea-lanes vital for the United States and is the main passageway between the Atlantic and Pacific oceans. According to U.S. definitions, security is combined with economic interests (the Caribbean is the source of raw materials supplies important to the U.S. economy) and with political interests (maintaining preeminence in an area that historically has been in the U.S. sphere of influence and where the loss of control could be interpreted as a sign of U.S. weakness.[6] Thus, the traditional view of the Caribbean as an area of high interest for U.S. security was reaffirmed.[7]

2. South America, in contrast, is not considered by the United States to be a separate regional group; instead, the various nations in the subcontinent are assessed in terms of security according to their particular geographic location, the nature of their power, or the U.S. functional interests. Venezuela and Colombia as well as Guyana and Surinam are considered to be part of a broad concept of the Caribbean area. Brazil, Venezuela, and to a certain extent, Argentina are considered emerging powers with increasingly autonomous interests.

Venezuela is viewed as a Caribbean subregional counterpower to Cuba. The U.S. sale of first-generation F-16s to the Venezuelan Air Force was meant to reinforce that role. Still, the policies of Venezuela with respect to Central America have not always coincided with U.S. positions, though Venezuela has been closer to Washington than has Mexico.[8]

Brazil has been a traditional U.S. ally in Latin America, but the privileged relationship in security matters was seriously eroded by the rupture in March 1977 of the Brazil-U.S. military pact. The Reagan administration followed a policy of rapprochement. President Reagan, during a visit to Brazilia in November 1982, signed a military technological and industrial cooperation memorandum as a token of this intention. Difficulties in implementing this agreement highlight the differences in the security interests of the two countries.[9]

Argentina, the South American nation that historically has had the most disagreements with the United States, was also the focus of a Reagan administration policy of rapprochement and military cooperation. The privileged relationship with the Galtieri government, which was starting to support the United States militarily in the Central American conflict, was voided by U.S. backing of Great Britain in the Falklands/ Malvinas war.[10]

The specific interests of the United States are not uniformly applied in South America. The U.S. distinction between the South Atlantic area and the west coast area of South America indicates the unequal values that the government places on the different regions of the subcontinent. In the South Atlantic, those interests include the maintenance of the main sea-lanes used for shipping oil and raw materials supplies vital to the United States and its West European allies; the stability of pro-Western regimes in that area, including South Africa; the lessening of the impact of a larger Soviet fleet and its presence in those seas, and the strengthening of complementary relations in security matters with the emerging powers of the region—Brazil, Argentina, Nigeria—relations that can potentially free U.S. forces for action in other areas in contingency situations. "The West Coast countries neither guard major ocean trade routes, nor provide the launching platform to the Pacific Ocean that the East Coast countries provide to the Atlantic."[11] For U.S. contingency planning, the east coast countries would provide access to ship repair and refueling facilities in the event of circumstances requiring the movement of ships between the Atlantic and Pacific oceans. In addition, they are an accessible source for the supply of vital raw materials for the U.S. economy, a source that could replace more distant suppliers in the event of a generalized conflict.[12] In sum, U.S. security interests in South America are focused on protecting sea lines of communication and preventing influence hostile to the United States in countries bordering the South Atlantic. To accomplish these objectives, the United States has engaged in a cooperative relationship with Argentina and Brazil.

3. In the United States, there is a consensus on what U.S. security interests are in Latin America. They are understood in terms of direct military threat. However, the way that radical regimes are perceived varies, particularly with respect to their level of threat to U.S. security. Protection against a direct military threat to the United States from Latin America, denial of third-country military bases in the region, protection of vital maritime passageways—including the Panama Canal—and assurances of U.S. access to strategic raw materials[13] are generally recognized as U.S. security interests in Latin America. Discussions can arise over the extent to which these interests are threatened, but not over their existence. It can be said that in defining U.S. security interests, there is a general consensus in the U.S. political system.

The existence of radical regimes is also generally viewed within the United States as contrary to national interests but is assessed differently by conservatives and liberals. Conservatives find the existence of such regimes to be a threat to U.S. security because these regimes are perceived as closely linked to the Soviet Union and not liable to change through a policy of economic ties. Consequently, these regimes should be actively opposed until they are removed. Liberals see them as nationalist regimes that can be separated from the Soviet Union by means of "constructive engagement" policies—through trade and economic aid—which may even promote pluralism and greater respect for human rights within their respective political systems. However, military pressures and economic sanctions would, in the liberal view, only tend to drive them closer to the Soviet Union.[14]

Since the 1962 Cuban missile crisis, there has been no direct threat to U.S. security from Latin America, according to the liberal viewpoint. However, supporters of the predominant conservative thinking have labeled regimes as different as the 1970–1973 Chilean government, the Bishop administration in Grenada, and the Sandinistas in Nicaragua as threats.

4. The relatively low strategic importance of South American countries make the subregion an area in which a regional security system can be established. Interstate conflicts in South America have not been associated with either extraregional or internal conflicts. Except for the case of the Falklands/Malvinas war, they have not become centers of global concern either. Thus, U.S. attention to South America, barring situations of imminent or open conflict, has not been very prominent. The narrow range of the U.S. security interests involved in some cases, and the deterioration of ties with certain South American military establishments in others, make U.S. influence less important, particularly in comparison to the situation of Central America and the Caribbean.

Though inter-American links still exist, they do not operate automatically in cases of conflict, as proven not only by the Falklands/ Malvinas war but also by other feuds among South American countries, for example, Argentina and Chile in 1978 and Ecuador and Peru in 1981. The increasing autonomy of South American security interests was not curtailed by the 1960s U.S. policy of restricting the flow of new generations of sophisticated weaponry into the region. The proliferation of supply sources allowed the purchasing independence of these countries vis-à-vis the United States. Hence, the challenge of establishing a regional security system that would allow the implementation of development processes within a peaceful international setting falls to the South American countries themselves.

5. In order to create such a regional security system, the interests of South American countries should be taken into account. First, countries located in northern South America have the dual nature of being both Caribbean and South American. *Venezuela* is the most important of these countries, since it is one of the emerging powers of the region that has used part of its enormous oil resources to modernize its armed forces.

Venezuela is projecting itself economically, politically, and militarily into the Caribbean, seeking to be a counterweight to Cuba, a situation favored by the United States. In the face of the Central American situation, Venezuela's participation in the Contadora Group has been guided by the common goal of avoiding U.S. interventionist policies and by the espousal of an internal political process in El Salvador and Nicaragua that is not very unlike that sought by the United States.[15] In relation to its South American neighbors, Venezuela has territorial and maritime boundary conflicts that influence its security strategies.

Colombia is also a nation that is both Caribbean and South American, although its external thrust is less significant than Venezuela's. President Belisario Betancur's policy of active international participation represented a change from the traditional "inward-oriented" posture of the nation.[16] Colombia's participation in the Contadora Group has been explained as an attempt to prevent the internationalization of the guerrilla conflict in Colombia, thus favoring an internal peace process. Although President Betancur's and President Virgilio Barco's initiatives have not resulted in internal peace, Colombia has continued to pursue its new foreign policy goals in order to avoid further internationalization and expansion of the internal warfare.[17]

Brazil is the main actor in the region. Its participation in South America's gross domestic product (GDP) rose from 26.4 percent in 1946 to 32.9 percent in 1966 and 52.7 percent in 1984.[18] This impressive economic growth supports the foreign policy of an emerging power seeking to increase its economic and political influence globally. Brazil pursues a conservative policy toward Latin America, which allows the country to keep its status as the top regional power without creating an image of hegemony.[19]

Since 1967, Brazil's foreign policy outside Latin America has moved away from its traditional automatic alignment with the United States. The new policy has led to confrontations with the United States, as in the case of Brazil's purchase of nuclear technology from West Germany, and to significant differences with the United States in the area of policy toward Africa. Brazilian African policy has revolved around economic interests, often without considering ideological differences. Its rapprochement with black African countries led to an early recognition of the Popular Movement for the Liberation of Angola (MPLA) government in Angola and the refusal to join a security system in the South Atlantic with the Republic of South Africa.[20]

In Latin America, Brazil's policy has been to maintain the regional status quo. It should be remembered that every South American nation except Chile and Ecuador has a common border with Brazil.[21] The main goal of Brazil is to seek cooperative solutions to bilateral and multilateral regional security problems.[22] The development of a local military industry has served as a basis for Brazil's security policy, without significantly stepping up military spending in relation to the GDP.

Argentina, another key regional actor, has followed a path that can be called the opposite of Brazil's. Argentina's share in the South American GDP has dropped from more than a third of the regional product in 1946 to a fourth in 1966 and 14.4 percent in 1984.[23] The economic slump has had an impact on political life; there were recurring crises, resulting in the political predominance of the military. The military regime's management of international conflicts was disastrous. It nearly caused a war with Chile in 1978 and brought about the Falklands/Malvinas war, which led to the downfall of the Galtieri government and the end of the military regime in 1983. The democratic government of President Raúl Alfonsín has changed security goals, trying to settle conflicts peacefully.

The *other countries* of the region define their security interests mainly through their relations with neighboring countries. Their security goals determine their resource allocation for national defense purposes; their foreign policies include alliances historically designed to create regional and subregional balances.

6. There is no consensus in South American countries about the definition of security interests. They are the result of the contrasting perspectives of domestic actors.

Geopolitics and national security doctrines are the main frameworks to define security interests in authoritarian regimes. To preserve and increase autonomy for national development projects are the main security goals in democratic regimes.[24] Latin American countries do not have high levels of social cohesion and are unstable. The determination of security interests depends on which sectors prevail within the political system; therefore, in order to understand security policy orientations, it is necessary to consider domestic power realities. The operational definition of security is affected in political systems where there is a relatively precarious balance between competing democratic and authoritarian forces.

Nevertheless, it is possible to find shared elements, such as territorial defense, when countries determine their security interests. Countries with participatory democracies, such as Venezuela, or with long-term economic expansion, such as Brazil, have generated more permanent interests and seem to achieve greater consensus on a definition of security interests. Finally, factors weakening the region's economic autonomy are seen, particularly in the debate on inter-American relations, as threats to regional security.[25]

Regional Security Issues

In order to give substantive meaning to the definition of a regional security area, it is necessary to go beyond merely distinguishing various security interests. In the present section I will briefly address the structure of conflicts in South America, in terms of confrontations among South American states and between South American states and states outside the region. I will also examine, on the one hand, the relationship between these disputes and global conflicts and, on the other hand, their linkage with the dynamics of domestic conflict. I will refer to the current state of *dispute settlement mechanisms* and to the actual and potential development of the *war capability* of these nations.

The purpose of this summary of the problems affecting South American security is to highlight those that could become points of conflict in the future and to note elements that could influence the development of the dynamics of those processes.

Interstate Conflicts

The reemergence of conflicts among Latin American states has been associated with the deemphasis on the cold war and the enthusiasm for détente, the deterioration of the inter-American system since the sixties, and the increase in international tension since the late seventies.[26] Although interstate conflicts in South America have increased in number, they have not become generalized, as in Central America. However, the Falklands/Malvinas war was a conflict that aroused world concern, and the Paquisha incident between Peru and Ecuador went beyond bilateral framework to involve the main countries of the area and the United States. The Argentine-Chilean situation in 1978 also shook the regional system of interstate relations.

What is the nature of these conflicts? Which of them can end in a war? How are they interrelated?

Interstate conflicts in South America arise from border disputes that in many cases go as far back as the colonial period (territorial conflicts), the securing of raw materials, energy sources, and commodities obtained from the sea (resource conflicts), displacement of populations across borders (migratory conflicts), attempts by one power to impose its supremacy in a particular region (hegemonic conflicts), or ideological differences between two states (systemic conflicts).[27] Nevertheless, it is more likely that they turn into armed conflicts if there is an element of territorial dispute involved.

When this typology is applied to the conflicts occurring in the area, the categories are not mutually exclusive. Indeed, the conflict between

Argentina and Great Britain over the Falklands/Malvinas Islands can be classified as both hegemonic—stemming from decolonization—and territorial. Disputes between Chile and Argentina and between Colombia and Venezuela combine territorial, resource, and migratory elements, and the conflicts between Chile and Bolivia, Ecuador and Peru, Venezuela and Guyana, are of territorial and resource origin. Only the Argentine-Brazilian dispute over the use of water from the Río de la Plata Basin to build the Itaipu dam—already settled—was exclusively a resource conflict.[28] A traditional dispute over borders that were not precisely determined during the colonial period or that were modified by subsequent occupations and wars can become a dispute over resources—whether presently or potentially exploitable—that exist or are supposed to exist in those territories. Thus, situations that have historically marked the thinking of certain groups in South America, such as the military, and that have served as an element of national identification through the educational system are reinforced by the economic value of the resources available in disputed territories. Conflicts over sovereignty based on the concept of "national honor" *also* become patrimonial disputes.

The new law of the sea, with the extension of the limit on territorial sea, and the creation of a coastal state economic zone for the exclusive exploitation of resources enhance the value of the resources that have been under dispute because of old, unsettled territorial conflicts. The same happens when oil or other new energy sources are present.

The overlapping of a traditional conflict with a resource conflict handicaps settlement methods and boosts the chances that the conflict escalates. When the main dispute is over resources, regardless of the importance of their patrimonial value, it is simpler to estimate the costs and benefits of the various solutions. In these cases, agreements are easier to reach and compensations are easier to calculate than in cases where elements of territorial sovereignty, loaded with historical meaning for the armed forces and the population as a whole, are involved.

A distinction should be made between a real or latent *conflict* among states, where the object of the dispute is known, and a rivalry among countries of the region, where although elements of mutual hostility may exist, they do not necessarily cause a specific dispute. Those situations of *competition* inherent to nation-states' practices in the international arena are less significant. These distinctions, usually not found in the literature on conflicts in the region, are essential for understanding the status of interstate relations in South America and for predicting the evolution of the conflicts that arise.

Interstate cooperation is, of course, possible at each of the levels of the dispute, although in cases of conflict such cooperation should certainly be directed primarily to settling the conflict—as happened in the Argentine-Chilean case from 1978 to 1985—and only afterwards take on a broader sense. Rivalry situations are perfectly compatible with cooperation mechanisms, as demonstrated by the Andean Pact. However, this integration scheme has not eliminated rivalries, which in one case turned into war. Nevertheless, the Andean process is a mechanism that can be used to de-escalate conflicts. Finally, mere competition is no hindrance to more profound interstate cooperation, as seen in Western Europe.

There is another element that should be included in the analysis of degrees of conflict and the steps from one stage to another: It is not enough to consider the actors directly involved; one must take into account all the relevant powers in the region. As Barros argued, although Argentina and Brazil, the two most important traditional rivals in South America, each with a sizeable weapons industry, could reach a conflict situation, both nations are too large and important internationally to confront each other militarily without inevitably inviting the intervention of other powers. This inhibits any prowar sentiments of the elites of these nations, and it could eventually lead them to indirect confrontations through other countries of the region.[29]

Conflicts among South American states should be understood within a system of rivalries, balances, and alliances with historical roots, but a system whose foundations have been significantly altered during recent years. According to the traditional structure of conflicts—originating in the nineteenth century—Argentina confronted Brazil, fighting for influence on Bolivia, Paraguay, and Uruguay; Argentina confronted Chile; and Chile, Peru and Bolivia. This gave birth to alliances between Brazil and Chile, on the one hand, and Argentina and Peru, on the other. The Peru-Ecuador conflict, in turn, led to the ties between Ecuador and Chile becoming closer.[30] Also, there were territorial disputes between Colombia and Venezuela and between Venezuela and Great Britain, the colonial power in Guyana. The Amazonia, an unconquered land, served to separate the alliance systems. Several of these traditional elements of conflict remain in current South American military thinking.

In all, the substantial variations produced in the relative importance of South American countries should be taken into account. An indicator such as participation in the South American GDP throughout a period of almost 40 years (from 1946 to 1984) shows that Argentina, which had more than one-third of the regional GDP in 1946, fell to less than 15 percent in 1984, while Brazil increased from a little over one-fourth of the regional product to more than one-half in the same time span (see Table 7.1). Three other countries show a decline in their contribution to the regional GDP: in descending order, Chile, from 8.7 to 4.9 percent; Colombia, from 10.2 to 7.4 percent; and Peru, from 5.7 to 4.6 percent.

Carlos Portales

TABLE 7.1

Participation in South America's Gross Domestic Product, 1946-1984
(in percentages)

	1946	1956	1966	1976	1984	1946-1984
Argentina	33.9	28.7	25.0	19.6	14.4	-57.5
Brazil	26.4	30.4	32.9	45.8	52.7	+99.6
Colombia	10.2	10.0	9.5	9.4	7.4	-27.5
Chile	8.7	7.4	7.5	4.6	4.9	-43.7
Peru	5.7	6.1	6.5	5.6	4.6	-19.3
Venezuela	6.4	9.7	10.9	9.9	9.8	+53.1
Others[a]	8.7	7.9	7.6	5.3	6.2	-28.7

[a]Includes Bolivia, Ecuador, Paraguay, and Uruguay.

Sources: For 1946, 1956, and 1976, prepared on the basis of data from
Cuadernos de la CEPAL, *Series históricas de crecimiento de América Latina,*
Santiago, Chile, 1978, pp. 30-34; for 1984, based on data contained in
Interamerican Development Bank, *Progreso Económico y Social en América
Latina Deuda Externa. Crisis y Ajuste,* 1985 Report, IDB, Washington, D.C.,
1985, p. 418.

Of the six largest South American nations, only Venezuela, besides
Brazil, enjoyed an increase, from 6.4 to 9.8 percent.

Let us compare these figures with those of the participation of the
same countries in the region's military spending (see Table 7.2). In order
to avoid the distortion that resource allocation for military purposes
may have on a calendar year, I have broken down the time span into
three-year periods to compare each country's participation in the regional
product.[31]

Brazil, a nation that doubled its participation in the regional GDP,
lowered its share of South American military spending by more than
half. Venezuela, another country that significantly increased its percentage
of the product, virtually maintained its share of military spending. The
same occurred with Argentina, despite a 57 percent drop in its participation in the product. However, Peru, Chile, and Colombia boosted
their participation in regional military spending by 157 percent, 75
percent, and 24 percent, respectively, from 1948-1950 to 1982-1984. If
we closely observe the Argentine case, we can see that the 1982-1984
period shows a noticeable increase in the participation in spending as
compared to the 1955-1957, 1965-1967, and 1975-1977 periods.

TABLE 7.2

Participation in South America's Military Expenditures, 1948-1984
(in percentages)

	48-50	55-57	65-67	75-77	82-84	48/50-82/84
Argentina	49.1	26.7	21.4	38.5	48.8	-0.6
Brazil	28.2	33.2	31.5	21.7	12.7	-55.0
Colombia	2.9	6.2	7.9	4.5	3.6	+24.1
Chile	9.0	13.0	9.1	11.1	15.8	+75.6
Peru	3.5	3.5	6.6	9.0	9.0	+157.1
Venezuela	6.5	12.7	18.3	8.5	6.4	-1.5
Others[a]	na	2.5[b]	5.1	6.7	3.8[c]	na

[a]Includes Bolivia, Ecuador, Paraguay, and Uruguay.
[b]No data available for Bolivia and Paraguay in 1955, nor for Uruguay for the
 three-year period.
[c]No data available for Paraguay in 1984, nor for Uruguay in 1983 and 1984.
na: Not available.

Sources: Stockholm International Peace Research Institute (SIPRI), *SIPRI
Yearbook*, London: Taylor and Francis, 1968-1969, 1972, and 1985.

Thus, there is an inverse relationship between the relative economic
growth and the relative step-up in military spending, leading to the
assumption that a reduction in relative economic power tends to be
compensated by greater participation in military expenditure.

Considering that Brazil has an important weapons industry and still
has the most developed armed forces in the region in absolute terms,
one cannot speak of old regional balances, but one can rather confirm
Brazil's preeminence, which underlies its conservative position in the
regional setting. In contrast, countries that have waned in terms of
product and raised their relative military spending are the ones that
have been involved in, or have been on the verge of, open conflicts.

Conflicts and Conflict-Settlement Mechanisms

What is the status of the main conflicts? Are there conflict-settlement
mechanisms in operation? Only a case-by-case approach will enable us
to make a more accurate evaluation of the dynamics and perspectives
of regional conflicts.

The *Falklands/Malvinas* conflict is the most important focal point of
interstate tension existing in South America. It has been the only major

conventional war in the region since the Chaco war in the thirties. The outbreak of the Falklands/Malvinas war threw into question all hemispheric security mechanisms, and many analysts saw it as the end of the inter-American security system.[32]

The Falklands/Malvinas conflict is still an unsettled territorial dispute between Argentina, a South American country struggling to put an end to a colonial situation,[33] and Great Britain, an extraregional power advocating respect for the principle of self-determination. However, with the surrender of Argentine forces and the end of armed combat in 1982, the conflict did not revert to its prewar state, but rather it precipitated an ongoing militarization of the South Atlantic. Because of the policy of the United Kingdom, these islands have become a military fortress, with more than 4,000 soldiers, a permanent fleet of frigates and destroyers equipped with the most modern weapons and radar systems, supported by submarines, auxiliary ships, and navy helicopters. These forces have been complemented with fighter planes, heavy helicopters, and transport airplanes.[34] The inauguration of the Mount Pleasant airport on May 12, 1985, facilitated an air connection via Ascension Island with the British Isles by means of airplanes with long-distance capability.[35] For its part, Argentina rebuilt its air and naval forces, which had suffered serious damage during the 1982 war.[36] According to SIPRI, this country's military spending reached $6.536 billion in 1983 and $5.226 billion in 1984 (at constant 1980 U.S. dollar value), higher than the 1976–1981 figure, which was nearly $4 billion per year, and lower only than the $8.784 billion of 1982, the year of the war.[37]

The situation is made even more complex by the facts that the United Kingdom enforces a 150-mile perimeter as an area of exclusion of Argentine-flag ships and that Argentina has not formally declared the suspension of hostilities. The Argentine government contends that a declaration of that sort is not necessary, based on a precedent established by the British after the Suez incident in 1956 and on Argentina's solemn promise to use only diplomatic methods to satisfy its claims of the sovereignty over the islands.[38]

During 1985, some incidents between vessels from the two nations were reported. This is a demonstration of the danger of not submitting the conflict to negotiated settlement channels. The British government has categorically refused to address the subject of sovereignty within an overall negotiation, as recommended by the UN General Assembly. Nevertheless, the United Kingdom seeks a gradual resumption of financial and trade links with Argentina, which has already been implemented through unilateral decisions and the eventual reestablishment of consular relations and finally diplomatic relations. The British premise is to rebuild mutual trust in order to resolve *practical* issues of common interest and to ignore explicitly the problem of the islands' sovereignty. The Argentine position advocates the consideration of all subjects, that is, not excluding sovereignty from the agenda, though without demanding its immediate discussion.[39]

For the time being, the debate has been carried out at the United Nations, where the subject has originated annual resolutions from the General Assembly, encouraging negotiations on the islands' sovereignty and requesting the secretary general's mediation between the two parties.[40]

As long as bilateral negotiations are not established, the South Atlantic situation can again become a focal point of international tension, aggravated by the existence of the "Falklands fortress." The Argentine government has argued that the military troops stationed there and the war apparatus constitute a strategic base whose purpose far exceeds the mere defense of the islands. The intention of that installation must be to project NATO's military might to this region of the world, which Buenos Aires has denounced as a way of introducing the East-West conflict into this area.[41] In any event, whatever the plans for the military base may be, its existence heightens the possibilities of a resumption of a major armed conflict. A new conflict between Argentina and the United Kingdom would again become a threat affecting the relations between Latin American and West European countries and between the latter and the United States.[42]

This does not seem likely with a democratic government like that of President Alfonsín. However, the persistence of an unresolved situation in the Falklands/Malvinas and the absence of an acceptable negotiating process can be used as justification for the internal military establishment's demands for renovation and strengthening. This could destabilize Argentina's democratic system in the future. At any rate, the maintenance of this situation affects the region; other countries in the area take into account the levels of spending, arms, and military training and demand resources in order to maintain a balance in the regional security system.[43] Moreover, the experience of the 1982 war led Brazil's armed forces to initiate a modernization process, raising them to the technological level of that conflict. Likewise, the presence of British nuclear submarines in the area was used to justify, soon after the war, the development of research projects like Argentina's nuclear submarine project, which should it materialize, would significantly increase the regional arms race through an action-reaction process. The preservation of the "Falklands fortress" and the refusal to negotiate all the problems related to the Malvinas contribute to maintaining a focal point of tension whose escalation would destabilize regional security.

Other interstate conflicts are still latent. In certain cases, the parties are in the process of searching for peaceful dispute settlement mechanisms.

In the dispute between *Venezuela and Guyana* over the Esequibo territory, which is claimed by Venezuela, alleging that the arbitration decision awarding this area to Great Britain in 1899 was invalid, both countries handed over to the UN secretary general the task of resolving the dispute by choosing one of the instruments set forth in Article 33 of the UN Charter. As long as the situation is not settled, tension could return, as happened in 1984 with Venezuela's continued opposition to Guyana's membership in the Organization of American States and the declaration of Cuban Foreign Minister Isidoro Malmierca supporting Guyana's territorial integrity, interpreted by Caracas as interference in bilateral affairs.[44] Nevertheless, bilateral relations improved during 1986 and 1987: Commercial ties were established and political dialogue took place at the top political level between Presidents Jaime Lusinchi and Hugh Desmond Hoyte.[45]

Another matter still pending is the delimitation of the Gulf of Venezuela between *Colombia and Venezuela*. The last attempt at negotiation culminated in 1980 with the Caraballeda Hypothesis, which failed because of the opposition of the Venezuelan armed forces. The idea of using a settlement mechanism for this situation has been explored, but an agreement on the formula between the two governments has not yet been reached.[46] The border problem generates tensions and is a powerful incentive for new arms acquisitions, such as the Venezuelan purchase of F-16s in 1982, which in turn may increase bilateral conflict.[47]

In two other cases, Ecuador-Peru and Bolivia-Chile, there are conflicts that are not recognized by one of the parties. One party invokes legal instruments that are either disavowed or to be reviewed by the other party. The Rio de Janeiro Protocol of 1942, which established the border between *Ecuador and Peru*, was not recognized by the latter country. The border incidents occurring in the Cordillera del Cóndor in 1981, a sector in which there is no boundary line, led Ecuador to seek an OAS settlement of the conflict. However, the mechanism of the Rio de Janeiro Protocol, which established that Argentina, Brazil, Chile, and the United States were to be guarantors of this agreement, prevailed. These countries carried out some sort of mediation that led to the separation of forces. However, although the dispute has been settled, Ecuador has not closed the book on the matter.[48]

Relations between *Bolivia and Chile* have been severed since 1978, when negotiations to cede to Bolivia a sovereign passageway to the sea through an exchange of territory with Chile failed. Later, the Bolivian government succeeded in having the OAS declare for a period of several years that the problem of Bolivia's landlocked status was of "interest to the hemisphere." The Chilean government has systematically refused to agree to the treatment of the problem in multilateral organisms. However, in 1983 an offer by Colombia opened up a dialogue between Santiago and La Paz; the offer was supported by an OAS recommendation accepted by both countries, with Colombia assisting. Bilateral exchanges faced an uphill battle, and finally the Chilean government decided not to attend a meeting held in early February 1985 in Bogota;[49] in March Chile reiterated that "Bolivia's quest for having access to the sea through Chilean territory can only be analyzed within a bilateral context."[50] Bolivia returned to the Organization of American States and the subject was included again in the agenda of the OAS General Assembly of December 1985, with the strong opposition of the Chilean government.[51] A new process of bilateral negotiations was initiated in 1986, with the support of the government of Uruguay, but negotiations abruptly failed in 1987.[52] The solution to Bolivia's landlocked status is complex, since according to the 1929 Lima Treaty between Peru and Chile, the latter country needs prior consent from Lima before handing over to a third party any territory formerly owned by Peru. Thus, Bolivia's passageway, without producing discontinuity in the Chilean territory, requires Peruvian approval.

It is worth mentioning two cases of conflicts that were settled. These settlements contributed to increasing security not only between the interested parties but also for the entire region. The dispute between *Argentina and Brazil* over the use of water resources in the Río de la Plata Basin culminated—after a long negotiating process—in the signature of the 1979 Technical-Operational Cooperation Agreement for Hydro-electric Uses of Itaipú and Corpus, which constitutes a very important framework for the relations among Brazil, Argentina, and Paraguay.[53]

The settlement of the *Argentine-Chilean* dispute over the Beagle islands and the maritime delimitation in the southern sea, in effect since May 2, 1985, with the exchange of ratification instruments of the 1984 Treaty of Peace and Friendship, put an end to a long-standing border dispute that nearly triggered a war in 1978. The settlement by means of peaceful dispute settlement—mediation of the pope—achieved the implicit recognition of the British arbitral decision of 1977—which had been rejected by the Argentine government, causing the escalation of the conflict. In line with the British decision, Chile was to grant compensation involving the demarcation of maritime spaces in the zone south of the Beagle Channel and in the eastern mouth of Magellan Strait.[54]

Finally, it is necessary to take into account that there are "security networks" forming part of the system currently operating in the region.[55] The weakening of the inter-American security system has not meant the disappearance of all mechanisms to prevent and settle conflicts. Many situations are governed by international legal agreements among the parties concerned or with the participation of third parties. In the case of the Ecuador-Peru controversy in 1981, the guarantors of the 1942 Rio de Janeiro Protocol—Argentina, Brazil, Chile, and the United States— acted diligently to limit the effect of the confrontation and obtain troop withdrawal. In the Argentine-Chilean conflict, a legal mechanism was ever present: the 1972 Treaty for the Legal Settlement of Disputes, which was revived exclusively to settle the southern dispute in September 1982 (after being denounced by Argentina that same year) should either the papal mediation or the arbitral procedure carried out by the Helvitic Confederation after the ratification of the Treaty of Peace and Friendship in 1985 fail. The first dispute settlement mechanism operated only partially in this conflict, inasmuch as Chile's intention was to appeal to the International Court of Justice in late 1978, which caused the Argentine military government to threaten war. At any rate, the armed conflict was avoided through the acceptance by both nations of the pope's mediation, an avenue not considered previously in the international agreements that bound the two nations.

External Links and Regional Conflicts

The international system influences the regional system from the outside. It has been pointed out that the combination of a weakened inter-American security system and a declining U.S. power has created a less controlled, more permissive international setting in which time-worn rules have been relaxed. This has occurred without the establishment of a new system with the same degree of structuring as the one instituted in the postwar period. Regional conflicts develop within this context.

Nevertheless, this does not mean that external actors are unimportant. On the contrary, they influence the regional system by means of political actions and military ties, but without entirely determining the events occurring in South America. Of these actors, the United States continues to be the most important. Its political influence is sizable, though it cannot impose settlements unilaterally. The case of the Falklands/ Malvinas war is significant. As one study on the U.S. role in the 1982 crisis showed, Washington's lack of clarity in transmitting its stands before and during the conflict, along with the Argentine government's misperception, contributed to the making of Argentina's decisions— particularly with regard to invading the islands—on the basis of false assumptions. Conversely, it was evident that the United States was unable to settle the conflict by imposing its viewpoints on the Galtieri government.[56]

Another line of linkages is related to the supply of arms and war equipment. The eclipse of the U.S. monopoly and the transformation of the arms trade into a competitive market have diversified the prospects for external influence in the region's security affairs, especially by facilitating the acquisition of arms, as will be seen further on.

South American countries are increasingly taking their own stands on world politics, weakening automatic alignments. East-West conflict is seen in more autonomous terms, determined by regional and national interests, less acceptance of military ties, a striving to transform the international economic system, and adherence to democratic values.

The first demonstration that the countries were establishing their own definitions of their roles in the global conflict was shown in their perception of Central American conflicts as a danger to South American security. Two South American countries—Colombia and Venezuela— participate in Contadora. Their proximity to the focal points of the conflict caused them to react energetically, to propose negotiations, and to develop a policy that has at the least contributed to curtailing the escalation of the conflicts. Despite the differences existing among the Contadora countries over Central American conflicts, each wants to prevent unilateral action by the United States and to enhance its settlement capability in the crisis.[57]

The remaining South American countries adopted a position more distant from the crisis, since the expression of firm support for negotiated settlement was neutralized by U.S. policy.[58] However, since 1985, several South American countries chose a more active position in favor of the Contadora negotiating process: The new democratic governments of Argentina, Brazil, Uruguay, and the Alan García administration in Peru established the Contadora Supporting Group.

Several South American countries have made a distinction between East-West and North-South conflicts, characterizing the first by ideological and strategic confrontations between the United States and the Soviet Union and the second by a controversy over the justness of international relations. Argentina's minister of foreign affairs, Dante Caputo, has pointed out that confusion has negative effects on Latin American countries, since the East-West conflict has progressively become more military and less ideological, and "claims for international justice are used in the war of propaganda and harassment being developed between the East and West," turning underdeveloped countries "into pawns caught in the confrontation of global interests between the two superpowers." Thus, new problems are added to those already burdening these countries. The use of the North-South conflict in the East-West controversy involves third parties "that do not belong to either of the two military alliances," such as Latin America. Caputo considered Argentina as part of the South but refused to let the claim for international justice "become an instrument of confrontation which, not because it is ideological, but because it is strategic, does not pertain to us."[59]

Thus, Latin America is abandoning automatic alignment with the United States by emphasizing that it does not belong to any military alliance and refusing to permit demands for international justice to make the region part of the East-West conflict. The recognition of North-South differences is coupled with the refusal to allow the South's demands to be used by the East against the West.

By refusing to accept the diagnosis of the Central American conflict in East-West terms, Latin America is rejecting the U.S. viewpoint, its hegemonic policy, and the means, especially military, it employs to achieve it; Latin America's acceptance of the conflict as an East-West one would facilitate the penetration of East-West dynamics into the area, thus magnifying the prospects of the conflict there.

The South American countries' shying away from the East-West conflict does not necessarily imply that they share a neutral or equidistant position from the blocs. Though the Rio Treaty has shown its ineffectiveness as a security mechanism to settle conflicts with an extraregional power, such as the situation between Argentina and Great Britain, and is not useful for settling disputes among the region's states, it is a legal instrument that is still in force and is complemented by a series of miltiary ties between the United States and the region's countries. These links may have deteriorated, but they have not disappeared, and, in the final analysis, the hypothesis is that they would work in a global conflict. The inter-American system's immediate support for the United States during the 1962 missile crisis is a precedent that goes beyond the changes occurring in the political and military fields during the past twenty years.

Internal Conflicts and Regional Security

Unlike Central America, where social conditions and internal divisions are at the root of the conflicts affecting the subregion, in South America internal armed conflicts are found only in Colombia and Peru. In these countries, the democratic governments seek to avert internal security problems by separating these conflicts—incited by guerrilla groups in Colombia and Sendero Luminoso in Peru—from the international conflict. The policy initiated by President Betancur has emphasized Colombia's international role within the Contadora Group; he has drawn closer to the group of nonaligned countries as a way of preventing the linkage with local guerrilla forces.[60] Thus, he tried to create conditions for implementing his internal peace policy, which has failed to end the armed conflict. Ultimately, Colombia's location adjacent to the Central American conflict has until now checked the internationalization of the internal conflict.

In the Peruvian case, a linkage between the serious internal conflicts and external security has not taken place either. During the Fernando Belaunde government a basically military approach to the problem prevailed. The administration of President García tried to combine economic and social development with military practices, but failure of economic policies increased the room for guerrilla activities. In both cases, defining the problem as military or as socioeconomic with security aspects has divided military and civilian sectors.

In the rest of South America, there are no armed conflicts, and social conflicts are regulated through democratic systems, with the exception of Chile and Paraguay. The national security doctrines that inspired the military regimes have ceased to be the bases for defining the state's security areas and policies. Nevertheless, the military powers' decline in South American countries does not imply the extinction of the national security doctrine and its replacement by a logic coherent with democratic principles. Subordinating the armed forces to civilian power is a long-range task that will depend on a complex set of factors, one of which, if not the most important, is the efficient functioning of the democratic political system. In turn, one of the factors that makes a democratic system stable is the peaceful settlement of internal conflicts and the prevention of their acquiring international links at the time they break out.

From 1964 on, Brazil, Argentina, Peru, Bolivia, Uruguay, Ecuador, and Chile fell under the rule of military regimes in which the armed forces exercised power—under differing modalities—occupying not only the government, but also interpenetrating state machinery, transforming it, and achieving a new presence that did not disappear in those cases in which the military regimes stepped down. The relations between civilians and the military cannot be characterized now as a "return to barracks"; the military, rather, seem to adopt new forms of participation in the ongoing functions of the state apparatus, controlling aspects critical to their institutional autonomy, such as military production, or exerting strong influence on related projects, such as the development of nuclear technology.

Early in the chapter, I pointed out that in South American countries there is not just one particular view of security that prevails and that defining interests in this field depends on the actors formulating it. Traditionally, a distinction was made according to whether civilian or military governments were in power. With the new types of relations between the armed forces and the state apparatus, that distinction is not clear-cut today. In order to understand what the resulting security definition would be in a given country, we should look at the ways the military has interpenetrated the rest of the state apparatus. Thus it is

TABLE 7.3
Annual Rates of Increase in Military Expenditure (in percentages)

	South America	Central America	World
1976	10.9	13.9	1.3
1977	6.7	27.0	1.8
1978	-1.0	6.5	2.7
1979	0.0	7.3	4.2
1980	1.5	0.0	0.7
1981	3.0	8.6	2.2
1982	48.0	5.1	5.7
1983	-10.9	6.4	2.1
1984	-7.5	4.7	4.2

Source: SIPRI, *SIPRI Yearbook 1985*, London: Taylor and Francis, 1985, p. 271.

not surprising that when the Ecuador-Peru incident erupted in 1981, both governments were civilian, but reflected the military power still existing in these nations. In any event, Belaunde's civilian government performed a role as moderator in the military response.[61]

South American armed forces' professionalization processes have improved their organization, and nearly two decades of incorporating more modern and sophisticated weapons have increased their war potential. The armed forces have become actors with a stabilizing influence in their countries and with a capacity to make demands of the political system to obtain more resources and further increase their war capability.

Military Expenditures and Arms Transfers

Another element shaping the structure of regional conflicts is the capacity to execute war actions, determined by the development of the armed forces, including the incorporation of weapons.

1. South America increased military expenditure at much higher rates than world-average increases between 1976 and 1982, except for 1978 and 1979 (see Table 7.3). A significantly greater proportion of its resources were allocated to military purposes. This ratio began to *decrease* only with the foreign debt crisis in 1983 and 1984. In the same period, Central America pushed its military spending over the world average, except during 1980 and 1982.

The resource allocation effort seems even more disproportionate when one notes that during the 1972–1982 period, the per capita income in Latin America grew at an annual average rate of 1.6 percent; central

TABLE 7.4

Value of Arms Transfers and Percentage of Participation in the South American Market, by Supplier Country (in millions of current dollars and percentages)

	1965-1974		1974-1977		1978-1982		1982-1986	
	$	%	$	%	$	%	$	%
U.S.	722	36.4	593	20.5	455	6.7	1,065	16.0
USSR	30	1.5	550	19.0	525	7.7	320	4.8
France	463	23.3	470	16.2	1,825	26.8	720	10.8
G. Britain	260	13.1	525	18.1	715	10.5	100	1.5
Canada	172	8.7	25	0.9	a		a	
W. Germany	135	6.8	325	11.2	405	5.9	2,360	35.4
Italy	b		130	4.5	950	13.9	b	
Others	200	10.2	280	9.6	1,940	28.5	2,095	31.5
Total	1,982	100.0	2,898	100.0	6,815	100.0	6,660	100.0

[a]In this period, Canada is included among "others."
[b]In this period, Italy is included among "others."

Sources: U.S. Arms Control and Disarmament Agency, World Military Expenditures and Arms Transfers, Washington, D.C.: U.S. Government Printing Office, 1965-1974, 1968-1977, 1972-1982, and 1987.

government expenditure, excluding military expenditure, at a yearly rate of 6 percent; and military expenditure at an annual average rate of 12.4 percent. The effort especially focused on arms imports, which rose at an average rate of 13.2 percent per year in this period.[62]

2. Latin America as a whole increased its participation in Third World major weapons imports: from 7.1 percent in the 1965–1969 period, to 9.1 percent in 1970–1974, 9.4 percent in 1975–1979, and 13.5 percent in 1980–1984.[63] In the last period, four of the region's countries were among the top twenty countries in the Third World to import heavy weaponry: Cuba (eighth), Argentina (ninth), Peru (seventeenth), and Venezuela (twentieth).[64] Nevertheless, during 1985–1987, the region decreased to 8.8 percent its participation in Third World major weapons imports.[65]

3. The increase in arms imports has been coupled with a diversification of suppliers and, up to the beginning of the 1980s, a diminishing U.S. role in the supply of weapons to South America (see Table 7.4). From being the main supplier during the 1965–1974 period, with 36.4 percent of the market, the United States fell to 20 percent in 1974–1977, to only

TABLE 7.5

Military Expenditure in South America's Main Countries (yearly average in millions of constant 1984 dollars)

	Argentina	Brazil	Chile	Colombia	Peru	Venezuela
1975-1978	2,164	1,678	632	256	957	806
1979-1982	3,176	1,493	701	374	881	738
1983-1985	2,473	1,851	720	480	1,208	716

Source: Data taken from U.S. Arms Control and Disarmament Agency, *World Military Expenditures and Arms Transfers 1987*, Washington, D.C.: U.S. Government Printing Office, ACDA Publication 128, March 1988.

6.7 percent in 1978–1982, and recovering to 16 percent in 1982–1986. In contrast, West Germany has become the main weapons supplier for the subregion, with 35.4 percent of the market, and along with France and Great Britain, controlled almost half of the South American market during 1982–1986.

4. The trend in the region is to incorporate new generations of sophisticated weaponry. As indicated by Mercado Jarrin, South America's weapons purchases during the 1970s were aimed at strengthening naval forces. Eight of the ten maritime countries of the region acquired modern submarines and four, missile-launching frigates. The decade of the 1980s has been the age of incorporating missiles. "The Malvinas war showed the need to reinforce naval forces in their antimissile and antiair defense with Exocet missiles, to strengthen the ground-to-air missile systems of ground forces, and equip air forces with air-to-ship missiles in particular."[66] Between 1982 and 1984, Brazil purchased 48 Exocets (ship-to-ship missiles); Chile, 8 Exocets, an undetermined number of Rapiers, and 16 Seacats; Argentina, 168 Exocets and 96 Aspides; Colombia, 32 Exocets and 64 Seasparrows; Ecuador, 36 Exocets and 72 Aspides; and Peru, 40 Exocets, 96 Aspides, and 96 Otomat-1s.[67]

5. Military expenditure has increased in the main South American countries (see Table 7.5). The average yearly military expenditure was higher in 1979–1982 in three countries (Argentina, Chile, and Colombia) and lower in three countries (Brazil, Peru, and Venezuela) than in the preceding four-year period. The average yearly military expenditure was higher in 1983–1985 in four countries (Brazil, Chile, Colombia, and Peru) and lower in two countries (Argentina and Venezuela) than in the 1978–1982 period.

Military imports (see Table 7.6) in the 1981–1983 period were higher than they were in the previous three-year period in Argentina, Chile,

TABLE 7.6
Arms Imports in the Main South American Countries (millions of constant 1984 dollars)

	Argentina	Brazil	Chile	Colombia	Peru	Venezuela
1978-1980	1,493	786	647	129	1,034	261
1981-1983	1,896	142	752	207	918	697
1984-1986	652	264	179	729	339	919

Source: U.S. Arms Control and Disarmament Agency, *World Military Expenditures and Arms Transfers 1987*, Washington, D.C.: U.S. Government Printing Office, ACDA Publication 128, March 1988.

Colombia, and Venezuela, and they were lower in Brazil and Peru. In 1984–1986, they fell sharply in Argentina, Chile, and Peru—countries severely affected by the debt crisis—and increased in Colombia and Venezuela and slightly in Brazil. The general trend was to hike spending, especially on weapons imports, up to the time of the debt crisis, which became the principal factor in slowing down imports.

6. The impact of military expenditures on the economies is not uniform (see Table 7.7). SIPRI estimated that in Chile they reached 9.6 percent (1984), and 8.3 percent (1986) of the GDP; in Peru, 9.6 percent (1983) and 8.7 percent (1986) of the GDP; and in Argentina, 6.2 percent (1981), and 4.5 percent (1986) of the GDP. In contrast, they were estimated at 1.7 percent (1979) and 2.2 percent (1986) for Colombia, and in Venezuela, 2.1 percent (1978) and 3.1 percent (1986). In the case of Brazil, military expenditure as a share of the GDP was calculated to be under 1.0 percent throughout the period, but recent evidence has suggested that the amount is considerably higher.

7. South America has not only been importing more weapons, but it has also started to produce and even to export them. Brazil and Argentina have an appreciable and diversified production; Chile and Peru manufacture various types of arms; Colombia has a limited production; Venezuela and Uruguay, marginal production, while Bolivia and Ecuador restrict their production to small arms.[68] An estimate of the potential base for arms production by Third World countries puts Brazil in first place; Argentina, fifth; Venezuela, eleventh; Chile, twelfth; Colombia, seventeenth; Peru, twenty-first, and Uruguay, twenty-fifth.[69]

Brazil is the most outstanding producer of weapons.[70] It is the major weapons manufacturer in the Third World and the most sophisticated from the technical viewpoint. There are estimates that the development of the military industry permits Brazil to cover over one-half of its arms

TABLE 7.7

Military Expenditure as a Percentage of Gross Domestic Product in the Main
South American Countries (1978-1986)

	Argentina	Brazil[a]	Chile	Colombia	Peru	Venezuela
1978	5.8	(0.8)	7.0	na	5.5	2.1
1979	5.4	(0.7)	6.9	(1.7)	3.9	2.4
1980	5.6	(0.7)	6.7	1.9[b]	(5.3)	2.7
1981	6.2	(0.7)	7.4	1.9[b]	(6.0)	3.1
1982	6.0[b]	(0.9)	9.5	1.8[b]	na	3.4
1983	4.5[b]	(0.8)	8.0	2.3[b]	(9.6)	2.9[b]
1984	4.3[b]	(0.8)	9.6	2.5[b]	(6.5)	2.8
1985	4.2	na	7.6	2.2[b]	(7.5)	3.0
1986	4.5	na	8.3[b]	2.2[b]	(8.7)	(3.1)

[a]The series is currently being revised because recent evidence suggests that
Brazilian military expenditure is considerably higher than the amount given
here.
[b]Uncertain data.
( ) Estimates with high degree of uncertainty.
na: Not available.

Source: SIPRI, SIPRI Yearbook 1987, London: Taylor and Francis, 1987, p. 172.

needs with war matériel produced internally.[71] Sophisticated fighter jets,
helicopters, missiles, tanks, and warships are produced. The country has
more than 60 weapons manufacturing companies and nearly 350 industries associated with the production of war matériel. Arms factories
directly employ 80,000 workers; another 200,000 people live off arms
production indirectly.[72]

The industry is geared toward exports (see Table 7.8), which currently
represent more than 90 percent of industrial invoicing. In 1984, Brazil's
weapons export revenue was estimated at between $1 billion and $2.6
billion, which in any case makes Brazil the top Third World arms
exporter.[73] Brazilian industry exports mainly to the Third World, reaching
more than thirty countries. The Middle East receives a third of its arms
export market, followed by Latin America and Africa.[74]

War production is strongly influenced by the armed forces; their
projects are developed in joint ventures with European and U.S. enterprises. Some of the more recent and sophisticated plans are the construction of the AMX supersonic bomber, a joint project of EMBRAER,
a Brazilian company, and the Italian firms, Aeritalia and Aermacchi,[75]

TABLE 7.8

Arms Exports in the Main South American Countries (in millions of constant 1984 dollars)

	Argentina	Brazil	Chile	Colombia	Peru	Venezuela
1978-1980	20	473	na	a	na	b
1981-1983	33	1,058	6	a	65	b
1984-1986	173	1,057	48	a	na	b

[a]Limited production.
[b]Marginal production.
na: Not available.

Source: U.S. Arms Control and Disarmament Agency, *World Military Expenditures and Arms Transfers 1987*, Washington, D.C.: U.S. Government Printing Office, ACDA Publication 128, March 1988.

construction of submarines in association with Ferrostal from West Germany,[76] and overseas projects like the assembling of Tucano airplanes, which EMBRAER will carry out in Egypt.[77] Brazil's industry is not completely autonomous but depends on a high proportion of imported technology. The projects contemplated by the Brazilian war industry for building missiles, defense systems, aircraft carriers, tanks, and artillery cannons include state-of-the-art Swiss, U.S., and British technologies, among others.[78]

Argentina's military industry started in the 1950s,[79] but its growth has been somewhat anarchic, and the new democratic regime has submitted it to a process of restructuring.[80] Some of its most sophisticated products, such as the Argentine medium tank (TAM), built with German technology, and the counterinsurgency plane, Pucara, have had difficulties in competing on the external market.[81] However, efforts are kept up to introduce new products, like the recently built IA-63 training plane, Pampa.[82] Having developed an important military industry, Argentina, like Brazil, has diversified production with export capacity.

Other countries of the region, including Chile, Colombia, and Peru, are developing arms production, though they are at a less advanced stage.[83] Chile has also started to develop an export industry.

Table 7.9 illustrates the type of war production in five countries of the region.

The goal of arms production is to be a substitute for imports; in order for the industry to sustain itself economically, it must find external markets so as to cut back the costs of the import substitution process.

TABLE 7.9
Development of Arms Production in South America (1984)

	Argentina	Brazil	Chile	Colombia	Peru
Fighter & training jets	L	L	c		c
Light & transport planes	L	L	c	c	
Helicopters	lic	c			
Guided missiles	L	L			
Large battleships and rapid attack ships	lic	L			lic
Small battleships	L	L	L	L	L
Submarines	c	c			
Large battle tanks	lic	L			
Artillery	L	lic			
Light tanks and armored vehicles	lic	L	L		
Small arms	L	L	L	a	L

Notes: L: local design and production; lic: production under license of the weapons system (with importation of sophisticated parts; c: component production under license; a: assembly.

Source: Stockholm International Peace Research Institute (SIPRI), *SIPRI Yearbook 1985*, London: Taylor and Francis, 1985, pp. 332-333.

There are no in-depth studies on the cost of this kind of industry in South American countries, but it can be assumed that the activity does represent a cost to countries developing it in cases where exports are not significant, since the size of the domestic market is small. Even for Brazil, where the arms industry is clearly export oriented, to calculate the benefits in terms of the balance of payments, it would be necessary to know the amount of foreign currency spent on input imports and the payment of patents and royalties.

At the level of intraregional rivalry, arms production is a component of relations between Argentina and Brazil, with Argentina's preeminence being reversed over recent years.

Nuclear Development

The development of nuclear energy and its potential military application influence the structure of regional conflicts. Basically, this involves the rivalry between Argentina and Brazil, since they are the only countries in the region with advanced technological development in these matters. Both have been reluctant to assume international commitments that prohibit them from becoming nuclear military powers. In order to manufacture nuclear weapons, both the capacity and the intention to make them must exist.[84]

1. In terms of *capacity*, nuclear energy development programs in Argentina date back to the 1950s and form the most stable sector of the state apparatus, a sector that has achieved great prestige in the Argentine society and has obtained substantial leeway for bureaucratic autonomy. In the case of Brazil, the nuclear development policy has received strong support only since the mid-1970s, when an agreement was negotiated with the Federal Republic of Germany. The Argentine program emphasizes the development of a technological capacity of its own and the acquisition of foreign technology needed to achieve progress in the field.[85] The Brazilian program is more dependent on German technology imports, though it has also developed its own research with the goal of attaining autonomy in the domain of nuclear technology. Brazilian research programs are being carried out at the Aeronautics Technical Institute at São Jose dos Campos and at the National Nuclear Energy Commission in São Paulo.[86]

2. In terms of *intentions*, both countries have refused to assume international commitments concerning nonproliferation of nuclear weapons. They have not signed the Nonproliferation Treaty (NPT), which they consider to be discriminatory, nor are they subject to the Tlatelolco Treaty, which established the denuclearization of Latin America. Argentina signed the Tlatelolco Treaty with the understanding that the treaty does not prohibit nuclear tests for peaceful purposes, but has not ratified it. Brazil signed and ratified the Tlatlelolco Treaty with the same understanding.

3. The *transition to democracy* and the *economic crisis* in Argentina and Brazil have led to the review of the nuclear development programs and international commitments of these countries. The end of authoritarian regimes and the inauguration of democratic processes in Argentina and Brazil produced debates on the subject of nuclear development due to its costs, submitting it to intense scrutiny during a time of a shortage of foreign exchange.

In Argentina, President Alfonsín adhered to the goal of achieving technological independence,[87] confirming the value of mastering the technology of the fuel cycle and gaining self-sufficiency in the production of heavy water and nuclear inputs and components, including a local uranium enrichment technology. The nuclear industry is considered to be a key element for forging an advanced technological development, which would have locomotive and transformation effects on the productive system.[88]

However, the National Atomic Energy Commission (CNEA) has experienced budget cuts, causing the postponement of the construction of the Atucha II nuclear plant,[89] while the areas of research and development geared toward achieving technological independence and training human resources have continued to receive priority treatment.[90] Budgetary restrictions have not forced the elimination of any program, according to CNEA President Alberto Constantini, although they have meant the deferral of programs, as is the case in the construction of a nuclear submarine.[91] It can be concluded that the domestic nuclear lobby, particularly CNEA, has not succeeded in obtaining its budget demands, but has been able to keep long-term projects alive.

In Brazil, the nuclear energy development program carried out in association with West Germany has been delayed by technical and cost problems. The Angra I nuclear energy plant is in operation, though not to full capacity, after being finished five years late. The lack of resources may thwart the main goals of the Brazilian nuclear program: to absorb, master, and reproduce nuclear technology.[92] In a discussion on the future of the program in early 1985, scientists argued that the country was acquiring inefficient, obsolete technology.[93] At any rate, the technological absorption capacity allowed by the Brazilian-German agreement is much lower than that of the projects under way in Argentina.[94]

In terms of intentions, the democratic government of Argentina has explicitly supported the peaceful uses of nuclear energy, as indicated by unilateral declarations, but has not altered its stand against endorsing the Nonproliferation Treaty and ratifying the Tlatelolco Treaty. At the meeting of the Organismo para la Proscripción de las Armas Nucleares en América latina (OPANAL—Organization for Banning Nuclear Weapons in Latin America), held on May 7, 1985, the Argentine representative argued that it was impossible to ratify the treaty, since "the IAEA [International Atomic Energy Agency] has improperly assimilated the commitments derived from our Latin American instrument into the discriminatory obligations provided for in the NPT," because "not only has the full ratification of the two protocols (annexed to the treaty) by all countries owning nuclear weapons not been obtained, but also the powers that have ratified it have voiced interpretations that are aimed at modifying the treaty's provisions, inserting discriminatory elements," due to the country's reservations over the protection of industrial secrets.[95] Thus, the peaceful use of nuclear energy depends upon the unilateral discretion of Argentina, a country that has declared itself to be a "civilian nuclear State."[96]

In the Brazilian case, there are also contradictory signals: In March 1984 a high military chief declared that within five years Brazil would be in a position to build a bomb, but that the technology would be applied only to producing electricity,[97] and in June 1985, he reported that the joint chiefs of staff of the armed forces were against including an article in the constitution that would prevent Brazil from building an atomic bomb.[98]

It can be concluded that in terms of intentions, Argentina and Brazil have kept their options open, as they are not bound by international agreements. Instead, since 1985, Argentina and Brazil have been negotiating a system of reciprocal inspections of nuclear facilities and have been establishing the basis for cooperative programs in the nuclear field.[99] One can conclude that development of nuclear capabilities has been hurt by the economic crisis in both countries, but no firm change has been made in Argentina or in Brazil in terms of intentions. In countries with political instability and sectors advocating the war application of nuclear technology, unilateral guarantees are not enough. Until now, the development of nuclear technology has required external support. The need for that support acts as a temporary stumbling block for a military nuclear option because of the risk of costly upsets if the technology becomes unobtainable.

Regional Security:
The Challenge of Cooperation

Relations among South American countries have been guided by a narrow notion of national interest, with exclusionist biases and a strong geopolitical influence. Failure at regional integration projects and autonomous management of international economic affairs, even in the foreign debt crisis, are examples of the narrow limits prevailing when defining a national interest. Regional security policies follow the same pattern: Ever since the military regimes of the 1960s and 1970s considered their "internal wars" ended, military thinking, organization, and arms acquisitions have been more directed toward the hypothesis of external conflict, focusing mainly on neighboring countries.

These competitive trends cannot be the bases for the regional security policies emphasizing common interests among South American countries. The regional economic crisis, and particularly the scarcity of foreign exchange, are a common limit for the development of military establishments, whose excessive growth would have a bearing on the intensification of the crisis. However, the processes of transition to and consolidation of democratic regimes in South America call for a new type of civilian-military relations; a disturbing growth of the armed forces would not contribute to its development.

Maximizing shared interests among countries in South America means defining certain preferences and dismissing other options. Since this is a sphere in which U.S. presence and policies have been very important to the region, it is also necessary to list the conditions that U.S.-South American links should have for security relations to materialize through cooperation.

Foundations for a Cooperative Security Regime in South America

Cooperation in the security area must consider:

1. A degree of relative autonomy of South America in terms of defining its own security problems, its positions vis-à-vis the global conflict, the processes to settle internal conflicts, means of supply, and so forth, must be recognized. Preservation of autonomy should be linked to increasing levels of security and requires cooperation with countries outside South America.

2. South American countries have sought to prevent the East-West conflict and particularly its hostile manifestations from reaching the region. This concern was evidenced at the 1985 Cartagena meeting held by the ministers of foreign affairs of the Contadora Group with the representatives of the Contadora Supporting Group (Argentina, Brazil, Peru, and Uruguay) to discuss the negative effects of the internationalization of Central American conflicts on the entire region.[100]

3. The definition of shared interests in the field of security. In order to make the policies designed effective, they should be formulated taking into account the region's economic development goals. This involves obtaining security at a reasonable cost.[101]

4. Regional security must be asserted through mechanisms compatible with political democracy, avoiding the militarization of the region. This does not mean that state security requirements should be reduced and diluted at a merely political level, but that the effects that a security framework could have in the political system should be taken into account.

5. A cooperative security system in South America should seek relations compatible with the United States. Such a system cannot assume that linkages established in the inter-American system are automatic, nor can it ignore the existence of concrete ties in the field of security, such as the Rio Treaty; relations among the different branches of the armed forces, i.e., conferences of com-

manders in chief; some inter-American military entities; bilateral linkages between South American countries and the United States; yearly joint operations among several South American and U.S. naval forces (Unitas), and so forth.

6. The relations between the United States and South American countries will not have the same intensity and importance in all cases. U.S. security priorities in South America may not correspond to those established by South American countries. Countries having greater regional power will tend toward greater autonomy in their own policies, making it difficult for them to accommodate to U.S. policies. The situation of smaller countries may receive less attention from the policymaking process in the United States, which could give them more room for maneuver.

U.S.-South American security relations in the 1990s should be built upon a framework that takes into consideration diverse interests, though they need not necessarily be antagonistic in nature; limited, though not unimportant, U.S. influence in the region; and growing autonomy of military links.

7. A cooperative scheme among countries in South America should not be dissociated from Central American problems nor abandon the existing inter-American and Latin American security mechanisms. South American concern over Central American conflicts has become very important during the 1980s, reinforcing proposals for a negotiated settlement. Other problems summarized in the previous section, such as nuclear proliferation, have security mechanisms that go beyond the realm of South America (for example, the Tlatelolco Treaty). A cooperative system among South American countries must make use of existing mechanisms as long as they are efficacious for conflict management and settlement.

Trends and Policies for Cooperation in the 1990s

How should a South American cooperative scheme be applied to security problems? To answer this question, we will return briefly to the problems mentioned in the preceding section, indicating probable trends, possible cooperative policies for managing the problems, and the types of relations with the United States required for the viability of such policies.

1. The reduction and elimination of focal points of conflict among states of the zone must be the first goal shared by South American countries. Although trends toward an intensification of these intraregional conflicts appeared to decline in comparison to tensions between Argentina and Chile, Ecuador and Peru, Colombia and Venezuela, and Venezuela

and Guyana in the late seventies and early eighties, the persistence of latent conflicts breeds the threat of escalation.[102] The search for solutions must be approached, not through merely one regional formula, but through an exploration of the different mechanisms available for settling each dispute, taking into account that only the involved parties' acceptance of the application of such mechanisms can lead to solving the problem.

A review of past experience indicates that security networks formed by both bilateral and multilateral mechanisms serve as a mainstay for settling disputes. The creation and strengthening of such networks must be a regional objective. The settlement of conflicts with a territorial element will be facilitated if incentives are created to transform the dispute from a zero-sum game into one in which both parties can gain benefits. Regional development projects and the common use of resources might serve as key elements to break a stalemate in this type of dispute.

A crucial factor for de-escalating conflicts and preventing their outbreak must be the development and application of mutual confidence-building measures among the South American armed forces.[103] Measures such as notifications of military maneuvers, the presence of observers, exchange of military information among neighboring countries, demilitarization of borders, and verification agreements may contribute to creating the climate for détente, facilitating negotiations to settle conflicts as well as to limit weapons.

The preceding analysis indicates the limitations of U.S. influence on the dynamics of intraregional conflicts. However, the U.S. role may be a very efficient element for cooperation in managing them, as confirmed by its unofficial participation in preventing war between Argentina and Chile in late 1978, as well as its participation as one of the guarantors of the Rio de Janeiro Protocol at the time of the incident between Ecuador and Peru in 1981.

It is just as important to prevent the creation of imbalances through arms transfers. This is a field in which U.S. participation is neither exclusive nor actually the most important; nevertheless, the adoption of a policy tending to use arms transfers as a means of restoring influence can cause problems among countries of the region; this was the case with Colombia's perception of the transfer of U.S. F-16s to Venezuela. Finally, the U.S. role in eventual settlements of territorial conflicts may be to finance regional development projects.

2. The management of intraregional rivalries and the elimination of hostile features in interstate competition must also be a common objective of South American countries. Let us consider the case of Brazil: Its growth, the colonization of its border areas, and its economic impact on neighboring countries, such as Bolivia, Paraguay, and Uruguay, have reinforced geopolitical views in states considered to be Brazil's potential

rivals. Thus, in Argentina, the actors that define its practices in competing with Brazil have sought compensation militarily and in the development of nuclear energy, where Argentina's scientific, technological, and industrial capacity is quite superior to that of Brazil.

The management of competitive relations goes beyond the realm of security, extending to all the spheres of interstate relations, particularly, economic integration and political cooperation. In matters of security relations, prevention of nuclear proliferation, coproduction of arms, joint military training exercises, and arms limitation agreements would all contribute to a relaxation of hostilities.[104]

As previously mentioned, conflicts and rivalries are interrelated within a regional structure, and consequently, tensions between two countries tend to spread. Hence, cooperation schemes must dedicate ongoing attention to security relations as a whole.

3. South American countries need the settlement of Central American conflicts through negotiations and a reduction in the militarization of that region in order to prevent the internationalization of those conflicts from affecting regional peace. The support granted by the democratic governments of Argentina, Brazil, Peru, and Uruguay to the Contadora Group reflects the fact that the region's countries have a different perspective from that of the United States in their assessment of the Central American situation. The persistence of the conflicts, as well as an eventual intensification of the hostilities and destabilization of governments due to the direct or indirect action of the United States, would contribute to a deterioration of the links between South America and that country.

Keeping South America beyond the reach of the East-West confrontation entails the settlement of the situation in Central America. From the South American perspective, the abatement of the conflict and its peaceful settlement are the factors that could prevent any incidents that could invite hostile extraregional presences.

4. In terms of regional security, closing down the "Falklands fortress" and starting a negotiating process between Argentina and Great Britain covering all issues involved, including sovereignty over the Malvinas Islands, are a requisite for demilitarizing the controversy. This not only has a bearing on bilateral relations but also affects the zone as a potential focal point of tension. The role of the United States in softening the British stand should be not discounted.

5. Legal mechanisms, the observance and respect for treaties and international law, must be revitalized in regional relations. The observance of the principles of nonintervention and nonuse of force or threat to use force is particularly relevant for governing the relations of South American and Latin American countries with extraregional powers,

particularly the United States. Discussion in the U.S. Congress and subsequent legislative approval of aid to fighters striving to overthrow a government with which the United States maintains diplomatic relations are viewed as a very dangerous deterioration in the legal principles of international coexistence in the region. Similarly, the U.S. government's disavowal of the compulsory jurisdiction of the International Court of Justice in The Hague so as to avoid submitting its potential actions in Central America to that court's judgment is a threat to regional security.

6. A cooperative scheme requires a decisive delinkage of external security and domestic armed conflicts. The settlement of conflicts considered to be domestic and social reintegration should be sought by democratic structures. Accordingly, nonintervention principles should be strictly enforced by both the countries of the zone and extraregional powers.

The problem of relations with the United States points to an unresolved historical issue: military relations between the United States and Latin America and their effect on domestic political behavior of the Latin American, and particularly South American, armed forces. The introduction of doctrines on internal defense and development and of counterinsurgency techniques by the U.S. armed forces in the sixties and their assimilation into the national security doctrines of South American military establishments had a perverse effect. It applied the logic of the East-West conflict to the assessment of internal social and political phenomena in South American societies, a misjudgment that led to the military governments, which are today in decline.

The U.S. reaction in the seventies—the human rights policy—and the application of military restrictions and sanctions damaged the links between the U.S. armed forces and almost all South American military establishments. Attempts to rebuild those military links have been carried out, within a context in which the South American armed forces are much more consolidated organizationally than they were in the sixties. Regardless of their withdrawal from government in several countries, they continue to be hierarchical institutions with a conservative view of society. The links that are reestablished with the U.S. armed forces will be more selective from the standpoint of the South American military establishments. There is a danger that the reintroduction of cold war notions—still existing from the U.S. standpoint and remaining in South American perspectives—may again have a negative impact on the domestic political behavior of the South American military.

7. A cooperative security policy must seek to restrict military expenditures and arms acquisition as well as to coordinate regional weapons production in order to provide for common security at an acceptable cost to economies in crisis.

Notwithstanding the economic restrictions, during late 1985 a military modernization plan was introduced and spending was increased in Colombia,[105] Peru purchased Mirage 2000 jets,[106] later reduced by 50 percent, and Brazil's military industry continued its development plans.[107] The downward trend of military expenditure was soon reversed (see Table 7.5), although arms imports tended to diminish in the second half of the eighties (see Table 7.6). Even before the financial crisis is over, a wave of import increases in certain countries would certainly sweep along other countries, as witnessed by Colombian-Venezuelan relations. In contrast, national efforts to develop an arms industry in countries like Brazil and Argentina will continue to emphasize exports as a way of making this type of industry acceptable—and even advantageous— for the balance of payments. The other countries of the region developing war industries would certainly have to continue to absorb the high costs through state subsidies; their external accounts would be affected until they achieved a significant export capacity.

The weapons production capability of the most advanced countries in the region would tend to be offset by those states having an incipient military industry through growing imports. This option would mean further detouring resources, limited by the country's financial capacity. Under a situation of external-resource crisis, like the current one, it is most probable that the gap will increase between producer-exporter countries—which obtain foreign exchange from the operation of the military industry—and the remaining countries, for which importation increases the balance-of-payments deficit.

A cooperative effort during a period of economic crisis reinforces the importance of a cutback in military spending and cooperative arms limitations. The limitations imposed on imports and eventually on the production of a given type of arms—especially the most sophisticated ones—must form part of this kind of initiative. The existence of producer countries poses the need to seek coproduction agreements among two or more of the region's countries as a way of substituting imports and avoiding intraregional rivalry.

The proliferation of arms suppliers has transformed any arms limitation agreement into an issue involving mainly recipient countries, which must restrict their imports. However, collaboration of suppliers may help to sustain a cooperative scheme. Among those supplier countries, the United States should be more interested than other arms dealers in contributing to a regional agreement to guarantee security in a neighboring area. The renewal of the policy of not being the first to introduce new generations of arms would be a step in this direction.

Nevertheless, it should be recalled that in the matter of arms transfer, the use of certain tools is at present much more complex: The technical approval by a U.S. Air Force commission to acquire 500 Brazilian T-27 Tucano military training planes[108] reveals that there are also incentives in the U.S. market to be a buyer of war matériel. This seems to be the most probable road for cooperation between Brazilian and U.S. armed forces and military industry.

8. Finally, a cooperative security system in South America requires the reinforcement of nuclear weapons nonproliferation mechanisms. The acquisition of nuclear arms by a South American country would greatly enhance regional rivalries, accelerate military competition to acquire status as a nuclear power, for those countries on that path, and conventional weaponry, for other states, as a way of compensation. This scenario would eventually destroy any possibility of an authentically cooperative security system in South America.

The goals set up by Tlatelolco are still alive: Presently there is a need to seek formulas that lead to progress in terms of international guarantees for nonproliferation. There are two fields immediately open in this respect: (1) development of mutual inspection and safeguard mechanisms of nuclear programs within the region, both bilaterally and multilaterally, as explored in the Argentinian-Brazilian integration agreements, and (2) the search for new safeguard formulas with the International Atomic Energy Agency, a path that has not been entirely closed off by Argentina.

Commonality is also found in this field between the positions held by the United States and by those countries in the region that consider nonproliferation to be a goal that should be pursued. The most complete guarantee of respect for the denuclearized zone by nuclear powers and for progress in the implementation of declared goals on nuclear disarmament would contribute to facilitating denuclearization in Latin America.

Notes

1. John Child, *Unequal Alliance: The Inter-American Military System, 1938–1978* (Boulder, Colo.: Westview Press, 1980), especially 143–187.

2. Alexandre S.C. Barros, "The Diplomacy of National Security: South American International Relations in a Defrosting World," in R. Hellman and H. Rosenblum (eds.), *Latin America: The Search for a New International Role* (New York: John Wiley, 1975), pp. 131–150.

3. Andrew Pierre, *The Global Politics of Arms Sales* (Princeton: Princeton University Press), 1982.

4. Child, op. cit., p. 189.

5. Josefina Cintron Tiryakian, "The Military and Security Dimensions of U.S. Caribbean Policy," in H. Michael Erisman (ed.), *The Caribbean Challenge: U.S. Policy in a Volatile Region* (Boulder, Colo.: Westview Press, 1984), p. 49.

6. Margaret Daly Hayes, *Latin America and the U.S. National Interest* (Boulder, Colo.: Westview Press, 1984), pp. 219–225.

7. For a view of the importance of the Caribbean as a vital area for U.S. security, see Abraham Lowenthal, *Rethinking U.S. Interest in the Western Hemisphere*, Center for National Policy, Washington, D.C., August 1984.

8. Tiryakian, op. cit., p. 52.

9. Paulo Kramer, "As Relaçoes Militares Brasil-Estados Unidos," *Textos*, Instituto de Relaçes Internacionais, Pontifícia Universidade Católica, Rio de Janeiro, no. 5, 1985.

10. Riordan Roett and Gunnar Wiegand, "The Role of Argentina and Brazil: A View from the United States," Center for Brazilian Studies, School of Advanced International Studies, Washington, D.C., 1986.

11. Margaret Daly Hayes, "Security to the South: U.S. Interests in Latin America," *International Security*, vol. 5, no. 1, Summer 1980, pp. 130–151; quotation, p. 144.

12. Ibid., pp. 144–145.

13. Lowenthal, op. cit., p. 4.

14. Anthony Lake, "Wrestling with Third World Radical Regimes: Theory and Practice," in John W. Sewell, Richard E. Feinberg, and Valeriana Kallab (eds.), *U.S. Foreign Policy and the Third World: Agenda 1985-86*, U.S.-Third World Policy Perspectives, No. 3, Overseas Development Council (New Brunswick, N.J.: Transaction Books, 1985), pp. 120–123.

15. Susan Kaufman Purcell, "Demystifying Contadora," *Foreign Affairs*, Fall 1985, pp. 82–83.

16. Alberto Van Klaveren, "Colombia: la reafirmación del nuevo perfil externo," in Heraldo Muñoz (ed.), *Las Politicas Exteriores Latinoamericanos frente a la crisis* (Buenos Aires, Grupo Editor Latinoamericano, 1985), pp. 157–178.

17. Fernando Cepeda Ulloa, "Contadora, Colombia y Centroamérica," paper presented at the seminar "Zona de Paz: Hacia una Alternativa de Seguridad Regional para América Latina," FLACSO, Santiago, Chile, June 5–7, 1987.

18. See Table 7.1.

19. Riordan Roett and Scott D. Tollefson, "Brazil's Status as an Intermediate Power," *Third World Affairs*, 1986 Annual Edition.

20. Shiguenoli Miyamoto, Consideraçoes sobre o pacto do Atlantico Sul," paper presented at the "VIII Encuentro Anual de la Associacao Nacional de Pós-Graduaçao e Pesquisa em Ciencias Sociais," (ANPOCS), Aguas de São Pedro, São Paulo, October 24–26, 1984.

21. The term has been used by Celso Lafer, "Una política externa para Tancredo," *Folha de São Paulo*, October 6, 1984.

22. Manfred Wilhelmy, "Brasil: cambio político y continuidad internacional," in Muñoz (ed.), op. cit., pp. 14–29.

23. See Table 7.1.

24. Howard T. Pittman, "Geopolitics and Conflict in the Southern Cone," paper presented at the Biennial Conference of the Military Studies Section of the International Studies Association, Durham, N.H., November 5–7, 1981.

25. Sergio Bitar, "Economics and Security: Contradictions in United States–Latin American Relations," Working Papers, No. 147, Latin American Program, The Wilson Center, Washington, D.C., 1984.

26. Jorge I. Domínguez, "Los conflictos internacionales en América Latina y la amenaza de guerra," *Foro Internacional*, vol. 25, no. 1, July-September 1984, pp. 1–13.

27. Typology created by Wolf Grabendorff, "Interstate Conflict Behaviour and Regional Potential for Conflict in Latin America," *Journal of Interamerican Studies and World Affairs*, vol. 24, no. 3, August 1982, pp. 267–294.

28. I have omitted the case between Peru and Chile cited by Grabendorff, since no territorial claims exist between these two countries and the fulfillment of the pending items of the Lima Treaty of 1929 that put an end to the border conflict generated by the War of the Pacific was being negotiated by the two countries in November 1985.

29. Alexandre S.C. Barros, "Arms and Conflict in South America," paper presented at the seminar "Paz, Desarme y Desarrollo," held during the RIAL annual meeting in Bogota, Colombia, November 4–6, 1985, p. 15.

30. Robert N. Burr, *By Reason or Force. Chile and the Balancing of Power in South America, 1830–1905* (Berkeley, University of California Press, 1974).

31. I have taken the same year in which I measured participation in the region's domestic product, the preceding, and following years. However, since there are no figures available on military spending for 1946, the participation in the regional product for that year is compared to the participation in the region's military spending in 1948, 1949, and 1950. Similarly, in the last period I compare participation in the 1984 product to spending in 1982, 1983, and 1984.

32. See works published in the "América Latina después de las Malvinas" issue of *Estudios Internacionales*, year 15, no. 60, October-December 1982.

33. Adrián F.J. Hope, "Soberanía y descolonización de las islas Malvinas Falkland Islands," *Boston College International and Comparative Law Review*, vol. 6, no. 2, 1983, pp. 391–445.

34. "Discurso pronunciado por el señor Ministro de Relaciones Exteriores y Culto Licenciado Dante Mario Caputo ante el Consejo Permanente de la Organización de Estados Americanos (Washington, mayo 15 de 1985)," version furnished by the Embassy of Argentina in Chile.

35. *Financial Times*, April 4, 1985.

36. Latin American Regional Reports, *Southern Cone Report*, February 1, 1985, and Foreign Broadcast Information Service, *Latin America*, June 19, 1984.

37. Stockholm International Peace Research Institute (SIPRI), *SIPRI Yearbook 1985*, London: Taylor and Francis, 1985), p. 276.

38. See "Declaración del Ministro de Relaciones Exteriores y Culto Licenciado Dante Mario Caputo ante el Movimiento de Países No-alineados (Nueva York, mayo 17 de 1985)," version provided by the Embassy of Argentina in Chile.

39. See "Mensaje Gobierno Argentino," July 10, 1985. Version of the Ministry of Foreign Affairs of Argentina.

40. See UN General Assembly Resolutions 37/9 of November 4, 1982, 38/12 of November 16, 1983, and 39/6 of November 1, 1984.

41. The position held by the government of Argentina is stated in the documents mentioned in notes 34 and 38 above, and in the "Nota presentada

por la República Argentina al Secretario General de las Naciones Unidas Javier Pérez de Cuéllar (Nueva York, mayo 16 de 1985)," version provided by the Embassy of Argentina in Chile.

42. Gabriel Marcella posed a different view, "The Malvinas/Falkland War of 1982. Lessons for the United States and Latin America," *Strategic Issues Research Memorandum*, Strategic Studies Institute, U.S. Army War College, Carlisle Barracks, Penn., August 1, 1983.

43. On the effects of the Malvinas conflict on other Latin American states, see Annegret Haffa and Nikolaus Werz, "The Falklands Conflict and Inter-American Relations," *Aussenpolitik*, 2/1983, pp. 185–201.

44. Taisa Medina, "Venezuela: rasgos centrales de la política exterior 1983–1984" in Muñoz (ed.), op. cit., pp. 73–74.

45. Manfred Wilhelmy, "Venezuela: política exterior en la adversidad," in Heraldo Muñoz (ed.), *Las políticas exteriores de América Latina y el Caribe: continuidad en la crisis* (Buenos Aires, Grupo Editor Latinoamericano, 1987), p. 102; and Marisabel Brás, "La política exterior de Venezuela en 1987," in Heraldo Muñoz (ed.), *Las políticas exteriores de América Latina y el Caribe: un balance de esperanzas* (Buenos Aires, Grupo Editor Latinoamericano, 1988), pp. 66–69.

46. Alberto Van Klaveren, "Colombia: la reafirmación del nuevo perfil externo," in Muñoz (ed.), op. cit., 1985, p. 170; Brás, op. cit., pp. 67–69; and Juan G. Tokatlián and Rodrigo Pardo, "Colombia: la reafirmación del pragmatismo en un escenario crecientemente conflictivo," in Muñoz (ed.), op. cit., 1988, pp. 170–174.

47. Gerhard Drekonja Kornat. "La política exterior de Colombia," in Juan Carlos Puig (ed.), *América Latina: Políticas Exteriores Comparadas* (Buenos Aires, Grupo Editor Latinoamericano, 1984), pp. 334–335.

48. Laura Madalengoitia U., "Los mecanismos de resolución en el case Perú-Ecuador (1981)," paper presented at the seminar "Zona de Paz: Hacia una Alternativa de Seguridad Regional para América Latina," FLACSO, Santiago, Chile, June 5–7, 1985.

49. *El Mercurio* (Santiago), January and February 1985, several issues.

50. *El Mercurio* (Santiago), March 3, 1985.

51. Heraldo Muñoz, "La política exterior de Chile: la crisis continúa," and Mladen Yopo, "Bolivia: democracia, inestabilidad interna y política exterior," in Muñoz, op. cit., 1985, pp. 359–362, and 174–194, respectively.

52. Edgar Camacho Omiste, "Bolivia en 1986: la política exterior del neo-liberalismo," and Heraldo Muñoz, "Chile: autoritarismo y política exterior en 1986," in Muñoz (ed.), op. cit., 1987, pp. 201–203, and pp. 443–449; and Mladen Yopo H., "Bolivia 1987: una política exterior de sobrevivencia," and Manfred Wilhelmy, "Chile: problemas externos y proyección del régimen," in Muñoz (ed.), op. cit., 1988, pp. 151–154, and pp. 299–304, respectively.

53. José Carlos Brandi Aleixo, "Líneas generales de la política exterior de Brasil" in Puig (ed.), op. cit., p. 224.

54. Michael Morris, "The 1984 Argentine-Chilean Pact of Peace and Friendship," *Oceanus*, vol. 28, no. 2, Summer 1985; and Oscar Pinochet de la Barra, "El Tratado de Paz y Amistad entre Chile y Argentina," *Revista de Ciencia Política*, Universidad Católica de Chile, vol. 7, no. 1, 1985.

55. The concept is taken from Oscar Camilion, "El conflicto Beagle," paper submitted to the seminar "Zona de Paz: Hacia una Alternativa de Seguridad Regional para América Latina," FLACSO, Santiago, Chile, June 5-7, 1985.

56. David Lewis Feldman, "The United States' Role in the Malvinas Crisis, 1982: Misguidance and Misperception in Argentina's Decision to go to War," and Alexander M. Haig, Jr., "Reply to David Lewis Feldman, *Journal of Interamerican Studies and World Affairs*, vol. 27, no. 2, Summer 1985, pp. 1-24.

57. Purcell, op. cit., p. 75.

58. Luis Maira, "El Grupo de Contadora y la Paz en Centroamérica," in Muñoz, op. cit., 1987, p. 380.

59. Interview with Dante Caputo, minister of foreign relations of Argentina, *La Nación* (Buenos Aires), August 14, 1985.

60. Cepeda Ulloa, op. cit.

61. Madalengoitia U., op. cit.

62. *SIPRI Yearbook 1985*, p. 452.

63. Ibid., p. 347.

64. Ibid., p. 351.

65. Calculated from *SIPRI Yearbook 1988*, pp. 202-203.

66. Edgardo Mercado Jarrin, "Perspectivas de los acuerdos de limitación y desarme en América Latina y el Caribe," paper presented at the seminar "Paz, Desarme y Desarrollo," held during the RIAL annual meeting in Bogota, Colombia, November 4-6, 1985, pp. 16-17.

67. Ibid., according to *SIPRI Yearbook 1985* data.

68. *SIPRI Yearbook 1985*, pp. 340-343.

69. Ibid., p. 340.

70. For a general view of Brazil's military industry, see Javier de Masarrasa, "La industria de defensa del Brasil," *Defensa*, year 7, no. 86, 1985; and Peter Lock, "Brazil: Arms for Export" in Michael Brzoska and Thomas Ohlson (eds.), *Arms Production in the Third World* (London and Philadelphia, Taylor and Francis, 1986), pp. 79-104.

71. Foreign Broadcast Information Service, *Latin America*, November 28, 1984.

72. Latin American Regional Report, *Brazil Report*, January 6, 1984, p. 4.

73. See note 69.

74. Roett and Tollefson, op. cit.

75. Foreign Broadcast Information Service, *Latin America*, June 12, 1985.

76. Foreign Broadcast Information Service, *Latin America*, February 8, 1984.

77. Foreign Broadcast Information Service, Latin America, February 28, 1984.

78. Latin American Regional Report, *Brazil Report*, August 9, 1985, p. 5.

79. Edward S. Milensky, "Arms Production and National Security in Argentina," *Journal of Interamerican Studies and World Affairs*, vol. 22, no. 3, August 1980, pp. 267-288; and Victor Millán, "Argentina: Schemes for Glory," in Brzoska and Ohlson (eds.), op. cit., pp. 35-54.

80. *Tiempo Argentino* (Buenos Aires), April 21, 1985.

81. *Tiempo Argentino* (Buenos Aires), June 16, 1984.

82. Javier Taibo Arias and Luis M. Maiz, "Por fin el IA-63 Pampa," *Defensa,* vol. 8, no. 81, January 1985, pp. 6–11.

83. See Michael Brzoska, "Other Countries: The Smaller Arms Producers" in Brzoska and Ohlson (eds.), op. cit., pp. 279–290.

84. See Daniel Poneman, "Nuclear Proliferation Prospects for Argentina," *Orbis,* vol. 27, no. 4, Winter 1984; David J. Myers, "Brazil: Reluctant Pursuit of the Nuclear Option," *Orbis,* vol. 27, no. 4, Winter 1984; and John Redick, "Non-Proliferation Initiatives for Latin America," paper prepared for the Inter-American Dialogue, March 1985.

85. Poneman, op. cit., p. 862.

86. Foreign Broadcast Information Service, *Latin America,* May 7, 1984.

87. Foreign Broadcast Information Service, *Latin America,* May 14, 1984.

88. Interview with Jorge Sábato, Foreign Affairs Secretary, *Clarín* (Buenos Aires), September 22, 1984.

89. There were two nuclear energy plants in operation in 1988: Atucha I and Embalse.

90. Foreign Broadcast Information Service, *Latin America,* May 2, 1985.

91. Foreign Broadcast Information Service, *Latin America,* May 22, 1985.

92. José Roberto Arruda, "Nuclear Program in Decisive Period," in *O Estado de São Paulo,* November 18, 1984, reprinted in Foreign Broadcast Information Service, *Latin America,* November 28, 1984.

93. Latin American Regional Reports, *Brazil Report,* January 9, 1985, pp. 4–5.

94. Myers, op. cit.

95. Organismo para la Proscripción de las Armas Nucleares en América Latina, *Discurso del señor Atilio N. Molteni, Representante de Argentina, ante el Noveno Período Ordinario de Sesiones de la Conferencia General de OPANAL,* Document S/Inf. 317, May 7, 1985.

96. Statement at the Conference on Disarmament in Geneva, May 1985.

97. Foreign Broadcast Information Service, *Latin America,* May 28, 1984.

98. *Folha de São Paulo,* June 22, 1985.

99. Bernardo Kucinski, "Dismantling the Timebomb," *South,* September 1985, p. 21.

100. Foreign Broadcast Information Service, *Latin America,* August 28, 1985.

101. This has been the purpose of the initiatives to limit military spending in the region, like the Ayacucho of 1974 and President García's initiative of 1984.

102. Gregory Treverton, "Interstate Conflict in Latin America," Working Papers, Latin American Program, The Wilson Center, Washington, D.C., No. 54, 1984.

103. Victor Millan, "Regional Confidence-Building in the Military Field: The Case of Latin America," in M. Morris and V. Millan, *Controlling Latin American Conflicts: Ten Approaches* (Boulder, Colo.: Westview Press, 1983).

104. For the case of Argentina and Brazil, see Wayne A. Selcher, "Brazilian-Argentine Relations in the 1980s: From Wary Rivalry to Friendly Competition,"

Journal of Interamerican Studies and World Affairs, vol. 27, no. 2, Summer 1985, pp. 25–54.

105. *El Mercurio* (Santiago, Chile), December 27, 1984, and May 21, 1985.
106. *El Mercurio* (Santiago, Chile), March 13, 1985.
107. *Ambito* (Buenos Aires), April 15, 1985.
108. *El Mercurio* (Santiago, Chile), November 1, 1985.

8

The Contadora Initiative, the United States, and the Concept of a Zone of Peace

Nina Maria Serafino

From the beginning, when the foreign ministers of Mexico, Venezuela, Colombia, and Panama met in January 1983 on Contadora Island off the Pacific coast of Panama to consider means to resolve conflicts in Central America, the Contadora process has attempted to meld several different concepts into a Contadora Act for Peace and Cooperation. The concepts were only vaguely defined when these four states began to mediate disagreements among the Central American countries, with the objective of arriving at a comprehensive agreement on political, economic, and security issues that all five Central American countries could sign. "Security" seemed to mean some permutation of a "zone of peace" among the five—Guatemala, El Salvador, Honduras, Nicaragua, and Costa Rica.

A wider definition was achieved in September 1983, when the four "Contadora Group" countries and the five Central American countries agreed on a Document of Objectives. This document, which was presented to the United Nations on October 6, 1983, listed what became known as the "21 points" of the Contadora process, setting forth the political, economic, social, and security goals that were to be worked out into a specific treaty.[1]

The security objectives were the most specific. These were as follows: (1) to halt the arms race in all its forms and to initiate negotiations on arms control, that is, the reduction of the current arms inventory and the actual number of arms; (2) to prohibit the establishment in the region of foreign military bases or any other form of foreign military interference; (3) to reach agreements to reduce, and eventually eliminate, the presence of foreign military advisers and other forms of foreign military and security actions; (4) to establish internal mechanisms of control for the prevention of the traffic of arms from the territory of one country of the region to another, and within the region from abroad, to persons, organizations, or groups attempting to undermine Central American governments; and (5) to prevent the use of their own territories for and to abstain from promoting or supporting acts of terrorism, subversion, or sabotage in the countries of the area.

Among the political goals were recommendations to respect and guarantee the observance of human, political, civil, economic, social, religious, and cultural rights; and for the countries to adopt measures conducive to the establishment and, in some cases, to the improvement of democratic, representative, and pluralistic systems. These measures would guarantee effective popular participation in decisionmaking and ensure free access of the different currents of opinion to honest and periodical electoral processes, which should be based on a total respect for citizens' rights. Additionally, national actions towards reconciliation in cases of deep social divisions were to be promoted, allowing participation in democratic political procedures according to the law.

In the economic and social area, the outlined goals included the following: (1) to continue with humanitarian aid directed to help Central American refugees who have been displaced from their country of origin and to provide conditions suitable for their voluntary repatriation; (2) to undertake economic and social development programs with the purpose of achieving a higher standard of living and a more equitable distribution of wealth; (3) to revitalize and normalize the mechanisms of economic integration in order to achieve a continuous economic development based on solidarity and mutual benefit; (4) to negotiate the acquisition of external monetary resources that will guarantee additional means to finance the reactivation of intraregional commerce, overcome the severe difficulties in the balance of payments, secure working capital funds, support programs for the expansion and restructuring of the systems of production, and to promote short- and long-term investment projects; (5) to search for a greater and wider access to international markets in order to expand the commercial flow between Central American countries and the rest of the world, especially with industrialized countries, through a revision of commercial practices and elimination of tariffs and nontariff barriers, while ensuring profitable and fair prices for the products exported by countries of the region; and (6) to promote mechanisms of technical cooperation to plan, program, and execute multisectorial projects of investment and promotion of commerce.

The drafting of these goals signaled a perception that lasting peace in Central America would require the creation of a mutual security zone, greater regional economic integration and union, and a certain consensus on political standards and values.[2] Thus, the central concept of the Contadora Initiative, as defined by the Document of Objectives, appeared to be that peace depended not only on the scaleback of levels of military development and the drastic reduction and eventual removal of foreign advisers, but also would require a degree of political and economic heterogeneity among the five Central American countries. As of June 1986, great progress had been made in arriving at a final treaty. However, the formulation of a final treaty and the conclusion of negotiations appears to have stumbled over differing opinions on the precise definition of Contadora's central concept, particularly the necessary interrelationships among the security and political aspects, and over whether the gradual rather than simultaneous implementation of all security aspects will diminish rather than enhance the possibilities of creating a "zone of peace."

Background of the Contadora Initiative

The Contadora Initiative was begun because of shared Mexican, Venezuelan, Colombia, and Panamanian concerns about the future of Central America. Their primary concern was that Central America had been defined, largely without justification, by the United States as a focal point of East-West tensions.[3] They viewed the increasing U.S. presence in El Salvador and Honduras, the activities of U.S.-backed anti-Sandinista guerrilla forces in Nicaragua, and the Reagan administration's hostile and volatile rhetoric against the Sandinista government as possible precursors to a regional war among the Central American states or a unilateral U.S. military action in Central America. U.S. policy at the time was seen as an overreaction to events in Nicaragua. However, some Contadora countries, particularly Panama, were also concerned about the drift of events in Nicaragua because Nicaragua had turned largely to the Soviet Union and Cuba to train and equip its expanding army.[4]

The escalating domestic conflicts in Nicaragua and El Salvador were seen as taking undesirable turns. Many concerned with the Central American situation were troubled by the radicalization of the Nicaraguan government and increasing restraints on the opposition there. (At the time the process began, the dominant perception among the Contadora nations appeared to be that U.S. actions and support of the anti-Sandinista guerrillas were radicalizing the Sandinista government, while the perceptions in Central American countries appeared to be split as to whether that radicalization was the product of U.S. policy or the result of the Sandinistas' inherent ideology.[5] In El Salvador, U.S. policy was seen as attempting to secure a military victory over leftist forces that were widely perceived in the Contadora countries as representatives of a significant minority of the Salvadoran population that should be rein-tegrated into the political system through negotiations.[6]

The end result of events, in the view of the Contadora countries and many in the region, would be a prolonged and substantial U.S. military presence in the area, if not an invasion. Any significant U.S. military presence, Contadora leaders appeared to reason, would strengthen the military and traditional political elites and exacerbate the economic conditions and social injustices that they perceived as the root cause of conflicts there. There were also indications that these conflicts were increasingly intensifying domestic economic problems, compounding the region's economic problems stemming from a drastic turnabout in the terms of trade in the mid-1970s.[7]

Those who desired a treaty thought that they would have greater success in achieving one if, initially at least, they excluded the United States from their deliberations. But they also recognized that the United States, as well as Cuba and the Soviet Union, was a protagonist in events in the area, exercised considerable control over some influential figures in Central American politics, and would eventually have to agree to the terms of any treaty if it were to last.[8] But some apparently thought that they could arrive at a solution that would ultimately be acceptable to the United States, as the ideas initially incorporated in documents as the goals, objectives, and principles of the Contadora Initiative largely echoed the position that the U.S. Department of State had set forth as its position on the means to achieve peace in Central America. The policy that the United States followed, however, seemed to many in the Contadora nations, and indeed within some sectors in the United States itself, to be aimed at blocking the achievement of peace.[9]

The Contadora Process Begins

As a result of their concerns, the Contadora countries undertook a mediation process that would first reduce tensions in the area by finding a formula to address what they viewed as both the legitimate security concerns of the United States and the Central American countries, and to create conditions for the domestic economic and political processes in each Central American country to begin to move to greater social justice and political pluralism. At first, the major problem seemed to be to get the representatives from all countries to sit down at the same table with each other. At the time the Contadora Initiative was announced and for the first six months of the process, the position of the Nicaraguan government was that its problems were of a bilateral nature and could be solved through bilateral agreements with Costa Rica, Honduras, and the United States.[10] According to participants in the process, Nicaragua would not then deal with all four other Central American countries at the same time in anything that looked like multilateral negotiations. The Contadora countries, which apparently had early hoped to deal with some questions on a bilateral basis and others on a multilateral basis in an effort to find some ground for common agreement, hailed it as an early achievement when representatives of all five countries agreed to gather in one room.[11]

Nicaraguan leader Daniel Ortega's announcement on July 19, 1983, that Nicaragua would be willing to discuss all its concerns on a multilateral basis[12] broke an impasse in what was beginning to be viewed as a stalled initiative. Shortly before Ortega's announcement, a news report cited a Mexican diplomat stating that the talks were hampered by a lack of "individual efforts" by the countries to resolve their problems.[13]

Another breakthrough was perceived a few months later when the Contadora Group countries made public the Document of Objectives, which they had drawn up in September 1983. (This outlined the goals of the process described earlier.) In January 1984, a document known as the Panama Resolution outlining principles for implementing the goals defined in the Document of Objectives and some procedures for doing so was adopted by the Central American countries. In accordance with the Panama Resolution's provisions, three working commissions were set up in the political, economic and social, and security areas to prepare studies, legal drafts, and recommendations to implement the goals. These commissions were to report to a joint meeting of the ministers of foreign affairs by April 30, 1984.[14]

The First Drafts of a Contadora Treaty

The Contadora process progressed through the summer of 1984. In July, a draft treaty was quietly presented to the Central American governments for their consideration and comments.[15] On September 7, 1984, Mexico, Colombia, Venezuela, and Panama sent to the Central American countries the "revised" version of a draft treaty. In the cover letter, the four foreign ministers wrote that they "had confidence that in the immediate future the Foreign Ministers of the Contadora Group and their colleagues from the Central American region, once the refinements that they deem pertinent are done, can sign the Act of Contadora for Peace and Cooperation in Central America." An October 15 deadline was set for comments and suggestions for revisions to be made on the draft.

The content of the treaty was divided into security, economic and social, and political commitments, which were a direct outgrowth of the 1983 Document of Objectives and the 1984 Panama Resolution. Under the political provisions, the Central American countries would commit themselves to adopt measures to further the development of representative and pluralistic democratic systems, to take specific steps to improve their electoral systems and to ensure honest and periodic elections, and to protect human rights. In countries suffering from civil strife, the governments would also promise to take steps to promote national reconciliation, and to create the mechanisms for a dialogue with and amnesty for their opponents. The provisions left the means and timing of achieving national reconciliation to the initiative of each country. The economic and social commitments set out provisions covering the protection, support, and voluntary repatriation of refugees. Commitments would be made to take specific steps to reactivate and strengthen the mechanisms for Central American integration and to jointly improve the region's economic conditions.

The security provisions outlined a framework for freezing arms imports, ending international military maneuvers, dismantling foreign military bases and schools, and ending arms trafficking and support for armed opposition movements in the region. It also set up conditions for further negotiations on the levels of arms and of military personnel and installations, and on the withdrawal of foreign military and security advisers.

On timing and conditions of negotiations, the September 7 draft called for an immediate and indefinite freeze on the acquisition of new weapons systems and a freeze on the acquisition of all military materiel within 30 days of signing, an end to the support of insurgent groups, and a halt to joint military maneuvers. This was to happen before the Central American countries began negotiations to set limits on the levels of arms, advisers, troop strength, and military installations. No firm deadline was set for completing those negotiations, and the arm freezes would remain in effect while negotiations were in progress.

The intent behind this arrangement was, according to Contadora Group officials, to reassure Nicaragua that it could participate in talks to reduce arms levels and troop strength without jeopardizing its security. The arrangement somewhat resembled a formula Nicaragua proposed in a series of treaties that it offered for consideration in October 1983. U.S. and Central American officials, however, thought that the draft gave Nicaragua at the outset an end to arms imports by its neighbors, to military maneuvers with U.S. participation, and to assistance to the anti-Sandinista guerrillas. They claimed that this removed incentives for Nicaragua to negotiate the other issues of concern to its neighbors, particularly reducing the size of Nicaragua's military forces.[16] U.S. officials also believed that since a team to verify implementation of the treaty would not be formed until 30 days after the treaty was signed, Nicaragua would be able to make clandestine materiel shipments to the Salvadoran guerrillas, while the freeze on arms purchases would require the United States to cut off immediately its more easily detectable assistance to the Salvadoran military.[17]

Initial reactions to the draft appeared from reports to be positive; officials in some of the Central American countries reportedly made statements indicating that their countries were willing to sign.[18] However, Daniel Ortega was the only head of state to announce that his country would sign. That announcement was made September 21; at the same time, Ortega said that it was mandatory for the United States to commit itself to abide by the treaty by signing the attached protocol. This in effect made the Nicaraguan agreement to sign conditional on a U.S. signature.[19]

Within weeks, the other Central American countries were discussing substantial changes in the draft, rather than just the "refinements" requested by the Contadora Group countries. On October 20, Costa Rica, El Salvador, and Honduras, issued the Act of Tegucigalpa, a proposed version of the treaty, which provided that a freeze on arms purchases would take effect immediately upon signing, and the freeze would last only 60 days during which time negotiations to set limits on arms, troops, foreign advisers, and military installations were to begin. Those negotiations were to be completed within 90 days. A temporary Ad Hoc Disarmament Group would verify compliance with the freeze from its start. The version also provided that all agreements would take effect simultaneously upon ratification of the treaty. In addition, the October 20 version eliminated the September 7 draft's outright prohibition on joint or "international" military maneuvers, and instead called for parties to give a 30-day notice before conducting them.

The September 1985 Draft Treaty

Dialogue over the next year led to the Contadora Group's drafting of their third version of the treaty, which combined elements of the 1984 draft and the Act of Tegucigalpa. Of the points under disagreement, the most important compromise was set out in the security area: the September 1985 draft proposed that a process of negotiations on acceptable levels of military arms, installations, and personnel begin simultaneously upon signature, at the same time that the parties were called upon to suspend the procurement of war materiel (except spare parts) and to refrain from increasing their military strength until maximum levels of military strength were negotiated. Parties were to decide on maximum levels within 90 days, or the provisional limits drafted by the Verification and Control Commission (VCC) set up by the treaty would go into effect.[20]

Other changes in the security area called for "international" military maneuvers to continue on a restricted basis until negotiations were completed on the acceptable levels of troop strength. In addition, the new draft required the parties to withdraw foreign military advisers and personnel capable of participating in military, paramilitary, and security activities within six months of signature. Acceptable levels of foreign advisers "performing technical duties related to the installation and maintenance of military equipment" were to be set, with suggestions from the VCC. On verification, the September 1985 draft responded to concerns about a weak verification mechanism by empowering the VCC to make on-site investigations on its own initiative. However, the procedures for resolving disputes did not take into account the proposal in the Act of Tegucigalpa that the Central American countries be allowed greater enforcement power by providing that both they and the Contadora Group countries constitute the first instance appeal panel. Most other provisions remained the same.

The June 1986 Draft Treaty

The draft of June 7, 1986, had few changes. The most important was that the time frame for the entire package of proposals on arms reduction—from arms freeze to negotiations on levels—would begin at the time the treaty took effect rather than upon signature.

As of this writing, Nicaragua had cautiously indicated its general approval of the June 7 draft (although press reports stated Nicaragua had agreed to sign, the wording of the Nicaraguan government's formal pronouncements were not that explicit), but conditioned the placing of Nicaragua's signature on any Contadora document on a U.S. signature of the protocol.[21] Nicaragua's position that it would only be willing to discuss as part of arms reduction negotiations a list of weapons and equipment that it submitted (which included foreign advisers, foreign bases and installations, and international military maneuvers, and excluded troops) indicated that it did not accept all the specifics of the draft treaty.

The other Central American countries were still formulating their responses to the June 1986 draft. It seemed likely that they would seek to either have comprehensive verification provisions incorporated into the treaty, or to have provisions under which they would be agreed to shortly after the treaty was signed but before it took effect. Although Nicaragua seemed to be coming closer to accepting a May 1986 Guatemalan and Costa Rican proposal that arms be reduced by establishing a "factorization" table, assigning each weapon a point value, and allowing each country to decide what weapons and equipment it wished to retain up to a maximum point value, they were likely to continue to insist that all weapons and troops be included in the reduction negotiations.[22] In addition, there were hints that the other Central American countries would seek to establish "benchmarks" (as they were called by Honduran President José Azcona) on the road to pluralism that Nicaragua would have to meet as part of the treaty.[23]

As of July 1986, it appeared unlikely that the Central American countries would reach agreement anytime soon on the outstanding differences on arms reduction, verification, and appropriate political processes.

Background to the U.S. Position on Contadora

The U.S. policy toward Central America, in particular Nicaragua, has been consistent in the manner in which U.S. goals for the region have been publicly expressed. What has appeared to vary over time within the Reagan administration has been the priorities attached to each of these goals, and the means that different groups within the administration have judged to be appropriate in attaining them.[24]

On August 20, 1982, then Assistant Secretary of State for Inter-American Affairs Thomas O. Enders outlined a four-point plan for peace in Central America during a speech at the Commonwealth Club in San Francisco, California. This encapsulated the various offers that the Reagan administration had made to Nicaragua for the improvement of bilateral relations during 1981 and 1982. In brief, Enders proposed the following: (1) a process of reconciliation in each country "in which adversaries can substitute political competition for armed competition," and the establishment and respect of democratic, or at least pluralistic, institutions; (2) the removal, subject to comprehensive verification, of headquarters, logistical support, and training camps of guerrilla movements installed outside the country of their origin; (3) a commitment, also subject to verification, to end the import of heavy weapons such as tanks and combat aircraft "that threaten neighbors and disrupt the traditional regional military equilibrium"; and (4) a limit to foreign involvement, particularly in the security areas, subject to reciprocity and full verification. Enders called for a common ceiling to be set for each country on the number of outside military and security advisers and troops, and asked, "Why not make it zero?"[25]

These proposals contained threads from previous suggestions, not only from the United States, but from both the Central American countries and from other interested countries made during 1981 and 1982. In his February 1982 speech in Managua, the president of Mexico at the time, José López Portillo, is most remembered for his offer to mediate negotiations between the United States and Nicaragua, and between the Salvadoran government and Salvadoran rebel forces. However, López Portillo also suggested that to ease tensions between Nicaragua and the United States, the United States needed to renounce any threat or use of force against Nicaragua; Nicaragua needed to reduce its arms level once Nicaraguan rebel groups were disarmed and forbidden to train in the United States; and that Nicaragua should sign a nonaggression pact with the United States and its neighbors.[26]

Two proposals by Central American officials took a slightly different tack. In March 1982, Honduran Foreign Minister Edgardo Paz Barnica presented a six-point plan to the Organization of American States. This called for general disarmament, a reduction in foreign advisers, an end to arms trafficking, respect for borders, mechanisms to ensure compliance, and a permanent multilateral dialogue to strengthen democratic and pluralist systems.[27]

A plan advanced by Costa Rican President Luis Alberto Monge at his inauguration in May 1982, and signed by the presidents of Panama, Colombia, Venezuela, Honduras, and Costa Rica, and a member of the Nicaraguan governing junta, was broader. It cited (1) the need to reach established goals in adjusting levels of military forces and materiel to those strictly necessary for the defense of national sovereignty and for territorial integrity, and for maintaining order, subject to the universally accepted requirements of a democratic society ruled by law; (2) an essential need for the adoption of effective political, economic, and social measures to eliminate the current climate of tension that affected the peace, security, and integral development of the area, with a recommendation that the Central American Common Market be reactivated; and (3) the establishment of a multilateral and permanent dialogue to analyze and discuss all matters of common interest.[28]

The importance to the United States of the differences between the Central American and the Mexican approaches became clear later in 1982. On September 7, 1982, the presidents of Mexico and Venezuela addressed a letter to President Reagan that proposed undertaking "a joint exploration of the paths still open to us in order to stop the actual and worrying escalation" and reach a "global peace" that would secure peace between Honduras and Nicaragua. The letter stated that the authors had already encouraged Nicaragua to take steps to avoid a military engagement with Honduras and also considered it "convenient to put an end to the support, organization, and emplacement of former Somoza guards." It also suggested that the United States raise the level of its discussions with Nicaragua to true negotiations. The letter referred to proposals already advanced for limiting armaments in the region under international control, in effect proposing this as one subject of "joint exploration."[29]

The Reagan administration received this initiative cordially, but indicated that it found the proposal too limited as it addressed only the bilateral problems between Honduras and Nicaragua and Nicaragua and the United States. Although Nicaragua was suggesting that all its problems could be solved by separate bilateral agreements with Honduras, Costa Rica, and the United States, the Reagan administration perceived the problems in Central America as requiring a multilateral approach, an attitude that was apparently intended to put pressure on Nicaragua.

The type of approach preferred by the Reagan administration was that signed in San José, Costa Rica, in October 1982, by the foreign ministers and other representatives of Belize, Colombia, Costa Rica, the Dominican Republic, El Salvador, Honduras, Jamaica, and the United States with the establishment of a Forum for Peace and Democracy. This approach called for the following:

1. prevention of the use of signatories' territory for the support, supply, training, or command of terrorist or subversive elements in other states;
2. limitations on arms and the size of military and security forces to levels strictly necessary for maintenance of public order and national defense;
3. international surveillance and supervision of all ports of entry, borders, and other strategic areas under reciprocal and fully verifiable arrangements;
4. withdrawal of all foreign military and security advisers and forces from the Central American area on the basis of full reciprocity and verification;
5. a ban on the importation of heavy weapons of manifest offensive capability through a guaranteed means of verification.[30]

The exact intent of these recommendations is difficult to measure, however. The initial exclusion of Nicaragua from the Forum for Peace and Democracy suggested that the forum would be meaningless unless its prime objective was, as many observers have pointed out, to isolate Nicaragua politically.

Obviously, these ideas all fed into the Contadora process, which began a few months later. Although the goals of the process had been rather straightforwardly adopted from previous proposals, early tensions in the Contadora process apparently stemmed from tactical differences between the Contadora countries and the United States over how to reach those goals.

Contadora vis-à-vis the United States

The Contadora Group countries hoped that by initially excluding the United States from their session, they could draw on common Latin American attitudes and interests to facilitate negotiations among the Central American countries. Even though the United States, as well as Cuba and the Soviet Union, were not to be directly involved at the beginning, the Contadora countries recognized that all were protagonists in the conflicts and would have to support any final accord if it were to last.[31] (Although any final treaty would be signed only by the five Central American countries, some participants in the process wanted to append a protocol in which other countries would pledge to abide by its provisions. Such a protocol was appended to the draft treaty presented by the Contadora countries in June 1984 and in all subsequent drafts.) Many also believed that the United States would have to take clear and unequivocal action in support of the Contadora process in order to convince all parties to negotiate seriously.[32]

During most of 1983, the first year of the process, the United States expressed its verbal support for it, but gave no overt signs of accommodation and appeared to pursue the policy that it already had in train without concern for its probable effect on the Contadora process. That apparent indifference appeared to stem from skepticism on the part of U.S. officials about the prospects for the process, and the different approaches of the Reagan administration and the Contadora countries on two issues.

The first issue was over how to conduct negotiations. Apparently, the Contadora countries were seeking early on for a formula that would manage to incorporate both the bilateral approach to negotiations preferred at least by Nicaragua and Mexico, and the multilateral approach on all subjects preferred at least by the United States and ostensibly Costa Rica. This disagreement was resolved in mid-1983, when on the fourth anniversary of the Sandinista revolution on July 19, 1984, Daniel Ortega announced that Nicaragua was willing to undertake multilateral negotiations.[33]

The second area at issue was the political situations in El Salvador and Nicaragua. The Reagan administration proposed that countries suffering civil armed conflicts establish reconciliation processes that would allow adversaries, in Enders's words, to "substitute political competition for armed competition." In Nicaragua, the administration believed that substantial pressure was necessary to induce the Sandinista government to broaden their narrowing political spectrum and hold elections,[34] while most Contadora Group officials publicly cited U.S. pressures as an obstacle to greater pluralism there.[35] In El Salvador, the administration's position was that it was sufficient to allow the left to participate in elections,[36] while Contadora Group officials in general appeared to prefer that active steps be taken toward reconciliation; some advocated creating a new temporary government of all groups in the conflict to set conditions for free and fair elections.[37]

The emphasis that the Reagan administration was beginning to place on addressing political issues was underscored by President Reagan's response on July 26, 1983, to the invitation of the Contadora presidents for the United States to make common cause with their initiative. In his letter, President Reagan expressed "strong support" for the Contadora process. But, he also wrote that he believed that "a solution to the crisis in Central America must encompass four basic principles." The first that he listed, and thus appeared to stress, was the establishment and strengthening of democratic institutions to ensure "free and open participation in the democratic process. . . . " The others were respect for nonintervention, including "a ban on support for subversive elements that seek to destabilize other countries"; the removal of the conflict in Central America "from the context of an East-West confrontation through such measures as a verifiable withdrawal of all foreign military and security advisers and a certifiable freeze on the acquisition of offensive armaments"; and the fostering of economic growth.[38]

Growing U.S. Attention

In late 1983, the Reagan administration began to take a more active interest in the Contadora process. This was a result of the growing international and U.S. congressional support for the initiative, as well as the October 1983 signing of the Contadora Document of Objectives, which gave material weight and direction to the process. At that point, when it became clear that the Contadora Initiative might have greater success than first anticipated, the Reagan administration, according to U.S. officials, began actively considering the terms it would find acceptable for a Contadora treaty.[39]

In early 1984, U.S. officials met with some Central American and Contadora leaders to propose verification criteria and procedures. Sometime in 1984, the Reagan administration also reportedly offered to fund a major part of verification activities and considered giving substantial financial assistance to help implement economic goals set forth in an agreement. It was hoped that this would increase the incentives for countries, particularly Nicaragua, to sign.[40]

At the request of the Contadora countries, transmitted personally to President Reagan by Mexican President Miguel de la Madrid, the United States and Nicaragua began a series of bilateral talks in mid-1984, most of which took place in Manzanillo, Mexico. The talks centered on the U.S. and Nicaraguan positions on the Contadora Initiative, but were suspended by the United States after nine rounds in January 1985. U.S. officials have stated that the talks were broken off because Nicaragua sought a bilateral agreement with the United States on security issues in lieu of a Contadora document.[41] Nicaraguan officials have stated that their aim in pursuing the talks was to secure a separate U.S. guarantee that the United States would abide by any Contadora treaty.[42] Since that time, the United States has held to the position that it would resume negotiations with the Nicaraguan government if that government would begin talks with its armed opposition.[43]

The Reagan administration's verbal endorsements in 1983 and participation in early 1984 appeared to many observers to fall short of the type of U.S. support for the Contadora process that they sought.[44] Rather than supporting the process, the United States was seen by many—including many members of the U.S. Congress—as subverting the Contadora process by a policy toward Central America that included increasing U.S. military presence in Honduras and assisting the anti-Sandinista guerrillas. The Reagan administration, however, argued that this policy was necessary in order to protect U.S. allies in the region.[45]

The January 1984 Report of the National Bipartisan Commission on Central America (the Kissinger commission) supported the argument that a separate U.S. policy complemented rather than contravened the Contadora process. The report stated that the "United States cannot use the Contadora process as a substitute for its own policies. Experience has shown that the process works most effectively when the United States acts purposely. When our policy stagnates, the Contadora process languishes. When we are decisive, the Contadora process gathers momentum." This position appears to be at least partially shared privately by certain important civilian and military sectors of the Central American countries, if not by the Contadora countries.[46]

Specific U.S. Differences, 1984 and 1985

U.S. differences with the direction of the Contadora process at that point surfaced in September 1984, when the Contadora Group presented its "revised" draft to the five Central American countries for "refinements" and signature. The United States, which reportedly had serious difficulties with the draft, began closely consulting with Honduras, El Salvador, Costa Rica, and Guatemala on changes that were proposed in the October 1984 Act of Tegucigalpa.

Accounts vary as to how close the cooperation was and what objective was sought by it. Many believed that the United States forced the other

Central American countries to reverse their previous statement that they would sign, and dictated the provisions of the Tegucigalpa act. A *Washington Post* report of what was described as a classified document of the U.S. National Security Council was widely interpreted as proving that the United States was singlehandedly attempting to stop the Contadora process. The news report, however, only stated that certain U.S. officials had taken credit for blocking the adoption of September 7 version of the treaty because of their objections to specific provisions. In effect, the report could also be read as an indication that the United States favored continued working with the process because the Reagan administration obviously was interested in changing certain portions of it.[47]

U.S. concerns, made amply public since then, were that the security provisions be implemented simultaneously; that complete verification provisions, including standards and procedures, be agreed to at the same time as the act; that enforcement mechanisms be strengthened; and, increasingly since late 1984, that the requirements and mechanisms for political reconciliation and the establishment of democratic practices be stiffened. Apparently, U.S. officials have also been concerned that the United States be allowed to keep a certain minimal "traditional" military presence in the region, including the practice of occasional maneuvers.[48]

Since 1984, the subsequent drafts and positions of the Contadora countries have come closer to the U.S. position on many specific treaty issues. However, the Contadora countries have also subsequently moved publicly to a position more critical of the Reagan administration argument, which has been supported by increasing numbers of the U.S. Congress, that substantial pressure on the Sandinistas, that is, military aid to the anti-Sandinista guerrillas, is necessary to induce the Sandinistas to negotiate within the Contadora framework.

The September 1985 Contadora draft treaty, the result of compromises between the positions of the September 1984 draft and the Act of Tegucigalpa, came somewhat closer to the U.S. position, as the open end on negotiations on arms reductions was closed. However, it was still far from the simultaneity preferred by the United States and its allies, apparently because the Contadora Group countries continued to believe that the military threat faced by Nicaragua must be substantially diminished before the Sandinista government could be expected to agree to reduce its weapons and troops. (In addition, Nicaragua responded to the September 1985 draft that Nicaragua, in addition to having problems with some provisions, was also unwilling to begin talks on military reductions called for by the treaty unless the United States made concrete commitments to provide a minimum degree of security for Nicaragua.[49]) Certain concessions were made on strengthening enforcement measures, but they still fell short of the complete enforcement and verification provisions desired by the United States. And the U.S. preference for strengthened political provisions went unheeded, although apparently sometime during or after 1984, the Contadora Group countries expressed a willingness to mediate talks between the Sandinista government and the unarmed internal "civic" opposition.[50] The Contadora Group position, however, continued to regard the armed opposition largely as a U.S. creation, at the same time as they were beginning to be more widely viewed in the United States as an indigenous product of legitimate grievances against the Sandinista government.

The United States, the Caraballeda Document, and the June 1986 Draft Treaty

In January 1986, to respark the faltering process, the Contadora Group and Support Group (Argentina, Brazil, Peru, and Uruguay) adopted the Caraballeda Document, which called for a climate of mutual trust to be established by the simultaneous implementation of nine points. These were (1) the conclusion of negotiations aimed at signing the Contadora act; (2) an end to support from abroad for irregular forces (the anti-Sandinista guerrillas); (3) an end to support for insurrectional forces (the other guerrilla groups in the region); (4) a freeze on the purchase and distribution of arms; (5) the suspension of international military maneuvers; (6) the progressive reduction with the aim of eliminating the presence of foreign military advisers and foreign military installations; (7) unilateral declarations of nonaggression by the Central American countries; (8) effective steps toward national reconciliation and the total observance of human rights and individual liberties; and (9) the promotion of regional and international social and economic cooperation.[51]

This also moved the process, on paper at least, a step closer to the U.S. position in calling for "simultaneous" actions on several fronts, including steps toward national reconciliation, but it did not mention arms reductions, which the United States also wanted to take place "simultaneously," nor the adoption of verification provisions. However, the June 1986 draft of the Contadora treaty, the latest issued as of this writing, moved several steps away from the "simultaneity" desired by the United States, as the arms freeze and reductions would under its provisions take place after the treaty takes effect. At the same time, an accompanying memo made clear that aid to "irregular forces" and "insurrectionist movements" would have to stop on signature if not sooner, as, it argued, such aid is already prohibited by international law. It is not clear from available public information as of this writing, however, whether the shift regarding the arms freeze and military reductions was due to changes desired by the Contadora Group countries or the Central American countries.

Implications for a Latin American
Zone of Peace

As I understand it, the proposal by Carlos Portales calls for the creation of a Latin American "zone of peace" that is designed eventually to (1) eliminate any superpower military presence in Latin America in order to exclude the hemisphere as a potential site of East-West conflict; (2) demilitarize the area by progressive steps that would eliminate the presence of nuclear weapons, establish mechanisms for conflict resolution and the greater establishment of mutual trust, limit military spending and the acquisition of conventional arms, and finally create a climate for regional disarmament; and (3) create the basis for greater economic cooperation among all Latin American countries and a respect for political pluralism within and among the countries of the hemisphere. In the following section, I will attempt to point out some of the lessons learned from the progress and pitfalls of the Contadora process that might be taken into account in planning the strategy for implementing a zone of peace in the entire hemisphere.[52]

In theory, the Contadora process has been working toward, and the Contadora draft treaties embody the concepts for the establishment of such a zone of peace in its entirety. In practice, however, the Contadora process has been seeking a way toward implementing portions of the concept of a comprehensive zone in stages, although there still is not a consensus on how these stages should be ordered.

The latest draft treaty calls for the establishment of a partial and limited security zone on signature and the subsequent gradual working out of further security elements. The removal of foreign military elements and outside military threats is called for in the first stages of the draft treaty. On signature, the security aspects that would go into effect would require the removal of much of the foreign military presence and establish an expanded mutual nonaggression pact that would provide not only pledges that a country would not invade another or intervene in another's affairs, but which would also prohibit each country from allowing the use of its territory for any activities aimed at overthrowing another government.

Steps toward demilitarization, that is, national disarmament, are not dealt with until a later phase of the process, which would begin on ratification. It is unclear when the verification provisions would be agreed upon and come into effect. Although the conceptual basis of the Contadora Initiative, as first made concrete in the Document of Objectives, recognizes the need for some degree of political heterogeneity, those drafting the latest treaty have been loathe to dictate the terms under which this is to be achieved. Thus, these provisions have been left vague, and, as now construed many claim, would work out to be largely exhortatory in practice.

Although the situations and U.S. strategic interests in Central America and in Latin America are distinct enough to preclude drawing direct parallels, an analysis of the Contadora process can be seen as offering three guidelines for the establishment of a comprehensive zone of peace in Latin America:

1. An implementation strategy must take into account the concrete circumstances in which the concept is being applied;
2. The strategy must take account of the particular interests of the various elites in each country whose support will be necessary to implement the concept, and it must treat as valid, and recognize the domestic political implications of the specific concerns and interpretations of national interests voiced by each country that would be expected to participate;
3. The strategy must be willing not only to take into account U.S. strategic concerns, but also to deal with such concerns without ambivalence, and be prepared to continuously reexamine the political assumptions and forces at play in U.S. domestic politics at various stages in the process.

Concrete Circumstances

The Contadora Document of Objectives, adopted in September 1983, was an ambitious document, outlining the objectives for a comprehensive political, economic and security system. Initially, however, the scheme for implementation lacked clarity. Eventually, the scheme that came to dominate the process was undermined by a mismatch of program and historical moment.

Part of the initial lack of clarity was undoubtedly due to the problems of developing a program that would constitute an acceptable outcome to as many as a dozen countries—the five Central American countries, the four Contadora Group countries, the United States, Cuba, and possibly the Soviet Union. Another part was due to the changing perspectives on the possibilities and intentions of various other Central American political forces, and thus of the relative desirability of a Contadora settlement.

The original intention of the Contadora Group countries appeared to be to start a mediation effort, with the limited objective of preventing greater United States and Soviet involvement in the area. Decreasing external involvement apparently was perceived as the first step toward establishing a climate of trust that would lead to other steps such as a scaleback of arms and troops and other demilitarization measures. As part of this, one of the primary immediate concerns seemed to be the creation of demilitarized zones on the borders of Nicaragua with Costa Rica and Honduras.

There were two problems with this scheme, however. The first is that while this may have been a viable approach in 1981 or perhaps even as late as 1982, by 1983 the situation in Central America was probably too complex and the degree of external involvement too great for this type of settlement. By 1984, when the Contadora process reached its first crucial stage, events appear, with hindsight, to have been wildly out of sync with the comprehensive strategy underlying the 1983 Document of Objectives.

In early 1981, the Salvadoran left looked shattered, most of the internal opposition within Nicaragua still held that a modus vivendi could be worked out with the Sandinistas, neither the United States nor the Soviet Union had contributed much in military equipment and prestige in the Central American region, and Nicaragua had not yet been perceived by the United States as rejecting a U.S. bilateral "détente" offer of August 1981. Apparently, by about mid-1982, the Reagan administration had decided that Nicaragua had no interest in meeting U.S. security concerns. In this context, Enders's August 1982 Commonwealth Club speech could be viewed as a final U.S. declaration of the terms Nicaragua would have to meet for any future U.S. consideration of reconciliation, before the United States drastically stepped up the pressures it had already begun to exert.

By 1983, however, both external superpowers had begun to commit a fair amount of hardware and political prestige to the internal disputes in El Salvador and Nicaragua, and the political situation within each of those countries had polarized highly. In 1984, Nicaragua and El Salvador could be viewed as facing guerrilla armies of comparable strength in proportion to their respective populations. Both sides in both countries also felt the possibilities were good that they would increase strength shortly and might win eventually or be in a better position to force concessions from the other side. In Nicaragua, the institution of the military draft in December 1983 reportedly had greatly increased the recruitment rates of the anti-Sandinista guerrillas, despite the fact that U.S. government funding expired sometime in mid-1984. In El Salvador, the guerrillas appeared in 1983 to be confident that their fortunes were turning for the better, according to some observers.

Thus, by the time the Contadora process had begun to seriously grapple with formulating a treaty based on objectives adopted earlier, the major problem it faced was the need to bring a halt to extensive internecine strife, not merely to establish a militarily neutralized area. A logical first step, in the opinion of some observers, would have been the establishment of a cease-fire in both countries, rather than designing an elaborate framework whose final result would be an end to the fighting. The adoption of a cease-fire would have implied, however, the start of a dialogue or negotiations between the parties in dispute. Although it may well have been impossible to convince all parties to participate, any attempts to do so seemed to have been blocked by the lack of an international consensus that both sides to the conflict in Nicaragua and El Salvador were equally legitimate. Some Contadora countries apparently still viewed the contras as largely a U.S. creation that would disappear if U.S. support ceased. Because of this, the Contadora countries were unwilling to press for such dialogue, at least in Nicaragua. And the United States appeared to squelch such a possibility for El Salvador, where it was unwilling to recognize the guerrillas as a representative force. An inability or, perhaps, the political impossibility of all sides recognizing the legitimate grievances of all parties to the two conflicts precluded cease-fires and/or parallel dialogues as starting places.[53]

Thus, it appears that the presumptions or political constraints that governed the process were not appropriate for dealing with the political realities in Central America. Unfortunately, neither the United States nor, more importantly, the Contadora countries, as mediators, seemed able to deal with this fact.

In 1984, the United States began to press one formula as the sole means of resolving the situation—a comprehensive, verifiable, and simultaneous implementation of a treaty. "Comprehensive" seemed to have developed into a code word that implied a much more specific political agenda concerning Nicaragua than intended by Enders, or adopted in the vague wording of the September 1984 Contadora treaty, or that the Contadora countries were willing to deal with. And, the idea of the "simultaneous" implementation of security and other provisions seemed, at best, unwieldy, as the many steps necessary to put the extensive security provisions in place in the midst of active conflicts could not be taken all at once.

Contadora's stance was to advocate a progressive implementation of the security portions of the treaty, the first step of which would be the removal of any foreign presence. The Contadora Group countries felt that disengaging the United States as an active participant in the struggles in both countries would decrease the threat facing Nicaragua and enable Nicaragua to negotiate the further provisions called for by the Document of Objectives. The United States, however, felt that a U.S. withdrawal first would amount to a capitulation that would only ensure that Nicaragua would continue what the United States viewed as Nicaragua's activities against the other countries in the region and to maintain the military advantage provided by the Soviets, particularly given the fact that no agreement had been reached on verification mechanisms.

The draft treaties subsequent to the 1984 draft have been variations on the 1984 themes, which constitute an order that now appears somewhat unrealistic given the degree of conflict in two Central American countries. With hindsight, the bitterness and frustration that accompanied the clash of perceptions of reality, plus a certain natural bureaucratic inertia of governments not to shift course in midstream, can be seen as preventing all parties from reevaluating the political realities involved in all countries concerned and redesigning the implementation strategy.

Thus, it would appear important that any strategy for a zone of peace be carefully crafted to the circumstances in which it would be implemented. Further, it should be flexible enough to take account of changing conditions.

Particular Interests

A second point to be considered in the establishment of a zone of peace is that a strategy should take into account the particular interests and viewpoints of each participating country in the process as well as the benefits to elites within those countries to maintaining the status quo. Although the concept may promote a vision of the "common good" of the region as a whole, the participating countries may be responding to other factors. These competing interests may be so grossly affected by the creation of a zone of peace, that individual countries or elites might resist an agreement on the zone, despite lip service to the concept.

There has been no comprehensive and objective study of the role the Central American nations have played and the interests at work in each of them in the Contadora process. Although some analysts have recognized significant domestic underpinnings for each Central American country's position in Contadora,[54] in general, most analysts have assumed these countries have bowed largely to U.S. pressures in assuming their positions within the process. Yet, at least one observer close to a Central American leader has noted the latter's expressed frustration with a perceived insensitivity of the Contadora Group countries to his country's attempts to ensure its own security through the process.[55]

It seems likely that while Central American leaders may feel themselves under pressure from the United States to take a certain position, they also share certain positions with the United States. Further, faced with what is increasingly viewed in Central America as a military and ideological threat from Nicaragua, many leaders in these countries could well have an interest in maintaining a U.S. presence and backing if the process should, in their opinion, fail to arrive at a formula that would guarantee their security.

To move from the specific to the general, formulas for agreement that do not recognize the full range of pressures on or interests at stake for each participating government seem destined to fail. Thus, the level of actual or potential interstate conflicts or threats may well have to be reduced before a country will be willing to give up its superpower ties. Fears about the intentions of one or more parties to a zone of peace may mean that a logical starting point for implementing such a zone may not be the removal of the superpower presence, but the resolution of what participating countries view as threats to their security.

On another point, there has not been a full examination of the interests of various elites in the Central American countries in resisting certain parts of the Contadora draft treaties. For instance, although Nicaragua is the only country that has publicly resisted immediate disarmament, it seems likely that resistance to the disarmament provisions have come from all Central American militaries. This may well be not only for military, but also for sociological reasons. Central American officers derive their social status from the power that their military instruments give them in the political system; decrease their weapons and troops, and their political influence and social status may decline. In addition, corruption has been assumed by some analysts to be an integral part of the military apparatus in certain Central America countries.[56] Thus, to the extent that this evaluation is an accurate one, one could expect a corresponding degree of resistance by at least some military officers to a formula that would reduce weapons inventories (and thus military materiel contracts) and the military role in the political system.

A similar scenario can be developed for other Latin American countries, even though the situations may not be analogous. The prospect of reducing ties to the United States and of demilitarization could well be resisted by the militaries, not only for genuine security concerns, but because it would eliminate various forms of social and psychic benefits. Some compensatory mechanisms may have to be developed to deal with this type of problem.

U.S. Concerns and Politics

The Contadora process has been characterized by a great ambivalence and ambiguity in the Contadora nations' dealings with the United States, as well as a great fatalism that has seemed to block an understanding of U.S. domestic politics at work concerning the U.S. position on the Contadora process. An examination of these factors should help in developing a strategy of how to approach the United States with proposals for its cooperation in promoting a zone of peace in Latin America.

On the one hand, the Latin American nations have affirmed that the implementation of any ultimate agreement would require the cooperation of the United States. In 1983, one official of a Contadora Group country publicly stated that the process would take into account the legitimate security concerns of the United States.[57] Even Sergio Ramirez, currently vice-president of Nicaragua, was quoted in September 1984 in the U.S. press as stating that "Nicaragua does not seek to contest the sphere of influence the U.S. purports to uphold in Central America."[58]

Yet, U.S. attempts in 1984 to advance its position by working with Honduras, Costa Rica, and El Salvador were regarded as attempts to block the treaty, not as a legitimate effort by the United States to protect its security interests. The reaction to this U.S. participation was so severe that, subsequently, reportedly neither the Contadora countries nor the Central American countries kept the United States fully informed on details of negotiations.[59] Although this may have been seen as necessary from the standpoint of the political processes in Latin America, it also seems contradictory if U.S. acceptance was viewed as necessary for the effective implementation of a treaty.

In addition, as viewed from the outside, the Contadora Group countries at times appeared publicly to exhibit a great and stifling fatalism about the U.S. position on the Contadora Initiative. Some Contadora Group participants have scolded the United States (and some also Nicaragua) for a lack of "political will" in adopting a treaty. Yet, the function of negotiations is to arrive at a formula that will prove acceptable to all countries, which implies that it will be acceptable to most relevant actors in the domestic political process of participating countries or countries whose support is necessary to implement a final agreement. Obviously, this entails advancing formulas that will change the perceptions, patterns of interaction, and the constellation of forces, both within and among the states involved, that originally had created the conflictual situation. A "political will" for peace is the product, not the precursor or an intermediary step, of a negotiating process.

True, there are undoubtedly some sectors of the U.S. government, particularly in the executive branch, that are implacably hostile to the concept of a Contadora treaty and would like to see the Sandinista government liquidated. And there are undoubtedly also many that have grave doubts about the process. Nevertheless, the continued public agony marking the debate among the branches of U.S. government on the nature of the conflict in Central America and the proper policy toward

Nicaragua should have made clear that the Contadora process enjoyed support not only within Congress, but within certain sectors of the executive branch as well. Furthermore, fairly influential U.S. officials might see a negotiated solution that would imply a continued Sandinista presence as the most viable U.S. option.[60]

From the point of view of this North American observer, there seemed to be a few major points on which the Contadora Group countries' failure to grasp the political realities in the United States led to unnecessary frictions or extremely unrealistic positions. In one respect, the Contadora Group countries seemed to expect more of the United States than could be delivered because they viewed a lack of highly visible U.S. public support for a draft treaty as denoting total U.S. disinterest in a negotiated settlement to conflict in Central America. It should have been evident that the divisions within the executive branch would preclude an unrestrained political embrace of a developing process in which the final shape of a settlement was very unclear. Further, the Contadora Group countries appeared to avoid treating seriously U.S. concerns about the ultimate shape of a Contadora treaty. Clearly, one could dispute whether permanently maintaining a certain level of military advisers and military maneuvers, as appeared to be the 1984 position of the administration, was necessary to meet "legitimate" U.S. security interests. This almost certainly was a matter of debate within the Reagan administration itself as even Enders had suggested their complete removal in 1982. Yet, one could argue that by reacting as if the presentation of these concerns was in itself illegitimate, the credibility of the process even among its supporters was weakened. Most importantly, and this cannot be over-emphasized, by failing to take into account the repeated and consistent concerns of the United States about verification, the Contadora process apparently began to be viewed by many former supporters in the State Department and Congress as devoid of the serious intent necessary to hammer out a structure that would ensure a lasting peace in Central America.

There is a possibility, too, that the early 1986 stance of the Contadora countries that an end to U.S. aid to the anti-Sandinista guerrillas was a prerequisite to the success of the treaty was ill-timed and counter-productive in terms of executive branch dynamics. Although some congressional supporters of the Contadora process welcomed the an-nouncement, the number of those who thought that the Contadora process would bring peace without the benefit of strong U.S. pressure was severely diminished by 1986. Given shifting opinions, this Contadora position at that time may have undermined proponents by highlighting the distance between the Contadora position and perceptions in the

United States, where the growing perception among relevant actors was that U.S. aid to the contras had to be viewed as a subject of the negotiation itself because that aid provided the principal incentive for Nicaragua to negotiate. In effect, the Contadora countries had asked the United States to abide by treaty provisions before the treaty was concluded. Although their position clearly had solid domestic appeal in the respective Latin American countries and certainly could be argued to be grounded in international law, it was not a politically realistic approach at the time it was taken.

These examples are merely illustrative of considerations meriting attention in developing a Latin American zone of peace. South America is generally viewed by the United States as having a different, and many argue lesser, strategic value to the United States than the Caribbean Basin area.[61] Yet, there still may be resistance by the United States to giving up all military ties with Latin American countries, both because of the fragmenting of the system of political solidarity that implies and advances, and because of a desire to maintain flexibility in case changes in technology, strategy, or geopolitical circumstances should provoke changes in strategic concepts and concerns. Nevertheless, other analysts in the United States may perceive that the United States is gaining as great an advantage from the denial of Soviet military access to any South American territory as it would be getting a setback from restriction of its own access.

Conclusion

For Latin America, advancing the concept of a zone of peace may prove to be a double-edged sword. On the one hand, the possibility of establishing such a zone might focus greater U.S. attention on Latin America. If certain sectors of the United States argue strenuously that the establishment of such a zone would be inimical to the security interests of the United States, that would provide Latin American governments with greater leverage to extract other types of concessions from the United States. On the other hand, the process of extracting those concessions could well set into play domestic politics in the Latin American countries and the United States that would tighten, rather than loosen, ties with the United States. This possible dynamic indicates that all the factors mentioned above must be considered, as well as others—including, perhaps, the state of relations between the United States and the Soviet Union—in planning a strategy to implement a Latin American zone of peace.

Notes

1. The Document of Objectives, signed in Panama City, September 9, 1983, was released by the Secretary General of the United Nations. Security Council Document S.16041, October 13, 1983. Reproduced in Bruce Bagley, Roberto Alvarez, and Katherine Haagendor, eds., *Contadora and the Central American Peace Process*, SAIS Papers in International Affairs, no. 8 (Boulder, Colo.: Westview Press, 1985).

2. See, for instance, the argument by Mexican Assistant Secretary of Foreign Relations Ricardo Valero in "Contadora: The Search for Peace in Central America," *Washington Quarterly* (Summer 1986):19–32.

3. See Susan Kaufman Purcell, "Demystifying Contadora," *Foreign Affairs* (Fall 1985):74–95. Also, Lydia Chavez, "U.S. Team Studying Latin Arms Pacts," *New York Times*, March 3, 1984.

4. Purcell, "Demystifying Contadora," p. 86.

5. See Frank J. Prial, "Honduras and Nicaragua Give Opposing Views at the U.N.," *New York Times*, October 9, 1982; and Tom J. Farer, "Contadora: The Hidden Agenda," *Foreign Policy* (Summer 1985):59–72.

6. See, for instance, former Mexican President López Portillo's Managua speech of February 21, 1982. Bagley, Alvarez, and Haagendor, eds., *Contadora and the Peace Process*, Document 1.29.

7. See, for example, Richard E. Feinberg and Robert A. Pastor, "Far from Hopeless: An Economic Program for Post-War Central America," in Robert S. Leiken, ed., *Central America: Anatomy of a Conflict* (New York: Pergamon, 1984), pp. 200–201. The authors cited estimates that $2.5 billion to $3 billion in private capital left the region between 1979 and 1982.

8. See Juan M. Vasquez, "Latin Peace Formula Urges Arms Freeze," *Los Angeles Times*, July 21, 1984. According to another author, at the outset of the process Colombian President Belisario Betancur advised the United States to distance itself from the negotiations in order to avoid being perceived as controlling the talks. See Christopher Madison, "U.S. Toleration of Nicaraguan Regime is Ticket to Contadora Treaty Success," *National Journal* (November 24, 1984):2257.

9. For one observer's assessment of a U.S. intransigent stance toward Contadora, see Eldon Kenworthy, "United States Policy in Central America: A Choice Denied," *Current History* (March 1985):97–100 and 137–138.

10. Christopher Dickey, "Latin Officials Meet to Discuss Central America," *Washington Post*, April 21, 1986; and Marlise Simons, "Nicaragua Offers to Join in Talks on Regional Peace," *New York Times*, July 20, 1983.

11. My interviews with Latin American officials, November and December 1984.

12. Speech by Daniel Ortega delivered in Leon, Nicaragua, July 19, 1983. Reproduced in Bagley, Alvarez, and Haagendor, eds., *Contadora and the Peace Process*, Document 1.17. In the speech, Ortega outlined a peace proposal that included immediate talks on several security matters and a nonaggression pact between Nicaragua and Honduras. Thus, although accepting a multilateral framework for negotiations, Nicaragua apparently was not abandoning efforts to secure separate bilateral security agreements as soon as possible.

13. AP dispatch, "Contadora Summit a Last-Ditch Effort," *Miami Herald*, July 15, 1983.

14. Panama Resolution (Information bulletin issued in Contadora Island, Panama, June 9, 1983). Reproduced in Bagley, Alvarez, and Haagendor, eds., *Contadora and the Peace Process*, Document 3.1.

15. The Nicaraguan Embassy in Washington put out a press release on July 10, 1984, quoting a Foreign Ministry communique of the previous day that stated that the draft contained elements on which consensus had not been reached and required further discussion. The release stated that there should be greater emphasis on the basic principles of international law and relations among states.

16. See the "Unclassified Summary of State Department Objections to September 7 draft of the Contadora Initiative," in an International Policy Report of the Center for International Policy, *Contadora: A Text for Peace* (November 1984), p. 7.

17. Ibid.

18. See, for example, Alma Guillermoprieto, "Central American Meet in Contadora Changes," *Washington Post*, October 20, 1984.

19. During my interviews with Central American officials later in the year, some stated they believed that Nicaragua had changed its position and agreed to sign only because Sandinista officials learned that the other Central American countries were planning to reject the new draft. Indications that the initial Nicaraguan reaction to the draft may have been negative appear in reported statements by Nicaraguan Foreign Minister Miguel D'Escoto. On September 8, 1984, he reportedly stated that Nicaragua "would not go along with any disarmament proposals unless the United States respects the independence of Central American nations." AP dispatch, "Nicaragua Spurns Disarmament Plea," *New York Times*, September 9, 1984.

20. The September 1985 draft treaty. An English translation appears in U.S. Congress, House of Representatives, "Supporting the Contadora Process," Report of the Committee on Foreign Affairs, 99th Cong., 2d sess., February 16, 1986.

21. Julia Preston, "Nicaraguan Leader Says Contras Are No Threat; Ortega Offers Weapons List for Contadora," *Washington Post*, June 22, 1986.

22. Reportage on Contadora Group meeting in Panama, Foreign Broadcast Information Service, *Daily Report*, Latin America (elsewhere referred to as FBIS Latin America), May 20, 1986, pp. A1-A4. Note especially "Quiñonez on Tinoco Accusations," from *Prensa Libre*, Guatemala City, May 19, 1986; also, author's own conversations with a Central American diplomat.

23. Joanne Omang, "U.S. Allies Press Nicaragua on Democracy, Reagan Told," *Washington Post*, May 28, 1986.

24. My interviews with U.S. officials. Also, see Madison, "U.S. Toleration is Ticket to Treaty"; and Roy Gutman, "America's Diplomatic Charade," *Foreign Policy* (Fall 1984):4.

25. Thomas O. Enders, "Building Peace in Central America," Address before the Commonwealth Club, San Francisco, Calif., August 20, 1982. (Department of State Bulletin, October 1982), pp. 66–69.

26. Speech of Mexican President José López Portillo in Managua, Nicaragua. Reproduced in Bagley, Alvarez, and Haagendor, eds., *Contadora and the Peace Process*, Document 1.29.

27. Speech of Honduran Minister of Foreign Affairs Edgardo Paz Barnica before the Permanent Council of the OAS on March 23, 1982. Bagley, Alvarez, and Haagendor, eds., *Contadora and the Peace Process*, Document 1.31.

28. "Text of Communiqué Issued at San José Summit," May 8, 1982, FBIS Latin America of May 17, 1982, reprinted from *Barricada*, Managua, May 11, 1982. Nicaraguan junta member Rafael Córdova Rivas was among the communiqué's signers.

29. Letter from Mexican President José López Portillo and Venezuelan President Luis Herrera Campins to U.S. President Ronald Reagan, September 7, 1982. Reprinted in Bagley, Alvarez, and Haagendor, eds., *Contadora and the Peace Process*, Document 2.2.

30. Declaration of San José on the creation of a "Forum for Peace and Democracy," October 4, 1982. Reprinted in Bagley, Alvarez, and Haagendor, eds., *Contadora and the Peace Process*, Document 2.3.

31. Vasquez, "Latin Peace Formula." Also see statements by former Colombian Foreign Minister Rodrigo Lloreda Caicedo in Stephen Kinzer, "Latin Officials Report Progress on Peace Pact," *New York Times*, May 2, 1984.

32. See Viron Vaky, "Reagan's Central American Policy: An Isthmus Restored," in Leiken, ed., *Anatomy of Conflict*. Vaky pointed out, however, that the Contadora countries saw the United States as "too much of a protagonist in the region's turmoil to be a credible mediator." The Contadora effort, he argued, "was thus deliberately structured and presented as one independent of the United States" (p. 243).

33. Daniel Ortega's speech on the fourth anniversary of the Sandinista revolution, July 19, 1983. Reproduced in Bagley, Alvarez, and Haagendor, eds., *Contadora and the Peace Process*, Document 1.21.

34. One of the earliest versions of this argument was made by Assistant Secretary of State for Inter-American Affairs Thomas O. Enders to the U.S. Senate Foreign Relations Committee on April 12, 1983. His speech was reproduced in the *Congressional Record* of that date, pp. S4347–S4349. In this speech, Enders provides a detailed account of U.S. attempts to negotiate its concerns with Nicaragua.

35. In September 1984, Mexican President Miguel de la Madrid was quoted stating that the U.S.-backed rebels were causing a climate of violence and repression in Nicaragua, making the Nicaraguan revolution "desperate" and radicalizing it. UPI dispatch, "Mexican Says Rebels Cause Managua Tone," *Washington Post*, September 7, 1984. The Contadora nations as a group began to publically urge the United States to cease support for the anti-Sandinista guerrillas in early 1985.

36. The argument for this position is developed in Nestor Sanchez, "The Communist Threat," *Foreign Policy* (Fall 1983):46–47.

37. "Mexicans Entice Washington Towards Détente in Central America," *Latin America Weekly Report*, March 19, 1982, p. 1.

38. Letter of President Ronald Reagan, July 26, 1983. Reprinted in Bagley, Alvarez, and Haagendor, eds., *Contadora and the Peace Process*, Document 1.6.

39. My interviews with U.S. officials, as referred to in Nina Maria Serafino, "The Contadora Initiative: Implications for Congress," Congressional Research Service (CRS), IB 85109, reprinted in U.S. Congress, "Supporting the Contadora Process."

40. Early U.S. interest in the verification aspect of a potential Contadora treaty were cited in a March 3, 1984, *New York Times* article, "U.S. Team Studying Latin Arms Pact," by Lydia Chavez, which stated that the State Department had sent a team of technicians to Central America to consult with those governments on how to verify compliance. U.S. concerns that adequate verification provisions accompany the treaty were cited in many news reports in late 1984. In one, U.S. Secretary of State George Shultz was quoted as stating that "There is a real difference between agreeing on the idea that verification is necessary and important, and agreeing in advance that it will be done and here is how it will be done." "Latin Diplomacy: U.S. Influence May be Limited," *New York Times*, October 15, 1984. The U.S. offer to fund verification activities was cited in Barbara Durr, "In Contadora Negotiation, U.S. Offers to Pay for Compliance Verification," *Baltimore Sun*, December 2, 1984. The report cites a "key Administration figure" stating that costs for a verification plan suggested by the United States would be between $20 million to $25 million per year.

41. See U.S. Department of State, *Revolution Beyond Our Border: Sandinista Intervention in Central America*, Special Report No. 132, September 1985, pp. 29–30.

42. My interviews with a Sandinista Foreign Ministry official, December 1984.

43. In a letter dated June 11, 1985, to three U.S. representatives, President Ronald Reagan wrote, "I intend to instruct our special Ambassador to consult with the governments of Central America, the Contadora countries, and other democratic governments, and the United Nicaraguan Opposition as to how and when the U.S. would resume direct bilateral talks with Nicaragua. However, such talks cannot be a substitute for a church-mediated dialogue between the contending factions and the achievement of a workable Contadora agreement. Therefore, I will have our representatives meet again with representatives of Nicaragua only when I determine that such a meeting will be helpful in promoting these ends." An excerpt from this letter is reproduced in the "White House Report on Nicaragua," November 6, 1985, submitted to Congress in compliance with Section 722(j) of the International Security and Development Cooperation Act of 1985 (P.L. 99-83), and Section 104 of Chapter V of the Supplemental Appropriations Act, 1985 (P.L. 99-88).

44. See, for example, Peter D. Bell, "The Search for Peace in Central America," *San Jose Mercury News*, June 17, 1984; and Robert J. McCartney, "Mexico Says Peace Moves at an Impasse," *Washington Post*, May 11, 1984.

45. Report to Congress by Secretary of State Shultz, March 15, 1984, pursuant to Section 109(f) of the Intelligence Authorization Act of 1984. Reproduced in the Department of State Bulletin, June 1984, pp. 67–74.

46. See, for example, Eduardo Ulibarri, "Costa Rica and Honduras Find Washington an Unreliable Ally," *Wall Street Journal*, January 25, 1985.

47. Alma Guillermoprieto, "Document Describes How U.S. 'Blocked' a Contadora Treaty," *Washington Post*, November 6, 1984. The article reports that the leaked National Security Council document stated that the October 20, 1984, Act of Tegucigalpa "'shifts concern within Contadora to a document broadly consistent with U.S. interests.'"

48. Joanne Omang, "Habib Called Wrong, Imprecise on Letter on U.S. Policy," *Washington Post*, May 24, 1986; and James Morrison, "Habib's Message: 'Press Managua,'" *Washington Times*, July 10, 1986.

49. Stephen Kinzer, "Nicaragua Balks at Latin Peace Accord," *New York Times*, May 12, 1986; and UPI dispatch, "Nicaragua Spurns Arms Limit Plan," *New York Times*, May 20, 1986.

50. Information from my own interviews, as referred to in "The Contadora Initiative," CRS IB 85109.

51. Caraballeda Document, as reproduced in U.S. Congress, "Supporting the Contadora Process."

52. Although this chapter does not deal with the subject, I am not unaware of and do not underestimate the role that the Contadora talks may well have played in limiting the degree of conflict in Central America.

53. In 1983, one journalist reported that one of the key (unstated) elements of the San José Declaration of 1982 was the following trade-off: "the Salvadoran government talks to its external opposition and the Sandinista government in Nicaragua does the same with its external opponents." Shirley Christian, "Talking's Only a Start in Salvador," *Wall Street Journal*, March 4, 1983. Subsequently, the Nicaraguan Democratic Force made a few cease-fire offers, but the conditions it set forth for the cease-fire led few analysts to consider the offer as serious. Most recently, in February 1986, leaders of six Nicaraguan internal opposition parties have called for a cease-fire leading to a new electoral process.

54. Johns Hopkins University's School of Advanced International Studies (SAIS) in Washington, D.C., hosted a two-day conference on the Contadora process on February 3 and 4, 1986. Two presentations on Central American interests and domestic politics concerning the process were outstanding. These were "Costa Rica, La Crisis Regional, y Contadora," by Francisco Rojas Aravena, and a presentation on Honduras by Richard Millet. SAIS plans to publish a version of the proceedings.

55. My interviews with Latin American officials, November and December 1984.

56. See, for example: Leonel Gómez, "Behind the Violence in El Salvador," *Boston Globe*, December 4, 1982.

57. Alfonso Chardy, "Leaders Worry That Force Will Replace Diplomacy," *Miami Herald*, International Edition, April 24, 1983.

58. "Q & A with Sergio Ramirez, 'How Can We Not Want Peace?'" *Washington Post*, September 7, 1984.

59. My interviews with Latin American officials, November and December 1984.

60. As cited in a June 30, 1985, *New York Times* article, the retiring commander of the U.S. Army and Air Force combat forces in the United States, General Wallace H. Nutting, stated that U.S. policy should seek to build a democratic coalition of states in Central America through political reform and economic development that would isolate Nicaragua and, ultimately, provide an example that would generate an internal opposition to the Sandinista government among Nicaraguans who saw the other countries were better off. He is directly quoted as stating, "'We have learned to live with Cuba for 25 years . . . I think we are going to have to learn to live with Nicaragua.'" He specifically opposed a U.S. invasion of Nicaragua. Richard Halloran, "General Opposes Nicaragua Attack," *New York Times*, June 30, 1985.

61. A synopsis of U.S. strategic interests in Latin America is presented in U.S. Congress, Senate Committee on Foreign Relations, "United States Foreign Policy Objectives and Overseas Military Installations," prepared for the committee by the Foreign Affairs and National Defense Division, Congressional Research Service, Library of Congress (Washington, D.C.: U.S. Government Printing Office, April 1979). The report cites a Fiscal Year 1979 Military Posture Report and congressional testimony of Rear Admiral Gordon J. Schuller before the House Subcommittee on Inter-American Affairs of June 28, 1978 (p. 198), as sources for the following statements on the subject. "The Joint Chiefs of Staff (JCS) define the primary security objectives of the United States in Latin America as precluding the establishment of military power bases hostile to U.S. interests, maintaining access to regional resources, ensuring the security, availability, and use of the Panama Canal, and avoiding interregional hostilities and the involvement of U.S. forces in internal security. In addition, the Department of Defense has expressed the view that the ability of the United States to control sea lines of communication which pass through the South Atlantic and connect NATO with the Middle East is affected by the general state of U.S./Latin American relations.

"While Latin America has decided strategic significance to the United States, this significance is manifested much more in the potentiality of various worst-case scenarios which might transpire rather than the actuality of current trends or threats. The United States has long regarded the principal threat to its security interests in Latin America as developing in the guise of internal subversion, most likely exacerbated by social or economic chaos, and not in the form of an overt threat by the Soviet Union or proxy forces to invade the region. As a result, the United States has in recent decades deemed economic development, political stability, and an orderly transition to more democratic rule as the best weapons for guaranteeing hemispheric security."

About the Editor
and Contributors

Raúl Benítez is a political scientist and director of research at the Centro de Estudios Latinoamericanos, Universidad Nacional Autónoma de México. He is coauthor of the book *Viejos Desafíos, Nuevas Perspectivas. México-Estados Unidos y América Latina (1988).*

Lilia Bermúdez is a political scientist and senior researcher in the strategic analysis area at the Centro de Estudios Latinoamericanos, Universidad Nacional Autónoma de México. She specializes in U.S. security policies and is the author of *Guerra de Baja Intensidad. Reagan Contra Centroamérica* (1987).

Thomas S. Bodenheimer, a physician practicing in San Francisco, California, is coauthor of *Rollback! Right-Wing Power in U.S. Foreign Policy* (1989). He has also written several articles on U.S. health policy, international health, and U.S. foreign policy.

Mark Falcoff, a resident scholar in foreign policy at the American Enterprise Institute in Washington, was a professional staff member with responsiblity for Latin America on the Senate Foreign Relations Committee in the Ninety-ninth Congress. He is coauthor of the book *Crisis and Opportunity. U.S. Policy in Central America and the Caribbean* (1984) and *Chile. Prospects for Democracy* (1988).

Robert Gould, a pathologist working at the Kaiser Foundation Hospital in San José, California, is coauthor of *Rollback! Right-Wing Power in U.S. Foreign Policy* (1989). He is also cochair of the American Public Health Association Peace Caucus and is active in Physicians for Social Responsibility.

Margaret Daly Hayes is a political scientist, former director of the Washington office of the Council of the Americas, and currently international relations adviser at the Inter-American Development Bank. She is the author of *Latin America and the U.S. National Interest* (Westview, 1984).

Carlos Portales is a political scientist and international relations researcher at the Facultad Latinoamericana de Ciencias Sociales (FLACSO) in Santiago, Chile. He is director of the international relations bimonthly journal *Cono Sur* and coauthor of *Global Militarization* (Westview, 1984).

Jorge Rodríguez Beruff is a political scientist and director of the strategic studies area at the Instituto de Estudios del Caribe, Universidad de Puerto Rico. He is the author of *Política Militar y Dominación* (1988).

Nina Maria Serafino is a Latin American specialist and head of the Asia/Latin America section of the Foreign Affairs and National Defense Division at the Congressional Research Service, Washington, D.C. She has written several articles on the Central American crisis.

Augusto Varas is a political sociologist and international relations analyst at the Facultad Latinoamericana de Ciencias Sociales (FLACSO) in Santiago, Chile. He is the author of *Militarization and the International Arms Race in Latin America* (Westview, 1985) and *Soviet-Latin American Relations in the 1980s* (Westview, 1987).

Index